claudia reiche / verena kuni, eds.

cyberfeminism. next protocols

autonomedia

Autonomedia
POB 568 Williamsburgh Station
Brooklyn, NY 11211-0568 USA
Fax/Phone: 718-963-2603
www.autonomedia.org

Claudia Reiche, Verena Kuni, Eds.
Cyberfeminism. Next Protocols, New York 2004

Graphic design and illustrations: Janine Sack

Cover image: courtesy of Prof. Peter Fromherz, Department of Membrane and
Neurophysics, Max-Planck-Institute for Biochemistry, D-82152 Martinsried/
München, Germany
Cf. Vassanelli, Stefano / Fromherz, Peter (1999): Transistor Probes Local
Potassium Conductances in the Adhesion Region of Cultured Rat Hippocampal
Neurons. In: *The Journal of Neuroscience*, August 15, 19(16), 6769, Figure 2:
Scanning electron micrograph showing neurons from rat hippocampus cultured
for 4 days in serum-free medium on a silicon chip with a silica surface coated in
poly-L-lysine.

Printed in Canada

ISBN 1-57027-149-6

004/contents/

Contributors   329

editorial

CLAUDIA REICHE

> Some books arrive at the printer's press after a long, adventurous journey. The adventures of this book in its making could fill books, but shall not fill this one.

In 1999, Autonomedia's Jim Fleming sent an invitation to the Old Boys Network for the development of "a cyberfeminist anthology." This invitation was seized as an opportunity for a cyberfeminist editing practice, the results of which are documented in this book. At this time, the Old Boys Network was happy to call itself the "first international cyberfeminist alliance," and the invitation didn't surprise us. 'Us' indicates the former core members of OBN, who believed – from very different points of view – in the power of such labelling. An editorial group was formed, including Verena Kuni, Yvonne Volkart, Faith Wilding, and myself. We collaborated on the 'Call for Contributions to a Book'[1], which was posted on mailing lists such as 'faces' and 'nettime' – and received many replies and proposals. It was one of the occasions when this "first international cyberfeminist alliance" provoked a multiple and multi-modal response from others who committed themselves to the suggestions of the 'Call' and the notion of 'Cyberfeminism.'

Faith Wilding and Yvonne Volkart left the Old Boys Network, and Verena Kuni and I were left to carry out the editorial work. Without speaking here of their reasons for leaving, it had become clear that the theoretical positioning and modi operandi of the individuals within the group tended to conflict.

I consider this breaking apart one consequence of the group's labelling itself as the "first international cyberfeminist alliance," an inherent conflict in this formula having been worked out through group dynamics. Without expanding on the consequences for the Old Boys Network itself[2], the relevance for publishing this book may be discussed.

The question is which concept of representation one advocates. Either you believe in representation as repetition of a preexisting concept infinitely aiming at identity (with the true meaning), or you see representation as articulation based on the principle of difference focusing on how such meaning emerges from signifiying practices. From this rather simple opposition between 'tradition' and 'in(ter)vention' two different ideas about cyberfeminism and styles of cyberfeminist editing were developing.

On the one hand, it was maintained that the editors were responsible towards history: they had to represent the 'true' heritage of (feminism and) cyberfeminism with the contemporary global landscape of the most influential cyberfeminists' works. On the other hand, it was argued that repeating such a global overview meant simply to obey mainstream tendencies and could – by no means – be a "cyberfeminist" way of working. I think cyberfeminism entails a subject's responsibility towards its political and conceptual desires or, more precisely put, towards ideas of what cyberfeminism shall be and do. Cyberfeminism is seen here as a policy of radical invention based on different experiences – thus abandoning trends of the art and theory markets, except if given the power to position cyberfeminism itself as a trend.

I don't think there would have been anything wrong with the OBN having been labelled as the "first international cyberfeminist alliance," if this was not read as 'Cyberfeminism 'r us'[3] in the sense of exclusive institutional and representative rights. It is everybody's right to coin the notion of what 'cyberfeminism' is. This creative ambivalence of the label only works if understood as a blank screen. Such emptiness serves to defend the non-institutional status of a group grounded in the principle of individual freedom and responsibility to follow one's idea of cyberfeminism. That is: a policy as an articulation of different cyberfeminisms, with one necessary exemption: to fulfill the general representation of cyberfeminism. It is a policy of respecting a singular condition for the multi-folded articulation of wishes: the empty place, that – by taking different positions and functions – facilitates the fluidly changing significations in the Freudian *Interpretations of Dreams* as the imaginary dance of calculations on the Turing Machine's strip. How was this analytical figure translated into a working Cyberfeminism? It'll have been about respecting the "missing chief" aka "empty stage principle" of the former Old Boys.[4] One institutionalized cyberfeminism would be as illusory as one "chief" of a cyberfeminist group. This tribute to the emptiness that a difference (in the mathematical sense) holds in its paradoxical core tried to transpose conceptual insight into political signification and cyberfeminist practice.

The 'Call for Contributions' was an attempt to operate according to these ideas. The phrase "IF 'Cyberfeminism' is a powerful label for some vague ideas…" was meant to set up a mode of imagination, to invite creative disrespect, to test existing cyberfeminist methods, to introduce new elements and experiments. "Can a word express a widespread intimation of something not yet articulated? Yes, […]."[5] The subject of this book is the challenge of critically analyzing and enhancing an imaginary object like cyberfeminism. The choice to send out an open call, rather than inviting individuals whose works had known cyberfeminist qualities, was part of this policy of acknowledging the competence of anyone who was committed enough to send a proposal. As long as the name heading the submission was feminine – regardless of the author's sex – because it was thought impossible to speak in the name of masculinity from a (cyber)feminist position.

Choosing amongst the great number of abstracts and suggestions was difficult, because – even from the differing standpoints of the editors – everybody agreed that the overall quality of the submissions was very good. To make selections was a complicitous process that involved the mentioned losses within our editorial team. All the questions of how to 'do' Cyberfeminism were coming up in high precision during these debates – like a seductive and dangerous endowment which emerged from the submitted works. For it seemed the editors tried to put into editorial and debating practice what they had read in their favorite contributions. Contributions were even used as arguments for backing one's own interests.

The difficulty was how to legitimate one's choices. Arguments were often sketches of one's own concept of cyberfeminism, and discussions amongst the editors sometimes led far away from the contributions themselves. The necessity of including works by the editors into the book quite soon became obvious. One would be able to be criticized on the same level as the authors. This helped to raise the concentration on the differentiated landscape formed by the individual contributions. Different interpretations were worked out resulting in questions, suggestions, and extensive e-mail exchanges with the authors. Of course the last word was always left to the author.

And what became of the question of responsibility: be it towards 'representativeness' or towards 'experiments' or even towards the 'empty place'? The book as it is now is the result of some insight: 'the empty place' has shifted to the differences of interpretations of the works included. The editors had to choose among the proposals and have taken full authority of structuring the book.

The arguments for the different ways of acting – focusing either on individual tradition and topics or on in(ter)vention and its theoretical/artistic ways of representation – could even be deciphered as styles and techniques to pursue one's interests and was not always to be believed literally. But one responsibility grew during the process of editing: it was transferred into the strong will to have these excellent works published. It can be said that every contribution has been chosen for its courageous experimental mode and none was included because it was considered 'historically influential,' which does not mean they aren't now or will not become so.

This book was made possible by the work of many, extremely dedicated and generous participants:

Jim Fleming and Ben Meyers for following through all the way on the long process of its making.

Cornelia Sollfrank, for giving support from a distance, who especially didn't shy away from conflict with the Old Boys Network, and for suggesting that not only one person from the Old Boys Network, but a team of Old Boys, should edit this book.

Yvonne Volkart and **Faith Wilding**, from the first editorial group, for their strong input and for questioning the Old Boys principles as methods for the editorial work.

Sabine Melchert, as competent German-to-English translator and thorough proofreader, who worked through some hundred pages of different styles and topics.

Brigitte Helbling, as spirited translator and for proofreading.

Tina Horne, as proofreader, intensely corresponding on lingual/logical questions with authors whose native language was not English.

Margaret Morse, as proofreader with questions to the text.

Erika Biddle, for the final proofreading.

Janine Sack, as powerful lay-out artist on this book, on whose great work you already have fixed your eyes.

Every author, for sharing and discussing her work – and everybody who sent a proposal.

Thank you all.

My special thanks go to co-editor **Verena Kuni**, not only for bringing in her enthusiasm, her skills and knowledge but also for sharing her untiring questioning[6]. <

1   See: **Old Boys Network** (1999): Call for Contributions, in this volume, 13–17.

2   See: **Von Oldenburg, Helene / Reiche, Claudia**, Eds. (2002), *very cyberfeminist international*, Berlin, chapter: 'The principle of disagreement.'

3   … An interpretation that even seems to invite the attitude 'OBN, c'est moi.'

4   "There is no chief.", see the Video by Janine Sack and the Old Boys Network (GER 1999): *OBN. Processing Cyberfeminism*; OBN homepage: http://www.obn.org. [last access: 01/27/2004]

5   See: **Old Boys Network** 2003: 18.

6   See: **Kuni, Verena** (2003): [if, else, next.], in this volume, 325–327.

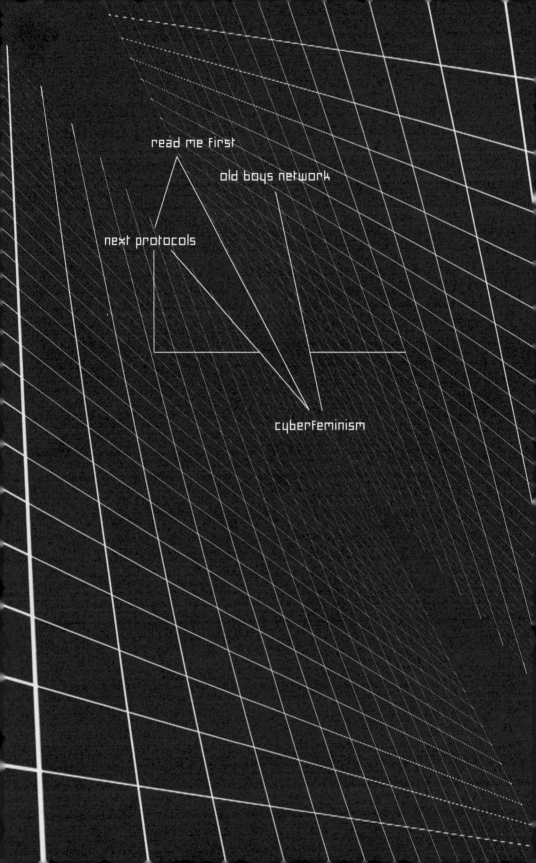

read me first

old boys network

next protocols

cyberfeminism

call for contributions

READ ME FIRST: invitation to contribute to
'cyberfeminism. next protocols'
The OLD BOYS NETWORK is especially interested
in texts which address the following:

Paradoxes of the digital medium

>   How do we judge the changes that the medium
of the computer has introduced in a historical way? And in the way it has
changed how we understand and use history? What are the everyday
embodied conditions of women's lives as they are being altered by the
new technologies and communications networks? What are the new
forms of oppression and of liberation? Has the digital medium – starting
with the indecisiveness of the Turing test, and in its latest form when cal-
culation-tasks have become autonomous data processing – taken the
place of the subject? Can you tell: Where do you or the machine 'end'?

Paradoxes of the body

"...there is an instability at the very heart of sex and bodies, the fact that the body is what it is capable of doing, and what any body is capable of doing is well beyond the tolerance of any given culture." (Elizabeth Grosz)

What is the experience of gender and femininity in the virtual medium? How do we describe these strange new bodies, these body doubles of virtuality and flesh? What are the effects of the biotech revolution on social constructions of gender, and on women? The manufacture and control of fertility/infertility and the medicalization of women's body processes are vital subjects for cyberfeminist scrutiny, critique, and activism. We need to examine the increasingly close links between medical and military technologies and the implications of these for women.

Paradoxes of the cross-breed: Net-condition

CYBERFEMINISM is not simply an evolution of historical feminism created as a more adequate answer to meet the changed conditions of the Information Age. CYBERFEMINISM can perhaps best be described as a feminist intervention into these new conditions, and an exploration of how they challenge the political and social conditions of feminism. What is the net-condition of women? What could cyberfeminist subversions and uses of the net consist of? What are the possibilities of the so-called networked body or the body on-line? In thinking beyond gender and gender discourses we find ourselves in the territory of the post-human, the cyborg, or the hyper-cyborg, the territory of the monstrous and the unrepresentable. With the advent of advanced biotechnology and genetic mapping, the field of teratology has acquired whole new meanings in medical and agricultural realms. How do things look in the physical and non-physical realms of virtual teratology?

READ.ME: IF/ELSE

If you would like to know more about the ideas leading to this project and go deeper into 'cyberfeminism. next protocols', then read this alternative invitation:

IF

CYBERFEMINISM is a powerful label for some vague ideas...

Can a word express a widespread intimation of something not yet articulated? Yes, condensations of some vague ideas have been a part of every genuine invention. For example, the digital computer emerged independently and in different places at about the same historic moment. Since about 1992 this has also been the case with CYBERFEMINISM. Yet the success story of this word seems unprecedented. As technical as the medium named above, CYBERFEMINISM indicates a diffusion through the hitherto thinkable and possible, like through a permeable membrane. Two masterpieces in male western cultural tradition: the 'woman' and the 'machine', worshipped in endless – mostly male – fantasies of mechanical women-automata or as female robots and cyborgs have in the meantime met elsewhere under strange new conditions: Not only have the male authors of these subjects disappeared from the stage of history, but authorship, stage and history may themselves have disappeared, or at least have changed their recognizable forms…

CYBERFEMINISM does not indicate the necessary "return of the repressed" in the male psyche of history, but a feed-back loop in a space-time named post-human. Like IF, the basic element of programming languages for case differentiation and ramification – CYBERFEMINISM indicates an operation. The feed-back loop: IF X THEN A ELSE B sets an unpredictable future for the machine's actions. Who would seriously trust such autonomous operations? Since the war-deciding programming of the 40's, almost everybody (preferably without knowing) trusts IF THEN commands as a means to prophesy the immediate future. Reported errors will already have predicted the unknown message, as a message is the transmission of certain calculable probabilities. Metaphorically (and incorrectly) spoken, a feminist bet could engage in the finding of some less predictable errors – one step beyond coding – in order to trigger a change in the immediate future of the machine's universe. Make a mess of the message? Count differently? Change the alphabet? Calculate faster? Re-arm the hardware to devices capable of all of the first four rules of arithmetic? Transmit viruses? Put the data of your genetic fingerprint in an Artificial Life environment to parody literary origin myths? Live new or ambiguous genders? The potential of this situation has not yet been realized in relation to patriarchally coded cultural systems: yet posing unresolvable decision problems, sometimes turning into infinite feedback-loops…

ELSE IF
CYBERFEMINISM is a simulation…
What will we have been wanting to say? We: some sort of strange new feminists, trying to work out this question theoretically and politically

with the foreseen result of changing or even demolishing 'feminism', or 'ourselves' in the way we conceive 'feminism' and 'ourselves' now. So: Cyborg Feminisms? Cyberfeminism with a Difference? Weaving automatic Feminism like Jaquard's loom? Tinkering with split or second selves? We think: IF you don't make your bets, THEN rien ne va plus… or worse: it continues in a way called progress. For IF the bet on what becomes reality is made by women with machines (they'll both win), THEN history can be deciphered in the mode of future perfect – and what will perhaps still be called 'women' continues to simulate.

At least that's what we are working with: the utopian space opened up between the meaning and the letter, between different lectures and practices, between desires and facts – that is working in a zone of passage between informational noise and modes of simulation. Coming out of the vague.

ELSE IF
CYBERFEMINISM is not a teleology…
If ideal and final concepts of history in cyberfeminist visions are not supported, there'll be alternatives to statements like the following: "[…] as machines get more autonomous, so do the women." or "It's not happening because people are trying to make it happen – or even because feminist politics are driving these changes […], but changes are occurring almost as an automatic process. […] It's beautifully effortless, it's an automatic process!" (Sadie Plant) Why should CYBERFEMINISM identify with philosophies of history that lead to any kind of historic fulfillment? No genuine simulation under the sign of 'women' would corrupt its open structure, like proposing a thermodynamic end of history as a law of nature.

ELSE IF
Gender is not obsolete…
Despite suggestions that one should put hope in a "monstrous world without gender" (Donna Haraway) – why not stick to the intimate monstrosities of sexual difference in an analytical, critical as well as an utopian sense? Assuming that the borders between humans and information processing machines, as between the physical and the non-physical world and some other identity granting convictions will have been shifting or down for quite a while – all this does not necessarily trigger wishes of getting rid of gender, including the most interesting monstrous female sex –

the vanishing point probably even of the perspective construction of a "world without gender". So – IF gender is not obsolete, there is a stake in reformulating it under contemporary conditions. How? CYBERFEMINISM encloses FEM in its very center – FEM that promising syllable which hints at gender, yet exceeds and eludes it.

ELSE IF

CYBERFEMINISM is a monster...

We think: CYBERFEMINISM is a monster born of net-conditions and cultural traditions, a hybrid concept of the strange new bodies of biotechnology and the new forms of simulation in the age of virtuality. If gender is not obsolete, but in process of changing, then how to describe these monstrous new sensibilities, identities, bodies – literally, conceptually, politically...? How to perceive and create the skin of the new hybrid existences, both physical and non-physical? As we live in a time of crass power consolidation through pancapitalism, as the gendered power formations and dominating structures are being spread to all corners of the earth by this globalization, and as information technologies are profoundly changing lives, all this can trigger 'women' to muster all their knowledge and cunning to find ways of creating active nodes of subversion and alternative processes on however tiny a scale. If CYBERFEMINISM uses the Net as a strategy and a medium for political, cultural, and social action within decentralized information and communication networks, what could the monstrous consequences be?

THEN send your proposal to the OLD BOYS NETWORK!

boys@obn.org

eating nothing

hunger

sexuality—desire—language—love—control—surrender

Cyber@rexia
Anorexia
and Cyberspace

MARIE-LUISE ANGERER

> In her book *How We Became Posthuman*[1], Katherine N. Hayles describes anorexia as the articulation of a time that was intent on governing, on controlling the body, on perceiving and documenting its every move. Anorexia is therefore the expression of a period known as modernism or enlightenment, a period that Michel Foucault, in his studies on the birth of the coupling of truth and sexuality, on the awakening of a thirst for knowledge and a new order of things, has found to establish a system of documentation that starts to take control of the body. The body is not only a dispositif for the rules of inscription, but also and above all an entity with depths that remain to be discovered. Its very own laws and lusts had to be dragged to light – in order to establish

a new dimension of eroticism and desire. Freud's studies on desire and drive as the forces which constitute human sexuality supported Foucault's viewpoint by confirming that desire is endless and drive can find fulfillment in every object.

Hayles also sees anorexia as an attitude towards the body that clings anachronistically to something which has lost its significance. The new era of the posthuman is seen as synonymous with a completely different attitude towards the body. Today, we can afford an uncontrolled, liberal, open attitude that no longer sets limits to the body. The anorectic person is intent on confining the space of the body, but these new spaces would define the limits of the body as open and in constant interaction. The literature on anorexia confirms Hayles' impression that the body is to be hindered in spreading itself out in or through space. This kind of expansionism is seen as bewildering and dangerous. Cyberspace as a new space, on the other hand, demands a broader differentiation.

Of course it is possible to establish parallels between anorexia and cyberspace – at least in a superficial-visual way. If, for example, Margaret Morse asks herself: "What do cyborgs eat?"[2] , she answers her question by pointing to the trend towards light food and vitamin pills, interpreting this as the weightlessness that users in cyberspace aspire to. Real food would not only interrupt contact (eating off-line or the cumbersome acquisition of nutrition), but also unduly burden the body in front of the screen.

Freeing oneself for mental mobility and incorporeal eternity is of course a major theme in mysticism. Fasting rituals and self-starvation play a large role in mysticism and are today retrospectively often seen as

1 Hayles, Katherine N. (1999): *How We Became Posthuman*, Chicago / London.

2 Morse, Margaret (1994): What do Cyborgs eat? Oral Logic in an Information Society. In: *Culture on the Brink. Ideologies of Technology*, Gretchen Bender / Timothy Druckrey, Eds., Seattle, 157–190.

3 Bell, Rudolph M. (1985): *Holy Anorexia*, Chicago / London.

4 Cf. Benedikt, Michael, Ed. (1991): *Cyberspace. First Steps*. Cambridge (Mass.) / London; Wood, John, Ed. (1998): *The Virtual Embodied. Presence / Practice / Technology*, London / New York.

5 Zizek, Slavoj (1997): *The Plague of Fantasies*, London / New York.

6 Zizek 1997: 155.

7 Lacan quoted by Shepherdson, Charles (1998): The Gift of Love and the Debt of Desire. In: *Differences*, vol. 10, 30–74, 30.

anorectic behavior. Rudolph Bell's *Holy Anorexia*[3] is one example among others. There is no doubt that the spiritual-theological dimension of cyberspace cannot be wholly ignored.[4]

In this sense, cyberspace and the anorectic concur in that the body is insignificant or even a burden. Hayles' deliberations, on the other hand, go in a completely different direction. Her conclusions see cyberspace as a place where bodies are made possible, and are no longer negated. There can be no doubt, however, that eternal freedom has not invaded cyberspace in its relationship to the body. Slavoj Zizek not only observes regressive tendencies in this area, he goes even further – in contrast to Hayles – by making cyberspace responsible for a new kind of anorexia: the anorexia of information. In *The Plague of Fantasies*[5] he wonders worriedly if a reaction to the excess of information in cyberspace could possibly be the refusal of information.

> "Is not one of the possible reactions to the excessive filling-in of the voids in cyberspace therefore informational anorexia, the desperate refusal to accept information, in so far as it occludes the presence of the Real?"[6]

Margaret Morse's comparison of light food with movement in cyberspace also clearly positions anorexia as the contemporary strategy of disappearance in an age of surplus and the unbearable intensity of being. I think one can accept a superficial parallel between anorexia and cyberspace insofar, as in both cases the body is denigrated/denied. But between the supposed dwindling (of the material body in cyber-culture) and the swindling (of the anorectic vis-à-vis the basic needs of her body) lies a far-reaching difference – if only of one letter.

Tracing the literal/letteral

My starting point for the statement of this difference is the psychoanalytical definition of anorexia. Psychoanalysis sees anorexia as "a failure of the gift of love." As Lacan states: "It is the child one feeds with most love who refuses food and plays with his refusal as with a desire (anorexia nervosa)."[7] This means that anorexia is seen here as a radically non-somatic disease which contains an obstinacy with a deadly potential. This is all the more remarkable, as the myriads of sociological-psychological attempts at explaining anorexia almost all tend towards seeing it as a typical Zeitgeist-phenomenon, as the wish to copy the needle-thin models in our audio-visual environment. All these studies have not however been able to find anything relevant, or even helpful on anorexia and eating disorders in general.

Only in psychoanalysis are those moments that are completely missing in other interpretations taken into account and proclaimed as central: sexuality – desire – language – love – control and surrender. When someone speaks, there is light, Lacan says, thereby letting speech act as communication and at the same time separating the two terms. Language is not the vehicle of information, it is a medium which contains above all an articulation of the desire to be loved. Since the beginning, Lacan says, language contains more articulation than communication, it formulates a desire, it appeals to the desire of the Other.

On this background, I would like to ask the following questions and try to suggest some answers to them:

1. *Can people who use the net to surf, chat, have relationships and so on – those users that seem to be hooked on their cyberspace – be described as anorectic? Anorectic, because they never achieve reality – are never touched, never see a face, never have sex?*

2. *Or does the virtuality of cyberspace perhaps contribute to the empowerment of desire that fuels this speech and these relationships?*

3. *Is it permissible to compare eating nothing with electronic spaces and its symptomatic hunger? Can the passion of cyberspace, using this definition of anorexia, make visible the link that, while it does not achieve the merging of the psychic space and the medial-social, at least shows how both are attracted to each other?*

Real scenarios

One could say that with cyberspace, the body has arrived. This might sound like a strange proposition after all those observations on its disappearance in a genetic data-pool. One thing however can be confirmed easily: in all social areas, talk about the body has become so prolific that there is no way to escape it. At the gym, in the pub, in magazines, in the supermarket, on vacation or at work – everywhere, there is talk about the body, one's own and other people's. More and more young people observe what they eat, which means that they court information on what to eat, how to combine nutrition, and what should or shouldn't be consumed. And to say it right off: Not only do more and more men frequent beauty salons in order to subject themselves to strategies of body-sculpting that were, up until now, the exclusive domain of women, but anorexia is well on its way to becoming a male disease. An alarming amount of men

---

8 Beside the german sense: 'agile', compare: They don't float, they don't sink, they flink. (See e.g. http://pbskids.org/zoom/sci/flinker.html [last access: 01/27/2004]). (C.R.)

9 Cf. **Scott, Melissa** (1994): *Trouble and Her Friends*. New York.

oscillate between obsessive muscle-training and radical denial of food. And – for more and more men and women – it is becoming normal to have one's body treated by a plastic surgeon.

Another important aspect is the fact that virtual reality addicts are often overweight or handicapped, or are people who occupy themselves with deviant sexual practices. The net allows them to establish contacts despite the abnormality of their bodies or their desires. The figures in cyberspace, on the other hand, are mostly light, flink[8] and ideal – they glide through the net like shadows (as Melissa Scott describes her protagonist *Trouble*).[9]

Media scenarios

Although cyberspace may seem ideal for a discussion of the disappearance of the body, this would mean an unnecessary restriction of possible view-points.

Other media and various art forms use the body in the same way – that is, the body is portrayed as a complex object, surrounded by the dual entities of To Have and To Be. In the movie theater, for example, a body is positioned in various ways – for one thing, there is the body of the viewer, then the identifying process of twofold bodies, the moment of leaving one's body behind and seeing the body elsewhere. Video plays excessively with the fragmented body, with the body as a mirror, with the body falling out of the frame. Furthermore, we have the body in cinema. Take, for example, *eXistenZ* (1999) by David Cronenberg, *The Matrix* (1999) by the Wachowski Brothers, and the Japanese anime *Ghost in the Shell* (1996). In all of these, the heroes and heroines switch realities, transport their body through different levels of reality, or are inscrutable bodies that resemble shells or a hull, that may be vulnerable, but can be replaced. Food or sexuality are impressively absent. Either they play no role at all, or they are seen as the same thing, as something slimy, formless, something that will always deform and destroy the body. Unconsciously, these cinematic examples state an anorectic short: the body must be closed, sealed, something that cannot be moved, either from within or from without.

Ideal bodies

In all the different scenarios that have been mentioned here, the crucial point is always space – space for the body, the body as a space. This space can also be interpreted in various ways. For one thing, as Henri Lefebvre and Gaston Bachelard have demonstrated beautifully, the body is above all space, is experienced as space and itself generates a spatial perception. Space is, primarily, my body. Space is my skin, a skin that expands and pulls itself together, a zone laid open for pleasure and pain – and pleasure and pain frame the body, dig trenches, inscribe traces. Freud called the Ego a skin-Ego, a skin-wrinkle or a skin-bag. He talks about the Ego as a border zone, the Ego as a psychic cover, as a zone of contact or a switchboard between the outside world and the psyche. This psychic cover is developed on the basis of the bodily cover, since the skin – according to Freud – is actually the body.

> One's own body and especially its surface is an area that emits inner and outer perceptions. It is seen as a different object, but it allows two kinds of sensations for tactile pressure, and one of them can be seen as an inner perception.[10]

Concrete space, or rather spatial perception, in this way is always bound to the psychic experience of space. One is not possible without the other. This means that the phenomenon of the largest room seeming too small, or a tiny room perceived as much too large, or the body seeming not to fit in one space and seeming lost in another, is only in a minor way a question of measurable impressions, and far more one of a feeling for oneself in space. Which brings us directly to the question of the ideal body, to the question of the ideal of a Body Ego.

Cyberspace is not the only place where humans set themselves in scene as they perceive themselves – uninhibited by an objective reality – rather, this phantasmatic creation of the Ego is produced in every situation. There is no non-phantasmatic interaction. However, this phantasmatic creation has nothing to do with the prescriptions of current beauty-ideals or other aesthetic classifications; rather, it just happens in, as one

10 **Freud, Sigmund** (1982 [1923]): Das Ich und Das Es. In: *Psychologie des Unbewußten*. Studienausgabe, vol. III., Alexander Mitscherlich / Angela Richards / James Strachey, eds., Frankfurt/M, 294.

11 Cf. **Callois, Roger** (1987²): Mimicry and Legendary Psychasthenia. In: *OCTOBER. The First Decade, 1976-1986*, Annette Michelson et al., eds., Cambridge (Mass.), 59–73.

12 Cf. **Copjec, Joan** (1995²): *Read my Desire. Lacan against the Historicists*, Cambridge (Mass.) / London, 37.

13 Cf. among others: **Winkler, Hartmut** (1997): *DOCUVERSE. Zur Medientheorie der Computer*, München.

could say, a double interpellation. One of these is the dictation of the Other (the symbolic order) that points towards the void of the ideal Ego. That means that the subject deports itself in a way that it believes will bring it love and admiration. And the other is the assimilation, the snuggling up to the other without any attempt at imitation. This mimetic moment that cannot only be observed perfectly with children, but is also more or less present in the most varied communicative situations, points towards a double structure of identification with the image and the so-called self-image. As Lacan stressed in his adaptation of Roger Callois' Mimesis-concept, the subject does not love its image, but the surplus in this image – the something that lies behind it. And this – as Callois himself describes mimetic behavior – can sometimes lead to a breakdown in the differentiation between the inner and the outside world, the border between one's own body and the environment. The body becomes double and is swallowed by the space around it.[11] This drama, or rather the stage of this drama has been defined by Joan Copjec as one between unconscious Being and conscious similarity.[12]

This brings us back to anorexia. Anorexia quite obviously does not pursue an ideal in the sense of a thin body, but rather an image that lies – one could say – behind the pictures of models and other bodies. It is most important to insist on the difference between the Ego-ideal and the ideal Ego, even if it is not really possible to separate the two and the distinction must seem largely artificial. But artificiality itself points towards the ideal Ego as retrospective, as something that has always been lost, as something that is lost, even though it was never in one's possession. The tactics of the Ego-Ideal cover this void, but fail in a moment of fracture – as with an anorectic. With the anorectic, a most important differentiation collapses, namely the distinction between desire and demand, thus allowing the drive to pursue its sometimes lethal satisfaction.

Symptomatic positions

Newer debates on the body, as can also be observed in the area of cyberspace, take the separation of language (as code or information) and materiality for granted. The body is seen on the side of the somatic, the material. The body does not only imply the border of the symbolic order, it is itself this border.[13]

However, psychoanalysis also operates with the type of drive that plays upon another border – the border between Soma and Psyche. With this demarcation of a threshold, Freud has tried to come to terms with the difficult relationship between language, sexuality and desire. Admittedly, there is nothing simple in Freud's definition of this thing, the drive, and Lacan's usage is even more complex. On the other hand, Lacan always underscored the unnaturalness of the drive, by radically differentiating it from that which is called instinct. The drive must be seen on the side of the corporeal, but cannot only be seen there; it demarcates exactly the threshold between the psychic and the somatic. The drive is always the symbolic demand of the Other that is registered within the flesh of the body itself. From the first, Freud saw the drive as something that represents the border between the somatic and the psychic, without itself being this border! The drive can only be seen as a psychic representation, and can only be imagined in this way. This psychic representation is called "object small a" by Lacan. In object small a, the drive finds its satisfaction, it wanders around in it. It marks the moment in which sexuality occurs in and through the symbolic order. Lacan has called the voice, the gaze, the phoneme, or the void a possible candidate for object small a. But sexuality is not only drive, but also that which can find no satisfaction in any object: desire.

In the context of anorexia, Lacan has spoken of an "oral demand," which is intimately coupled with incorporation and identification. The basic moments of incorporation and spitting out point towards a vital cut that introduces the border between subject and world. The distinction between having and being is fought out in the zone of the mouth. In many cases of anorexia, the image of one's own body seems to be unending, very difficult to limit, and one way of attempting a cut-off point is by closing one's mouth. This image is spanned in the emotional triangle of need – demand – desire. In anorexia, therefore, the vital distinction

---

14 **Shepherdson** 1998: 66.

15 **Lacan** quoted by Shepherdson 1998: 47.

16 Cf. **Stone, Allucquère R.** (1991): Will the Real Body Please Stand Up? Boundary Stories about Virtual Cultures. In: *Cyberspace. First Steps*, Michael Benedikt , Ed., Cambridge (Mass.) / London, 81–118.

17 "Etymology: Latin, female animal used for breeding, parent plant, from *matr-, mater*." Merriam-Webster OnLine, Collegiate Dictionary http://www.m-w.com [last access: 01/27/2004].

18 Cf. **Plant, Sadie** (1995): The Future Looms: Weaving Women and Cybernetics. In: *Body & Society*, vol. 1, no. 3–4, Mike Featherstone / Bryan S. Turner, Eds., 45–64.

between need and demand/desire has not been made, the difference has not inscribed itself, and instead, demand is stifled with food (need), so that the only possible answer for an anorectic is "to close her mouth in order to voice her demand."[14] This point is echoed in Lacan's differentiation between drive and desire: the drive can be satisfied, but desire, never.

> "As far as the oral drive is concerned, [...] it is obvious that it is not a question of food, nor of the memory of food, nor of the echo of food, nor the mother's care, but of something that is called the breast. [...] To this breast in its function as object, object is a cause of desire – we must give a function that will explain its place in the satisfaction of the drive."[15]

That is, the drive finds its satisfaction in not eating (eating nothing) – an oral jouissance, a jouissance beyond the pleasure principle.

The matrix of the female

But how can all this be tied in with cyberspace? Is it enough to refer to informational anorexia, as Zizek has done? Or is it that which Allucquère R. Stone means, when she defines cyberspace as an entrance into femininity, an incorporation of femininity?[16] Both may be true.

Matrix means uterus[17] and matrix defines the non-linear structure of cyberspace, wherein women supposedly feel more at home than in linear, hierarchical structures. Interestingly enough, this – albeit supremely ambivalent – metaphor of the matrix also introduces the one moment that is not mentioned in either the discourse on cyberspace or on anorexia: that of sexual difference. That is why both images can be brought together – matrix as an incorporation of the feminine and informational anorexia as the denial to open one's mouth.

In her expositions on the matrix of cyberspace, Sadie Plant[18] has cited Sigmund Freud, who in his cultural theory famously saw weaving as the only cultural achievement of women. In a crass leap, he then equates this technique with the female genitals, proclaiming them tangled and incapable of insight. That which is missing is not shown and generates the effect of a deficit. Sexual difference in its relevance to cyberspace, as well as for anorexia, is positioned exactly at the suture of not-seeing, of knowledge and denial. That means that sexual difference cannot be seen as a binary relationship – between the genders – but as something belonging to the site of the Real – it is that "rock of impossibility." It is not a transcendental event which simply cannot be symbolized adequately, but is, according to Zizek, deeply pathologic:

> "[...] a contingent stain that all symbolic fictions of symmetrical kinship

positions try in vain to obliterate. Far from constraining the variety of sexual arrangements in advance, the Real of sexual difference is the traumatic cause which sets their contingent proliferation in motion."[19]

Both gender positions must be seen as the expression of specific strategies as a way of coping with the original loss, which does not stand for something lost but for the emergence of loss as such. Lacan, in his works, sees masquerade as the female strategy, and imposture as the male strategy. "To be One" is male, "to be something different" is female. The female way is to cover, to mask the loss, the male way is to deny it, by acting as if it were the One, as if it were everything. Original loss then means the fact that each subject, in order to become subjectified, to appear as male and female, must separate itself from the mother as the first Other. With the entrance of the father as the Third – the law of language – the subject is hindered from melting with the primary undivided.[20]

Freud and Lacan have both described how food becomes demand and finds a desire for itself. This developmental process is directed and accompanied by language, by the law, by culture. Sexuality is not possible without language, sexuality must be seen in a position where what is not said is heard and what is heard is not said. With this I have returned to the issue of literal difference. In his "Return to Freud,"[21] Lacan has turned the Saussureian sign upside down by placing the signifier above the signified. He has also denied this sign its unity by introducing the "barre," the bar. Language, therefore, is not representation, insofar as a signified appears throughout language; rather, language is articulation. In this way, the object is represented by the signifier, the object is "chose" and "cause" of the signifier.

> "The object functions as a cause insofar as every signifier points toward a signified and must point towards it, according to form; but the later

19 **Zizek, Slavoj** (2000): Holding the Place. In: *Contingency, Hegemony, Universality*. Contemporary Dialogues on the Left, Judith Butler / Ernesto Laclau / Slavoj Zizek, London / New York, 310.

20 See: **Angerer, Marie-Luise** (2000): To be the ONE. Männlichkeit als obsessionale Reihe. In: *Männlichkeit und Gewalt*, Ingo Bieringer / Walter Buchacher / Edgar Forster, eds., Opladen, 94.

21 **Weber, Samuel** (1978): *Rückkehr zu Freud. Jacques Lacans Ent-stellung der Psychoanalyse*, Frankfurt/M / Berlin / Wien.

22 **Weber** 1978: 41–42.

23 **Weber** 1978: 40.

priority of the signifier as difference and articulation is engraved into the signified and introduces it into a structure of radical heterogeneity, which can never be completely swallowed by one identity. Concerning the fulfilled identity of an object, this heterogeneity of the signification can be seen as a hole or a void, as a 'trou' that one must always keep in mind, since only in the difference – only through the difference – is it possible to see anything. The other question is of course, if one wants to see this hole at all […]."[22]

It is no accident that Lacan demonstrates this with his train station game – an example that obviously plays with the idea of sexual difference. A boy and a girl are sitting in a train entering a train station. The boy says, look, we have arrived in Ladies. His sister says, no stupid, don't you see we are in Men?[23] According to Lacan, the important thing here is the fact that the location of the subjects are rails, and that the sexual difference in question is a loo, an "Ab-ort," a place apart, a word game that is of course only possible in German. But let us return once more to the signifier, the hole in the object that can be seen or not seen, the signified that is holed by the signifier.... An in-depth discussion of these particularities would lead too far at this point, however, I would like to stress the materiality of the sexual difference as a literal order. The important difference between Nothing and No thing also makes it impossible to simply equate cyberspace and anorexia.

If we go back to Zizek's description of cyberspace as an informational anorectic space, it is possible to demonstrate where the misunderstanding lies. Zizek declares that it is possible to see a reaction to the omnipotence of cyberspace, its abundant offers, the fact that everything is on offer and can immediately be procured; namely, exhaustion, listlessness, boredom, denial. The important hole, the important difference that allows an escape from immobility, is no longer there.

The anorectic does not eat nothing. She eats Nothing. She eats Nothing in order to appear in the space that is thereby opened up, even if this entails a fatal disappearance. In cyberspace, the situation is not as dramatic. Different desires and different demands meet each other. Possibly, there is the anorectic moment, a moment when Nothing is in demand, which can be found in "nothing," but it is also possible that suffering attaches itself exactly to this "nothing."

With this, I would especially like to speak against those interpretations that place psychic attitudes – as with the anorectic – on one level with the social-communicative, as with life on the net. It is not possible to identify modernism with anorectic behavior – as Hayles tried to do – nor can the posthuman age be defined as a period in which the borders of the body have been freed. Rather, it is important – also in the case of cyberspace – to see not only the plurality, but also the distemporality of *causes/choses*. <

BIBLIOGRAPHY
Print

Angerer, Marie-Luise (2000): To be the ONE. Männlichkeit als obsession-ale Reihe. In: *Männlichkeit und Gewalt*, Ingo Bieringer / Walter Buchacher / Edgar Forster, eds., Opladen, 91–95 **Bachelard, Gaston** (1992): *Poetik des Raumes*, Frankfurt/M **Bell, Rudolph M.** (1985): *Holy Anorexia*, Chicago / London **Benedikt, Michael, Ed.** (1991): *Cyberspace. First Steps*. Cambridge (Mass.) / London **Callois, Roger** (1987[2]): Mimicry and Legendary Psychasthenia. In: *OCTOBER. The First Decade, 1976–1986*, Annette Michelson et al., eds., Cambridge (Mass.), 59–73 **Copjec, Joan** (1995[2]): *Read my Desire. Lacan against the Historicists*, Cambridge (Mass.) / London **Freud, Sigmund** (1982 [1923]): Das Ich und Das Es. In: *Psychologie des Unbewußten*. Studienausgabe, vol. III, Alexander Mitscherlich / Angela Richards / James Strachey, eds., Frankfurt/M, 273–330 **Hayles, Katherine N.** (1999): *How We Became Posthuman*, Chicago / London **Lefebvre, Henri** (1999): *The Production of Space*, Oxford **Morse, Margaret** (1994): What do Cyborgs eat? Oral Logic in an Information Society. In: *Culture on the Brink. Ideologies of Technology*, Gretchen Bender / Timothy Druckrey, eds., Seattle, 157–190 **Plant, Sadie** (1995): The Future Looms: Weaving Women and Cybernetics. In: *Body & Society*, vol. 1, no. 3–4, Mike Featherstone / Bryan S. Turner, eds., 45–64 **Scott, Melissa** (1994): *Trouble and Her Friends*. New York **Shepherdson, Charles** (1998): The Gift of Love and the Debt of Desire. In: *Differences*, vol. 10, 30–74 **Stone, Allucquère R.** (1991): Will the Real Body Please Stand Up? Boundary Stories about Virtual Cultures. In: *Cyberspace. First Steps*, Michael Benedikt, ed., Cambridge (Mass.) / London, 81–118 **Weber, Samuel** (1978): *Rückkehr zu Freud. Jacques Lacans Ent-stellung der Psychoanalyse*, Frankfurt/M / Berlin / Wien **Winkler, Hartmut** (1997): DOCUVERSE. *Zur Medientheorie der Computer*, München **Wood, John, Ed.** (1998): *The Virtual Embodied. Presence / Practice / Technology*, London / New York **Zizek, Slavoj** (1997): *The Plague of Fantasies*, London / New York **Zizek, Slavoj** (2000): Holding the Place. In: *Contingency, Hegemony, Universality. Contemporary Dialogues on the Left*, Judith Butler / Ernesto Laclau / Slavoj Zizek, London / New York, 308–329

Film | **eXistenZ** (US 1999),1'36'', Production: Miramax Films / Robert Lantos, Andras Hamori, David Cronenberg, Director: David Cronenberg, Screenwriter: David Cronenberg, Performers: Jennifer Jason Leigh, Jude Law, Ian Holm, Willem Dafoe, Don McKellar, Callum Keith Rennie, Sarah Polley, Christopher Eccleston et al., Cinematography: Peter Suschitzky, Editor: Ronald Sanders, Music: Howard Shore

Ghost in the Shell / Kokaku kidotai (Japan 1995 / US 1996) 1'22'', Animated Film, Production: Yoshimasa Mizuo, Shigeru Watanabe, Ken Iyadomi, Mitsunisu Ishikawa, Director: Mamoru Oshii, Screenwriter: Kazunori Itô, Masamune Shirow (comic), Editor: Shiuchi Kakesu, Music: Kenji Kawai

The Matrix (US 1999) 2'16'', Production: Groucho II Film Partnership, Silver Pictures, Village Roadshow Productions, Directors: Andy Wachowski, Larry Wachowski, Screenwriter: Andy Wachowski, Larry Wachowski, Performers: Laurence Fishburne, Carrie-Anne Moss, Keanu Reeves, Hugo Weaving, Marcus Chong, Matt Doran, Gloria Foster, Joe Pantoliano,Cinematography: Bill Pope, Editor: Zach Staenberg, Music: Don Davi

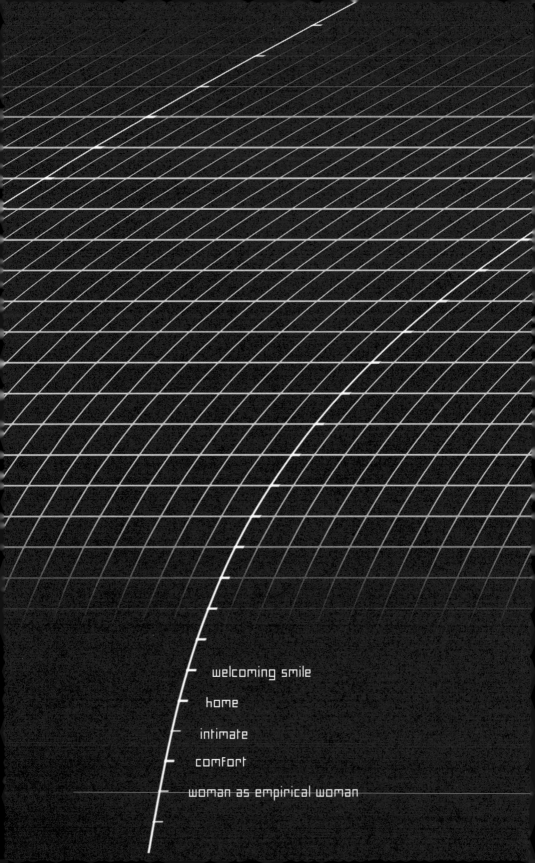

welcoming smile

home

intimate

comfort

woman as empirical woman

Feminity community hospitality: towards a cyberethics

IRINA ARISTARKHOVA

introduction

> Historically, the notion of community has been theorised as collective consensus based on homogeneity, thus forming the ground for unity and harmonious social interaction. The structural, practical and discursive conditions of communities are centered on notions of association by homogeneity, exclusivity and closure. One common thread in all criticisms of (net) communities is that the ideal of community is itself desirable and that the removal of disruptive conditions would make free communication possible within them. The structural and cultural differences between sociopolitical entities exemplified by their specific national borders, languages and identities are seen as temporary impediments deriving from their post-colonial conditions and global capitalism. The technological limits to community formation are bemoaned as significant but surmountable problems on the road to dynamic global net communities. However, throughout such conceptions of communities and their shortcomings, the notion of community itself remains 'unthought.' The question of whether the notion of community itself is constitutively incompatible with the formation of free and heterogeneous social formations in real life and on the net has

yet to be posed. The problems of closure and exclusivity are not unique to net communities. As I have argued elsewhere[1], insofar as they are communities they are exclusive. The associative conditions that have historically been deemed fundamental to community formation need to be re-examined. In the first part of my paper I will, using Derrida's notion of hospitality, deliberate on the notion of community by posing difference, heterogeneity and otherness as the very constitutive and dissociative conditions of community formations, both net and real. Following this, the article proceeds to critique of this notion of hospitality with regards to its relationship to femininity. The final part of the article will call for a radical revision of the place of the feminine within communities by a hospitable ethical agency.

diSSociation and hoSpitality

Jacques Derrida has presented several scathing critiques of unity-based notions of community in many of his works. He claims that

"if by community one implies, as is often the case, a harmonious group, consensus, and fundamental agreement beneath the phenomenon of discord or war, then I don't believe in it very much and I sense in it as much threat as promise."[2]

He says that "the privilege granted to unity, to totality, to organic ensembles, to community as a homogenised whole [...] is a danger for responsibility, for decision, for

1 **Aristarkhova, Irina** (1999): Hosting the Other: Cyberfeminist Strategies for Net Communities. In: *Next Cyberfeminist International, Rotterdam, March 8-11, 1999,* Cornelia Sollfrank / OBN, Eds. Hamburg.

2 **Weber, Elisabeth**, Ed. (1995): *Derrida, Jacques Points ... Interviews, 1974–94*, transl. Peggy Kamuf et. al., Stanford, 355.

3 **Derrida, Jacques** (1997): *The Villanova Roundtable: A Conversation with Jacques Derrida*. In: *Deconstruction in a Nutshell*, John Caputo, Ed., Fordham, 13.

4 **Derrida** 1997: 14.

5 **Caputo, John**, Ed. (1997): *Deconstruction in a Nutshell*, Fordham, 111.

ethics, for politics"[3] exactly because of their negative implications for "the relation to the other." Derrida consequently presents the possibility of thinking of a community based not on unity but on dissociation instead. "Dissociation is the condition of community, the condition of any unity as such."[4] However, dissociation only provides the initial condition for any community since it establishes heterogeneity as a necessary ground upon which to build community. What is required, he proposes, is a whole new way of thinking about and constituting communities; Derrida seeks to articulate this through another concept – that of hospitality.

In his article 'Questions of Responsibility: Hostility/Hospitality,' Derrida critiques the community based on unity that results from fusion and identification, and is therefore necessarily opposed to some 'other.' For him the community of unity is based on 'unity-against.' It invokes an etymological connection between 'communio' as a gathering of people and a fortification (munnis); an arming of oneself in opposition to some other. As such, the building of a community is inherently allied to the construction of a defense mechanism vigilant to and exclusive of *some* other as foreigner and outsider. The homogenizing logic of community development is constantly attentive to those heterogeneous elements within itself only to enable their effective elimination or assimilation. Community based on unity, fusion, identification, defense, closure and exclusivity needs to be redefined, through what he calls hospitality.

Derrida points out that etymologically the term 'hospitality' is related to the notion of 'hostility' since the root of the former, 'hospes' is allied to an earlier root of the latter, 'hostis,' which interestingly meant both 'stranger' and 'enemy.' Thus hospitality, as in *hostilis*, 'stranger/enemy' and *potes*, '(of having) power,' eventually came to mean the power the host had over the stranger/enemy. John Caputo, in an interesting commentary on Derrida's notion of hospitality, notes that "the 'host' is someone who takes on or receives strangers, who gives to the stranger even while remaining in control."[5] It is clear that the 'host' is in a necessary position of power insofar as he (she?) circumscribes the parameters within which the needs and comforts of the stranger/enemy are attended to. In addition to this circumscription, the host's 'power over' the stranger, Derrida suggests, results from his (her?) ownership of the premises that is thus offered. Given the fact that hospitality is dependent on ownership before it is offered to the other, Derrida argues, an essential tension is built into its structure. This is because it is difficult to give over to the other when you continue to own. The aporia for the one giving is the tension of wanting to give but also needing to have what is given away, for it is having that makes possible the giving. Derrida says that this aporia which could well paralyze any efforts at hosting the other is exactly what needs to be worked through rather than be denied. In fact, hospitality is only possible when one resists this paralysis by moving towards what Derrida calls a "hospitality beyond hospitality," wherein the very impossibility of a hospitality based on ownership as limit-condition is pushed to/at the limits. In having built its possibilities on their very impossibility, Derrida claims, hospitality, like deconstruction, is to come (avenir). The aporia of a hospitality to come is constituted by one's inability to know entirely or surely its specific qualities and as such, it is to be struggled with performatively.

hospitality as femininity

I have argued elsewhere[6] that the aporia of hospitality based on ownership would be highly problematic due to the legal and cultural dimensions of ownership. This problem of ownership is even further complicated by the issue of sexual difference. We must be especially careful when the issue of sexual difference is at stake. Traditionally women have been closely associated with the "welcoming smile" that greets one at the entrance of the home owned usually by someone else. What if the host is a hostess who does not own the home? The relationship between hosting and femininity has been addressed by Derrida in his essay "A Word of Welcome" from

the book *Adieu to Emmanuel Levinas*.[7] Here, Derrida claims that Levinas' book *Totality and Infinity* is in fact "a treatise on hospitality," and the notion of "feminine alterity" is the cornerstone of the architecture of Levinas' entire argument.

According to Derrida, hospitality, as it is conceived by Levinas, is primarily and essentially tied to sexual difference, and its very possibility depends on it. Furthermore, the (con-

6 Aristarkhova 1999.

7 Derrida, Jacques (1999): *Adieu to Emmanuel Levinas*, transl. Pascale-Anne Brault / Michael Naas, Stanford.

cept/metaphor of) Woman undermines any claim on safe ownership since she serves as a pre-condition for the hospitality and welcoming of the home for its potential or actual owner. In this case, fundamentally, the master of the property is always already in a situation of being received at his own home by some, so-called, feminine alterity, understood as a 'feminine welcoming being.' It is noteworthy though that for Levinas the actual presence of a woman in a given house does not determine or undermine the feminine essence of hospitality. In fact, the presence of empirical women is inconsequential to the femininity of hospitality. Thus, for Levinas hospitality is necessarily associated with the question of Woman, essentially, but without reference to empirical women as such. Before embarking on a critique of Levinas' notion of hospitality, it would be useful to outline some important constitutive elements of hospitality for both Levinas and Derrida.

First of all, hospitality is about welcoming. It can be a word of welcome, a welcoming smile, a welcome understood in its utmost openness and passivity – openness to the other, smile at the threshold of the house, unconditional acceptance of the other. Second, hospitality is about receptivity, an ability of reason to receive, to be "more passive than any given passivity." The owner is being received in his own house; he is being welcomed there prior to any language proper, to linguistic communication. Third, hospitality demands discretion. It is the manifestation and withdrawal of the face; indirect communication and at the same time a silent discreet presence without the transgression of interiority. Furthermore, hospitality is more than discreet, it is also intimate. Hospitality is about comfort, it is about the serenity of being 'at home' with oneself. Thus, it is absolute 'defenselessness,' a conscious and enjoyable vulnerability of feeling in a total refuge at home with oneself. This feeling of being at home with oneself refers necessarily to memory, though here without any psychoanalytic gesture, but understood as recollection: the recollection as a relation to the language of the host, recollection of meaning. And of course, following from all previous formulations, hospitality is posed through habitation. This relation to habitation, to home, to the interiority of the house, is a reminder of the self's relation to its own corporeality, in some sense, since "there is not yet the 'you' of the face, but the 'thou' of familiarity" (Levinas). Woman comes into the realm of hospitality at, as and through home:

"the other whose presence is discreetly an absence, with which is accomplished the hospitable welcome par excellence which describes the field of intimacy, is the Woman. The Woman is the condition for recollection, the interiority of the Home, and inhabitation."[8]

Derrida himself is fully aware of the problems associated with such definition of femininity, what he calls "traditional and androcentric attribution of certain characteristics to woman," however here, he calls for

"another reading of these lines," one "that would not oppose in a polemical or dialectical fashion either this first reading or this interpretation of Levinas".[9] For Derrida,

8 **Levinas**, cited in Derrida 1999: 36.

9 **Derrida** cites the following definition in Levinas: "The home that founds possession is not a possession in the same sense as the movable goods it can collect and keep. It is possessed because it already and henceforth is hospitable for its owner. This refers us to its essential interiority, and to the inhabitant that inhabits it before every inhabitant, the welcoming one par excellence, welcoming in itself – the feminine being." (Levinas, cited in: **Derrida, Jacques** (1999): *Adieu To Emmanuel Levinas*, transl. Pascale-Anne Brault / Michael Naas, Stanford, 43) He further proposes to make of this text of Levinas "a sort of feminist manifesto." (**Derrida** 1999: 44). His reasons for this sudden and somewhat forced gesture of "taking sides" are the following: "For this text defines the welcome par excellence, the welcome or welcoming of absolute, absolutely originary, or even pre-originary hospitality, nothing less than the pre-ethical origin of ethics, on the basis of femininity. That gesture reaches a depth of essential or meta-empirical radicality that takes sexual difference into account in an ethics of emancipated from ontology. It confers the opening, if the welcome is upon the "feminine being" and not upon the fact of empirical women. The welcome, the anarchic origin of ethics, belongs to 'the dimension of femininity' and not to the empirical presence of a human being of the 'feminine sex.'" (**Derrida** 1999: 44). After this Derrida immediately asks: "Need one choose between the two incompatible readings, between an androcentric hyperbole and a feminist one?" and then notes "whatever we might speak about later, and whatever we might say about it, we would do well to remember, even if silently, that this thought of welcome, there at the opening of ethics, is indeed marked by sexual difference."

the moment of hospitality as feminine par excellence is fundamental, if (male) hospitality based on ownership would be at all possible to perform. There are at least two implications to Derrida's argument here. First, by positioning Woman at the centre of the 'pre-ethical,' as a function and condition for any ethics, Levinas denies any necessity, and hence possibility for her own independent ethical position. Woman is a vessel that would elevate man to the ethical dimension, thus, giving no thought or effort to her own ethics. Here, at the question of home or refuge, some kind of primordial ethics is being raised in its fullest, most abstract form, as a function of femininity. There is no need to deny that this is a highly honourable, sacrificial role for feminine being, – to make possible a passage to the highest ethical and otherwise impossible dimensions within a community of men – for example, friendship and a word of welcome. Shall we create a feminist manifesto from it, as Derrida proposes? Take it as a gift from man? Seductive offer, but it has no sexual relation here, no 'us – empirical women,' as Derrida and Levinas suggest. And there is a second implication: this hospitality owes nothing to the actions of embodied women. It is born out of feminine being that might well come from either woman or man (as in the interpretation of Peperzak), or from the dimension of femininity that has nothing to do with the ontological category of Women as such. Only a smile of welcome remains of the hostess herself.

As we shall see in a moment, this kind of understanding of sexual difference, when femininity or Woman is disembodied and ontologically emptied to perform a particular function, being a 'symptom' of a man's project/ion, is developed by Hegel in his foundational discussion of community. Thus, the next question we will discuss is the role of sexual difference for the possibility of community as such, and its implications for net-communities.

community FEmininity cyBErSpacE

The Hegelian notion of community, especially as exemplified in his discussion of Sophocles' Antigone, has established the dialectic between divine law (family, home, the law of female gender/womankind) and human law (city, community, state, the law of male gender/mankind). Hegel's general argument is well-known and cannot be rehearsed here in detail. What is required, however, is to outline the grip of the Hegelian system on sexual difference, for as many claim, it is still in full force in Western thought and culture.

According to Hegel, Woman plays a crucial role when she follows her family duties and defends its divine law; she presents herself as a challenge to the human law, to community and the state of men, who aspire to transgress the family and its laws. Her challenge, in effect, produces the conditions for the human (man's) law to exercise and reproduce itself. The human law, at the moment of its birth, negates the family and its laws, in order to establish itself. Thus, in the next stage, it produces it in order to repress it, to negate it as its worse enemy. In Hegel's words:

> "Since the community gets its subsistence only by breaking it upon family happiness and dissolving self-consciousness into the universal, it creates itself on what is represses [erzeugt es sich an dem, was es unterdrückt] and what is at the same time essential to it – womankind in general, its inner enemy. Womankind – the eternal irony of the community – alters by intrigue the universal purpose of government into a private end."[10]

According to Kelly Oliver, "Hegel calls womankind the everlasting irony of the community because the feminine threat is necessary to sustain the community." Since "within Hegel's scenario, the community is possible only by virtue of the sacrifice and repression of the feminine."[11]

However, while challenging the state, Hegel argues, woman does not properly comprehend her act, since for herself, she is simply and naturally performing her family duty. In a fashion somewhat resembling that of Levinas' argument regarding the hospitality of feminine being, Hegel denies woman the highest level of ethical agency – conscious ethical action – since she acts from within the realm of the family, which is the realm of the unconscious, irrational desires and duties based on blood relations. For Hegel, woman, especially the sister (Antigone), propels to act by blood ties, not out of ethical consciousness. For example, he claims that:

> "The feminine, in the form of the sister, has the highest intuitive awareness of what is ethical. She does not attain to consciousness of it, or to the objective existence of it, because the law of the family is an implicit, inner essence which is not exposed to the daylight of consciousness, but remains an inner feeling and the divine element that is exempt from an existence in the real world."[12]

10 Hegel, Georg Wilhelm Friedrich (1977[1807]): *Phenomenology of Spirit*, Oxford, 496.

11 Oliver, Kelly (1997): *Family Values: Subjects Between Nature and Culture*, London, 48.

12 Hegel 1977: 274, §457, cited in Oliver 1997: 49.

Consequently, it seems as if it is the adherence of women to the intimacy and the interiority of home that enables men to transcend it and enter the community.[13] In her early book *Speculum, Of the Other Woman*, Irigaray suggested that the Hegelian positioning of sexual difference within community weaves itself into a tautological web, in its consumption and assimilation of the feminine:

"What an amazing vicious circle in a single syllogistic system. Whereby the unconscious, while remaining unconscious, is yet supposed to know the laws of the consciousness – which is permitted to remain ignorant of it and will become even more repressed as a result of failing to respect those laws."[14]

Thus, according to Irigaray, the feminine is nothing more than the other of the same, that is, the negation of the masculine,

13 **Slavoj Zizek** transforms Hegel's position almost into 'heroic feminism': "It may seem that Hegel simply ascribes to woman the narrowness of a private point of view: woman is the community's 'inner enemy' insofar as she misapprehends the true weight of the universal purposes of public life, and is capable to conceive of them only as a means of realizing private ends. This, however, is far from being the entire picture: it is this same position of society's 'inner enemy' that renders possible the sublime ethical act of exposing the inherent limitation of the standpoint of social totality itself (Antigone)." **Zizek, Slavoj** (1995²): *The Metastases of Enjoyment: Six Essays on Woman and Causality*, New York, 148.

14 **Irigaray, Luce** (1985 [1974]): *Speculum, Of the Other Woman*, transl. Gillian Gill, Ithaca, 223.

15 **Irigaray, Luce** (1993): *Sexes and Genealogies*, transl. Gillian Gill, New York.

16 **Irigaray** 1993: 110–111.

17 See, among others, **Featherstone, Mike / Burrows, Roger**, Eds., (1996): *Cyberspace/Cyberbodies/Cyberpunk: Cultures of Technological Embodiment*, London; **Kirkup, Gill**, et. al., eds. (1999): *The Gendered Cyborg: A Reader*, London; **Braidotti, Rosi** (1997): Cyberfeminism With a Difference, see: http://www.let.ruu.nl/womens_studies/rosi/braidot1.htm [last access: 11/12/2000]; **Stone, Allucquère Rosanne** (1995): *The War of Desire and Technology at the Close of the Mechanical Age*, London.

produced by him to attain a higher order of community and ethical relation to god. And the constant reminder of her only fuels his obsession to
negate her once and again. In her essay "The Female Gender"[15] from the
collection *Sexes and Genealogies*, Irigaray evaluates the action of Antigone
as anti-woman's gesture, since in fulfilling her family duty, protecting 'the
home,' Antigone no longer serves her female gender, but

> "is working in the service of men and their pathos. [...] She already
> serves the state in that she tries to wipe away the blood shed by the state.
> The female has been taken along, taken in by the passage out of divine
> law, out of the law of nature, of life, into male human law. Antigone is
> already the desexualised representative of the other of the same. Faithful
> to her task of respecting and loving the home, careful not to pollute the
> hearth flame, she now performs only the dark side of that task, the side needed
> to establish the male order as it moves toward absolute affirmation."[16]

In the first part of this essay it was suggested that net-communities reproduce rather than modify the homogenizing tendencies of flesh communities, based on assimilation and negation of otherness despite promises of
a 'borderless bodiless internet.' Moreover, the somatophobic tendencies
of cyber-utopias indicate their negation of living and breathing otherness,
while celebrating endless multiplication of sexual, ethnic, cultural and
species' difference. This again draws them closer to flesh communities by
their homogenizing logic. Such cyber-differences are taken as symmetrical and others of the same – black, white, male, female, animal, alien,
human – are all equal and supposedly of the same dimension, that is, easily
interchangeable and replaceable. In recent literature, these disembodied
visions of cyberspace and net-communities have been extensively criticized by a number of cyber-theorists, science and cultural critics, without
technophobic overtones.[17] As we discussed earlier in this essay, it is not
simply a question of "raising consciousness" of net-community's members, for homogenizing logic as such has been a constitutive part of the
notion of community. In this section, we have seen that this homoge-
nization is based on the negation of sexual difference at its roots, of negation of the other gender's own ethical dimension.

It was initially suggested, following Derrida, that the notion of hospitality can serve as an intervention that could allow us to sustain and
nourish heterogeneous elements within community without eliminating
them. However, Derrida's notion of hospitality, following Levinas, seems
to exclude feminine otherness as an embodied and living difference, once
again denying the living and breathing feminine other to be a

heterogeneous member of the community of men and women, women and men. We have analyzed the Hegelian notion of community and its implications for the feminine other that are largely in tune with those of hospitality by Levinas and Derrida. Now the question arises as to how we can inject a living feminine other back into community, if we want it to be welcoming to the living and embodied others, and thus allowing it to practice heterogeneity? And what especially interests us is whether or not net-communities have more potential than flesh communities in relation to such a re-formulated notion of hospitality.

Injecting hospitality into community would not alter its homogenizing logic, if woman (once again) is not welcomed there as woman, but only as a "feminine dimension always already at home." Femininity modeled for men and by men to carry out a smooth passage into heterogeneous community of men, would not wash off 'solidarity-in-guilt' for this femininity of home is invited on one condition: to be the femininity of an imagined woman. And if 'empirical women' are not needed for the formation of such new heterogeneous communities, then what kind of heterogeneity are we talking about, especially since sexual difference is conceived to be the founding pre-condition for any community?

conclusion

In a few concluding remarks, I would like to propose a way of entering into this problematic of community and hospitality that would radically shift our discussion into new directions and create a new opening. When Hegel discussed community, he positioned it outside the realm of family, that is, into public space, necessarily outside of the home. When Levinas and Derrida discuss hos-

18 Irigaray, Luce (1992): *Elemental Passions*, transl. Joanne Collie / Judith Still, London, 47.

19 Irigaray 1992: 71.

pitality as feminine par excellence, they also position it spatially, territorially, within private space vis-à-vis communal, public space. Coming back to the question of community it is of special interest for us here, how the split between communal and domestic is being maintained by Levinas' discussion of hospitality, and Derrida does not seem to question the separation as well. If the other of the community is also feminine, "woman as other par excellence," she does not have any place in the sphere of community. She silently prepares a ground for community only to disappear from it. Hospitality, community and femininity seem to be linked most of all by their spatial dimension. Hence, only by re-thinking the space of femininity as home, as intimacy and refuge, and as abyssal interiority (Levinas, Hegel, Derrida, among others), can hospitality and community be again mobilized as critical categories.

In traditional formulations of space, woman is not simply assigned a place (for example, at home) – ultimately, she is home, as we have seen from Derrida's arguments. Thus, she has no space herself, for she is it, she takes any form and place. As Irigaray writes:

> "Always you assign a place to me. [...] You close me up in home and family, final, fixed walls [...] You grant me space. You grant me my space. But in so doing you have always already taken me away from my expanding place. What you intend for me is the place which is appropriate for the need you have of me. What you reveal to me is the place where you have positioned me, so that I remain available for your needs. Even if you should evict me, I have to stay there so that you can continue to be settled in your universe."[18]

Given the spatial exclusions that frustrate women's participation in the community, Irigaray suggests an alternative framework for thinking the space of and for the feminine. A crucial element in this reformulation of feminine space is the notion of mobility and 'movement as woman's habitat.'

By positioning movement as habitat, as mobile home for a possibility of feminine being to become herself again, and for the first time, it is necessary to reformulate sedentary definitions of domestic and intimate, not so much to embrace them in a new light, but rather to make it become a part of community without compromising our lives and hospitalities, to break a vicious circle of public and private spaces. To think of mobile place is to shift the question of hospitality as femininity as home into new dimensions, different from what man projects for a woman: "For me infinity means movement, the mobility of place."[19] Cyberspace and the net-communities that arise therein interestingly problematize the classical distinctions between private and public. As such, they could provide the basis for a radical and systematic re-thinking of the relationship between femininity and space. Net communities that are enacted through a radical linking of the private home and the public realm of communities outside could provide the basis for Irigaray's notion of mobile space. The mobility is afforded by the frustration of any systematic effort to demarcate the private and the public. In these mobile spaces, hospitality has to be articulated by the active ethical agency of an embodied being rather than by one who is always already hospitable.   <

BIBLIOGRAPHY
Print

Anderson, Benedict (1983): *Imagined Communities*, New York **Aristarkhova, Irina** (1999): Hosting the Other: Cyberfeminist Strategies for Net Communities. In: *Next Cyberfeminist International, Rotterdam, March 8-11, 1999*, Cornelia Sollfrank / OBN, Eds., Hamburg **Caputo, John**, Ed. (1997): *Deconstruction in a Nutshell*, Fordham **Derrida, Jacques** (1992); *The Other Heading: Reflections on Today's Europe*, transl. Pascale-Anne Brault / Michael Naas, Indiana **Derrida, Jacques** (1997): *The Villanova Roundtable: A Conversation with Jacques Derrida*. In: *Deconstruction in a Nutshell*, John Caputo, Ed., Fordham **Derrida, Jacques** (1999): *Adieu To Emmanuel Levinas*, transl. Pascale-Anne Brault / Michael Naas, Stanford **Featherstone, Mike / Burrows, Roger**, Eds., (1996): *Cyberspace/Cyberbodies/Cyberpunk: Cultures of Technological Embodiment*, London **Harpold, Terry** (1999): Dark Continents: A Critique of Internet Metageographies, In: *Postmodern Culture*, 9/2, January **Hegel, Georg Wilhelm Friedrich** (1977[1807]): *Phenomenology of Spirit*, Oxford **Irigaray, Luce** (1992): *Elemental Passions*, transl. Joanne Collie / Judith Still, London **Irigaray, Luce** (1985 [1974]): *Speculum, Of the Other Woman*, transl. Gillian Gill, Ithaca

Irigaray, Luce (1993): *Sexes and Genealogies*, transl. Gillian Gill, New York **Kirkup, Gill**, et. al., Eds. (1999): *The Gendered Cyborg: A Reader*, London **Oliver, Kelly** (1997): Family Values: Subjects Between Nature and Culture, London **Peperzak, Adriaan** (1992): *To the Other: An Introduction to the Philosophy of Emmanuel Levinas*, Purdue **Rheingold, Howard** (1993): *The Virtual Community: Homesteading on the Electronic Frontier*, New York **Stone, Allucquère Rosanne** (1995): *The War of Desire and Technology at the Close of the Mechanical Age*, London **Weber, Elisabeth**, Ed. (1995): *Derrida, Jacques Points ... Interviews*, 1974-94, transl. Peggy Kamuf et. al., Stanford **Zizek, Slavoj** (1995[2]): *The Metastases of Enjoyment: Six Essays on Woman and Causality*, New York

Web

Braidotti, Rosi (1997): Cyberfeminism With a Difference, see http://www.let.ruu.nl/womens_studies/rosi/braidot1.htm [last access: 11/12/2000]

Illustration

All Illustrations are results from a WWW search with the GOOGLE engine, entering the words: "image female smile welcome". The first site with images was the "Esprit Gala" site, announcing "an annual convention for trans-gendered folks to get together, share ideas and support, learn new skills, gain new insights and friendships and generally to have a great deal of fun." (see http://www.espritgala.org/whatis.htm [last access: 07/07/2002].) All images http://www.espritgala.com/2002_presenters.htm [last access: 07/07/2002]. (C.R.)

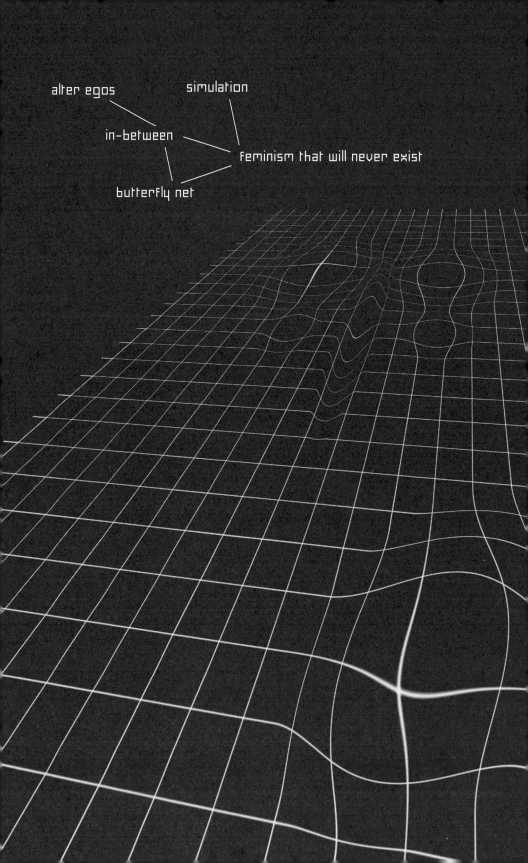

alter egos

simulation

in-between

feminism that will never exist

butterfly net

Dream-machine: Cyberfeminism

ANDREA SICK

> One might rephrase the question "where does the machine end?" to "where does reality begin and dreaming end?", if we thought of dreams as a machine that functions like a computer. Virtual Reality (VR) or so-called Cyberspace then corresponds to a dream; and dreams, according to Freud, are always present in two different states – one manifest, the other latent – even though both continuously fertilize each other.

> "Der Trauminhalt ist gleichsam in einer Bilderschrift gegeben, deren Zeichen einzeln in die Sprache der Traumgedanken zu übertragen sind."
> ["The dream-content is, as it were, presented in hieroglyphics, which symbols must be translated, one by one, into the language of the dream-thoughts."][1]

How can a translation between these two states (between perception and consciousness in Freud's terminology) be thought? And how can we translate what Freud calls dream into the world of VR or Cyberspace? These, and the question of how the "in-between" may engender the powerful label Cyberfeminism, constitute the objective of our analysis.

Dream and Computer

The suggested translation between dream and VR is by no means new –
our argument is based on tradition. As early as 1832 Ralph Waldo Emerson remarked in his diary: "Dreams and beasts are two keys by which we
are to find out the secrets of our nature. All mystics use them. They are
like comparative anatomy. They are our test objects."[2] Both are considered
as experimental objects to explore what Emerson calls "nature" but
which, in the wake of Artificial Intelligence, may also be referred to as
"model or structure" and in terms of psychoanalysis, "the Unconscious."

Taking this assumption as her starting point, the popular sociologist
of science at MIT Sherry Turkle claims that if Emerson had lived in the
20th century, he would definitely have added the computer as another test
object apart from dreams and beasts:

> "Dreams and beasts were the test objects for Freud and Darwin, the test
> objects for modernism. In the past decade, the computer has become the
> test object for postmodernism. The computer takes us beyond a world of
> dreams and beasts because it enables us to contemplate mental life that
> exists apart from bodies. It enables us to contemplate dreams that do not
> need beasts. The computer is an evocative object that causes boundaries
> to be renegotiated."[3]

If this were the case, the computer would be the key to explore the
"secrets of nature," which is what the suggested translation, transferred to
Emerson's test structure, implicates.

---

1 **Freud, Sigmund** (1972 [1900]): *Die Traumdeutung*, Studienausgabe, vol. 2,
   Alexander Mitscherlich / Angela Richards / James Strachey, Eds., Frankfurt/M,
   280; **Freud, Sigmund** (1913 [1900]), *The Interpretation of Dreams*, transl. A.
   A. Brill, online version, http://www.psywww.com/books/interp/toc.htm [last
   access: 01/27/2004].

2 **Porte, Joel** (1982): *Emerson in His Journals*, Cambridge, Mass., 81; quoted
   in: **Turkle, Sherry** (1995): *Life on the Screen, Identity in the Age of the Internet*,
   New York / London / Toronto / Sydney / Tokyo /Singapore, 22, 274.

3 **Turkle** 1995: 22.

4 "It (Computer, A.S.) is a mind, that is not yet a mind. It is inanimate yet
   interactive. It does not think, yet neither is it external to thought […] we
   think we can think. But can it think?" **Turkle** 1995: 22.

5 **Turkle** 1995: 26.

6 "We have used our relationships with technology to reflect on the human."
   Turkle 1995: 25.

01

Turkle's assumption therefore is that dreams, beasts and the computer enable us to learn more about the "secrets of nature" – including the thought processes of our brain[4]. In this construction, beasts are thought of as the embodiment of these processes, their representation. Whereas dream and beast seem to be bound to a "body" in Turkle's conception, the computer makes an experience possible which is beyond that of beast and even dream: it enables the contemplation of mental life, which as a result reveals itself as detached from the body. Her notion that the computer can broaden our horizon and open up new realms of experience is further underlined in the following statement:

> "Computer screens are the new location for our fantasies, both erotic and intellectual, we are using life on computer screens to become comfortable with new ways of thinking about evolution, relationships, sexuality, politics, and identity."[5]

As a logically consistent development of this thought, the computer is recreated as an autonomous machine. Because of its potential for "non-physical" experience, as Turkle calls it, it is particularly well suited for "reflection on the human,"[6] thereby going beyond the possibilities of both dream and beast.

The overlapping comparison between brain and computer on the one hand, while positioning the computer as a mechanism apart from the body in opposition to dream and beast on the other (thus intersecting the biological and the logical model), is however not reflected upon. The opposition of body and bodilessness is here as questionable as the exponentiation of experience ascribed to the computer. Is it not true that both dream and computer are confronted with the question of identity in much the same way? Who is the dreamer in this constellation? Who actually creates this "experience of nature," a concept that

02

Turkle first attaches to dream and beast and then transfers to the computer? And what is meant by "nature"?[7]

If "nature" (like the soul) is the mechanical construction of a dream – the dream potentially being a computer – then the dream will have to be considered, in the context dream-work and its technical proceedings, as an assembled (therefore to be disassembled as well) and productive machine. The connection between dream and beast would only be given if "the beast" is thought of as practically instinct-driven, acting without law or morals – just as compulsive as a machine (imbued with spirit). Such a link between machine/computer, beast and dream could only function in an

7 In Turkle's design nature appears, aptly, as a model for the computer. As a simultaneously biological and logical concept (derived from the ability to learn), it remains vague however. From here follows, not only for Turkle "the question of whether an artifact can be a life." **Turkle** 1995: 25.

8 On the amalgam of human-machine in the cyborg, see: **Hayles, Katherine** (1995): The life cycle of cyborgs, in: *The Cyborg Handbook*, Hables Gray, Bris, ed., New York / London, 323ff.

9 **Stryker, Tim** (1991): Ist die Wirklichkeit etwas Virtuelles. In: *Cyberspace, Ausflüge in Virtuelle Wirklichkeiten*, Manfred Waffender, ed., Reinbek/ Hamburg, 240.

10 **Lacan, Jacques** (1996): Der Blick als Objekt klein a, Die Spaltung von Auge und Blick. In: *Die vier Grundbegriffe der Psychoanalyse*, transl. into German Norbert Haas, Freiburg, 82.

"if…then" mode: a distinction to the human would always be a constitutive precondition for such a connection. The mechanisms that differentiate human and machine, as well as their "amalgamation"[8] might be exposed by means that classify them as body or machine.

The Butterfly Dream: Who does the flying here?

A dream vision frequently quoted in psychoanalytic and media theory shall illustrate the problem of constituting the subject and the impossibility of giving an unambiguous answer to the question "who does the dreaming here?" It is apparent that the question, here directed at the "nature" of the dream, could be translated into "who does the surfing/playing here?" or even better "where does the machine end?", again under the condition that the computer functions like a dream. In this dream, the subject is a butterfly:

03

> "Once upon a time, Zhuang Zhou dreamt he was a butterfly, aimlessly fluttering here and there, following his intuition. Of Zhuang Zhou he knew nothing. Suddenly he awoke and immediately he was Zhuang Zhou again. Now he [who now?, A.S.] can't tell whether Zhou had dreamt he was a butterfly or the butterfly had dreamt he was Zhou."[9]

Tschuang-Tse, as the protagonist is also called by Lacan, can, on waking up, ask himself whether the butterfly was not dreaming he was Tschuang-Tse. To Lacan the preconditions are given:

> "Der Beweis, daß solange er Schmetterling ist, ihm nicht in den Sinn kommt, sich zu fragen, ob er als aufgewachter Tschuang-Tse nicht der Schmetterling sei, der zu sein er eben träumt." ["Proof is that as long as he is the butterfly it does not occur to him to ask whether he might no longer be – as the awakened Tschuang Tse – the very same butterfly he is dreaming of being."][10]

The question that imposes itself is therefore: who is dreaming here? Is it Zhou (Tse) or the butterfly? There is no position from which the question can be definitively answered. Therefore, Lacan can also say for Tschuang-Tse: "Aufgewacht ist er Tschuang-Tse für die anderen und ist in deren Schmetterlingsnetz gefangen." ["He woke up as Tschuang-Tse for the others and is caught in their butterfly net."][11]

So there seems to be no certainty as to where so-called reality begins and dream ends. The existence of an identity seems even less certain: Tschuang-Tse (or Zhuang Zhou) dreams he is a butterfly or the butterfly dreams he is Tschuang-Tse. It always depends on the position for the others in the "butterfly net." In psychoanalysis however they are never one: Tschuang-Tse and the butterfly always consist of their mutual translation and perception as such.

Masquerades in MUDs Multi User Domains

This precarious constellation with respect to constituting a subject in dreams shall now be compared to the structure of MUDs, which also served as the starting point for Turkle's argument. MUDs are regarded as

---

11 **Lacan** 1996: 83.

12 **Turkle** 1995: 15.

13 See **Spreen, Dirk** (1997): Was verspricht der Cyborg? In: *Ästhetik und Kommunikation – Online-Verstrickungen, Immanenzen und Ambivalenzen*, Dieter Hofmann-Axthelm, ed., no. 96, vol. 26, Berlin, 86.

14 **Kuni, Verena** (2000): Arbeiten an der "Schnittstelle Geschlecht": Trans/Gender – Utopien dies- und jenseits der Interfaces, in: *Frauen Kunst Wissenschaft – Alternative Körper*, Angela Rosenthal / Christina Threuter, eds., Marburg, 13ff.

15 See **Ackers, Susanne** (1999): Cyberspace is empty – who's afraid of avatars? In: *Next Cyberfeminist International, Old Boys Network, Rotterdam, March 8-11, 1999*, Cornelia Sollfrank / Old Boys Network, eds., Hamburg, 100.

16 Turkle supposes that identity for gender is the starting point for identity in the net and does not originate in the "novel." This would imply that an original identity of gender exits. See: **Angerer, Marie-Luise** (1999): *Body Options*, Vienna, 93–94. To Angerer it here becomes clear that discourse introduces a decisive distinction between self and subject. The subject is here split, even though it is traced back to a unified one. But such a retraction is a belated construction.

17 See **Angerer** 1999: 94.

a new type of community in the computer-related world of communication, particularly the Internet. These worlds were originally text-based, but are now frequently represented graphically as well. After logging in, the participant must first create an avatar which then interacts with the avatars of other participants. New identities are continuously established with such avatars. They can also communicate in the shape of autonomous bots (a word derived from robot), small programs that act and write as semi-autonomous alter egos, also known as "agents," in the MUD.[12] In this respect they can also be understood as cyborgs, which denote in terms of information technology the reproduction of what is defined as a human being.[13] It is imagined that these new identities circulate in a multi-layered net in which the dissolution, or rather amalgamation, of the dividing line between VR and RL (Real Life), between user and machine, old and new is implored. It is precisely this prognosis that makes the game so appealing. Masquerades can take place: avatar meets avatar.[14] The term avatar though, can be applied more generally to the fictional figures in chat rooms, fake names in e-mail correspondences and similar constructions.[15] Here it is possible to create ever-newer identities, sometimes using a pre-defined selection – those specified in style sheets for example – partly to facilitate a more bureaucratic management of these created identities.

It is frequently argued that users create multiple personalities in MUDs, personalities they would like to be in so-called RL. Turkle also designs a structure of multiple net-personalities and Marie-Luise Angerer has interpreted this construction in a psychoanalytic context as relating to an "ideal self."[16] At first these structures seem comparable to the tangle in the butterfly net of the dream. However, neither the net, nor the dream figures simply correspond to an ideal self.[17] For then it would always have to be clarified from which position it is appropriate to speak, Tschuang-Tse's or from the butterfly's.[18] An original identity would have to be assumed. Yet, if the one (identity) is caught in the net of the other, the figures in a dream cannot be interpreted as an 'ideal self' just like that.

Butterfly Net

What could be the meaning of a butterfly net? Independent of any biological definitions, the net might be what the butterfly uses to capture Tschuang-Tse or a net consisting of many different butterflies. If it is defined always as that of the others, then Tschuang-Tse can not derive his identity as Tschuang-Tse from his butterfly.

04

From the impossibility of answering the question "who is dreaming?", it can also be concluded that dream and putative reality are as indistinguishable from each another as Cyberspace is from "true reality." At best, they can only be constituted by means of the other's discourse, a discourse that knows how to articulate the desire to be indistinguishable. For questions pertaining to what is 'real' already appear somewhat misplaced with respect to the dream – at least not specifiable, since in the dream everything is 'ever so real'. Consequently, we can say that translation events can be articulated and deciphered. However, such a decoding always participates in the process of transition – between perception and consciousness – and sides, however briefly, with one or the other.

So with the dream we establish a theoretical platform and an experiment: a place where dividing lines become impossible to define, identities and gender dissolve, fuse or present themselves more clearly in translation, only then becoming possible to represent and identifiable. A stage constituting the in-between as a space *"between perception and consciousness."*[19] This stage can emerge in dreams as well as in Cyberspace

---

18 More suitable to the idea of the butterfly net is the image of Zizek, where identities are associated with onion skins that have at their center nothing but more onion skins.

19 **Lacan** 1996: 82.

20 **Lacan** 1996: 82.

21 **Lacan** 1996: 83.

22 E.g. **Tipler, Frank** (1992): *Die Physik der Unsterblichkeit*, Munich.

– with Lacan a reality in waiting, "en souffrance."[20] A place of displacement and metaphor – translations in other words.

The means of representation in dream and so-called VR are also comparable: neither can be thought independently of a translating process and both are capable of disclosing "the longing of the subject" in the context of dream construction. Lacan asks:

> "Wie kann der Traum als Träger des Begehrens des Subjekts etwas produzieren, was das Trauma immer wieder hochkommen läßt – wenn nicht sein Wahres, so doch jener Schirm, der auf es hindeutet als auf ein hinter ihm Liegendes?" ["How can the dream, as vehicle of desire/longing, produce what the trauma keeps conjuring up – if not its true object then the screen that envelops it and points towards it as something underneath?"][21]

Particularly in Freud's analysis of dreams, a process emerges within the process of deciphering – that translates sign by sign almost like pictographic writing – a stage for the "between" where continuous translations never work out one to one. For the distinction between dream and reality, waking and sleeping/dreaming can only be described as a process of translation that "condenses" and "displaces." The dream can only be thought in translation, not in the hallucination of synthesis. A synthesis could only be remembered as part of the manifest dream-content. The same can be said of VR, the screen of which also raises great expectations that would disappear in synthesis.

Avatars and Dream Figures

Concrete examples of the means of representation that are utilized in Freud's work on dreams may serve to illustrate this – namely the dream figures which, transferred to the context of Cyberspace are here known as bots and avatars, similar to dream figures not only in their presentation but in their mode of construction as well. In the case of Freudian dream-work, different identities are also called upon, but here they are fused, condensed and layered in turn to produce another "collective person" whose various layers (or aspects) are only exposed in analysis (i.e., in the discourse of the dream). Such a reconstruction is possible in the case of MUDs, if it were related to an "identity" intended to remain concealed. In the presentations and visions of a "between," cyborgs are also described as dream figures: kids dream of morphing cyber-reptiles, scientists dream of immortality (e.g. Tipler[22]). Although the model of the butterfly net could apply to both cyberspace and dream, there are important distinctions to be made: Freud's concept of dream is layered and condensed and his amalgams always have a typification in mind, at least if one thinks of the amalgamated photographs of Galton that Freud uses to illustrate his ideas by means of comparison. In the Internet on the other hand, we are confronted with a circulating net of repetitive identities: avatars and bots, made concrete in the idea of the "cyborg" as an amalgam of human and machine. For this type of layering the constructions are merged, and thus are not imagined as freely circulating.

> "Das Gesicht, das ich im Traume sehe, ist gleichzeitig das meines Freundes R. und das meines Onkels. Es ist wie eine Mischphotographie von Galton, der, um Familienähnlichkeiten zu eruieren, mehrere Gesichter auf die nämliche Platte photographieren ließ." ["The face that I saw in the dream was at once my friend R.'s and my uncle's. It was like one of Galton's composite photographs. (In order to bring out family likeness, Galton used to photograph several faces on the same plate.)"][23]

In order to further specify this constellation (here transferred to photography) in the context of dreams let us look at an example: one of the dreams Freud himself dreamt, and one that has been analyzed and retold again and again, has itself produced detailed composites. It is the so-called "Irma dream":

> "*Irmas Klagen. Schmerzen im Hals, Leib und Magen, es schnürt sie zusammen.* Schmerzen im Magen gehörten zum Symptomkomplex meiner Patientin (sie ist Irma, A.S.), sie waren aber nicht vordringlich; sie klagte eher über Empfindungen von Übelkeit und Ekel. Schmerzen im Hals, Schnüren in der Kehle spielt bei ihr keine Rolle. Ich wundere mich, warum ich mich zu dieser Auswahl der Symptome entschlossen habe, kann es auch für den Moment nicht finden. *Sie sieht bleich und gedunsen aus.* Meine Patientin (Irma, A.S.) war immer rosig. Ich vermute, daß sich hier eine andere Person ihr vorschiebt." ["*Irma's complaint: pains in her throat and abdomen and stomach; it was choking her.* Pains in the stomach were among my patient's symptoms but were not very prominent; she complained more of feelings of nausea and disgust. Pains in the throat and abdomen and constriction of the throat played scarcely any part in her illness. I wondered why I decided upon this choice of symptoms in the dream but could not think of an explanation at the moment. *She looked*

---

23 **Freud** 1972: 155; **Freud, Sigmund** (1976 [1900]), *The Interpretation of Dreams*, The Pelican Freud Library, transl. James Strachey, 219.

24 **Freud** 1972: 128–129; **Freud** 1976: 284.

25 **Freud** 1972: 294; **Freud** 1976: 399, emphasis A.S.

pale and fluffy. My patient always had a rosy complexion. I began to suspect that someone else was being substituted for her."][24]

Freud himself interprets this composite construction even more precisely:

"Die Hauptperson des Trauminhalts ist die Patientin Irma, die mit den ihr im Leben zukommenden Zügen gesehen wurde und also zunächst *sich selbst* darstellt. Die Stellung aber, in welcher ich sie beim Fenster untersuchte, ist von einer Erinnerung an eine andere Person hergenommen, von jener Dame, mit der ich meine Patientin vertauschen möchte, wie die Traumgedanken zeigen…" ["The principle figure in the dream-content was my patient Irma. She appeared with the features which were hers in real life, and thus, in the first instance, *represented herself.* But the position in which I examined her by the window was derived from someone else, the lady for whom, as the dream-thoughts showed, I wanted to exchange my patient."][25]

The persons that will act in this dream are condensed into the composite image 'Irma'. Irma becomes the representative of these other "sacrificed persons."

Freud now introduces a second possibility: particular features of two or more persons are contracted in the dream-image.

"Solcherart ist der Dr. M. meines Traumes entstanden, er trägt den Namen des Dr. M., spricht und handelt wie er, seine leibliche Charakteristik und seine Leiden sind die einer andere Person, meines ältesten Bruders; ein einziger Zug, das blasse Aussehen, ist doppelt determiniert, indem er in der Realität beider Personen gemeinsam ist." ["Such is the nature of Dr. M. of my dream; his name is that of Dr. M., he speaks and acts like him, but his physical attributes and ailments are those of a different person, my elder brother's; a single attribute, the pale appearance, is determined twice over in that they apply to both in reality."][26]

As seen, two different procedures can be detected: identification and composition. According to Freud, identification consists of the fact that only a single person, joined by a common attribute to another in dreams, is represented in the content of a dream, while the second or other person is suppressed with respect to the dream: "The screening person however enters into all the relations and situations that originate in the person who is being screened."[27] An example of this is the composite image of Irma. Could this mean, transferred to the world of communication on the net, that persons are created which disguise completely different persons? Perhaps the composite image of the participants and the disguised persons is the very one that is discovered in the world of communication. These two models can only be dismantled by means of deciphering these supposed composite images.

A composite construction, and hence a new entity with respect to the concept of dream work, is created by contracting features that are not common. Freud calls this entity a "mixed" or "composite person" in the sense of a nodal point from which a number of different persons can be "activated." A dream figure, for example, can have the name of one person and the features of another. Thus the figure could well be imagined as having different sexes. The purpose of these composites is threefold according to Freud: something in common is represented, something in common and displaced is represented, something desired as common is represented. Despite these differences, both composite images and identifications can be seen as means of representation the dream utilizes to emphasize similarity, agreement and community. One could also be so bold as to describe them with the Freudian concept of "exchange" in the

---

26 Freud 1972: 318; Freud 1911, online-version.
27 Freud 1972: 318; Freud 1911, online-version.
28 Freud 1972: 320; Freud 1911, online-version.

sense of barter. Supposing that the "I" is a person, "I" can also enter into the exchange:

> "Wo im Trauminhalt nicht mein Ich, sondern nur eine fremde Person vorkommt, darf ich ruhig annehmen, daß mein Ich durch Identifizierung hinter jener Person versteckt ist. Ich darf mein Ich ergänzen. [...] Es gibt auch andere Träume, in denen mein Ich nebst anderen Personen vorkommt, die sich durch Lösung der Identifizierung wiederum als mein Ich enthüllen." ["In cases where not my ego but only a strange person occurs in the dream-content, I may safely assume that by means of identification my ego is concealed behind that person. I am permitted to supplement my ego [...] There are also dreams in which my ego appears together with other persons who, when the identification is resolved, once more show themselves to be my ego."][28]

The "interchange" enables an almost infinite circulation. One might think that the computer, or rather what VR has to offer, imitates what the dream has managed to do for a long time already. Strategies of simulation manifest in the dream where they aspire to being interchangeable (where they can no longer be distinguished) and boundless.

07

08

How Dreams Come True

During this process of screening, disguise and exchange however, nodal points are created in the manifest content, dream-figures related by a common feature are peeled in analysis, lines are drawn, strings are isolated, the infinite regress is briefly interrupted. Translation processes are specified through condensation and displacement, revealed through the relation between manifest dream-content and dream-thought. The thesis of Freud's book on dreams would be that in the dream, a wish-fulfillment in disguise always seeks to find its way.

Avatars in Cyberspace, whether they are layered and circulating or always have been circulating, can thus be understood as representations of such a wish-fulfillment. It can therefore be assumed that all the identities with their disguised, displaced and censored facets are wish-fulfillments. Not wish-fulfillment of a user, as Turkle suggests, but wish-fulfillments that are only revealed in the process of a continuous, infinite peeling, that can never be attached to central unit or heart and which only present themselves in disguise. If the disguise is lifted, the wish will disappear, as will the possibility to represent its fulfillment. For even in the figurative sense we can never know who flutters into the butterfly net of the other. Crashed into consciousness, the dream figures that circulate in the dream-machine of Cyberspace are hardly ever conceived as wish-fulfillment; here they revolve, censored and disguised by a mechanism that constantly seeks to withhold the wish-fulfillment, and the secret desires threaten to reveal, from consciousness. In the discourse that summons their story for analysis, the figures become inscribed into a wish for indistinguishability and boundlessness that on the other hand presupposes the possibility to distinguish, and plants coordinates into the butterfly net.

The wish therefore figures in the dream as something that "shows" and represents as well – though in disguise.[29] What remains is the question, how this disguise of the wish and its fulfillment is accomplished in the dream. According to Freud's theory, all impulses of desire have their origin in the unconscious. Dream-work succeeds in substituting all embarrassing fantasies with opposite ones, and in suppressing the uncomfortable effects that go with it. When the dream derives from a comparative relation to its own latent content – a displacement into the opposite for example – we can speak of a disguise or censorship as Freud calls it elsewhere, a disguise that intends to conceal the other emotion.[30] How does the wish disguise itself? In "friend R.'s" dream the same is equipped with an exaggerated affection that verges on the embarrassing. This embarrassment prevents any further questioning and thus a revelation of the dreamer's actual wish to abuse friend R. as an idiot.[31] Wish-fulfillment here presents itself in the guise of affection. In this manner,

29 **Freud** 1972: 525; **Freud** 1911, online-version. Freud distinguishes between dreams that present themselves as obvious wish-fulfillment (i.e., dreams of children) and those where the wish-fulfillment is disguised, often with all available means.
30 **Freud** 1972: 158; **Freud** 1976: 217.
31 **Freud** 1972: 161; **Freud** 1976: 220.
32 **Freud** 1972: 527; **Freud** 1976: 704.

analysis can present the masquerade to discourse and reading matter. It is the engine for translation-work. The embarrassing fantasies that can be part of a wish-fulfillment therefore issue, in altered shape, into the manifest dream-content.

If dream and Cyberspace are wish-fulfillment, then the wish – to revolve without limitations in space for example – is also a trigger for dreams, a trigger for virtual worlds. However, Freud says,

> "[…] der bewußte Wunsch (ist) nur dann Traumerreger, wenn es ihm gelingt, einen gleichlautenden unbewußten zu wecken, durch den er sich verstärkt." ["[…] a conscious wish can only become a dream-instigator if it succeeds in awakening an unconscious wish with the same tenor and in obtaining reinforcement from it."][32]

And the screen is up again.

Dream-Machine Cyberfeminism

If dream and Cyberspace were wish-fulfillment, then Cyberfeminism could reveal itself as a platform that disguises, displaces and represents the wishes of feminism, a feminism that, as such, has never existed nor will it ever exist, in whatever varied shapes it might present itself. The masquerade of a masquerade would be born. Cyberfeminism would be more than an up-to-date version of feminism in the age of New Media.

"We are all dreaming cyborg dreams" one might sum up, and Cyberfeminism is one of them. However, it is also the dream-machine that lets all the dreams and figures circulate, the machine that deciphers and constitutes wishes: Cyberfeminism might make explicit what will have been implicit in feminism. Cyberspace, like the dream, would not be thinkable without wish-fulfillment as its engine. Freud's dream-work, which puts into words a reading between wishes and "facts," offers a diverse instrument to decipher cyberfeminist disguises, to discover the screen, put up new ones and bravely keep the (dream-)machine running. That is what this text wishes to prove.   <

TRANSLATION: Michael Timmermann

BIBLIOGRAPHY
Print

Angerer, Marie-Luise (1999): *Body Options*, Vienna **Ackers, Susanne** (1999): Cyberspace is empty – who's afraid of avatars? In: *Next Cyberfeminist International, Old Boys Network, Rotterdam, March 8-11, 1999*, Hamburg, Cornelia Sollfrank / Old Boys Network, Eds., Hamburg **Freud, Sigmund** (1972 [1900]): *Die Traumdeutung*, Studienaugabe, vol. 2, Alexander Mitscherlich / Angela Richards / James Strachey, Eds., Frankfurt/M, **Freud, Sigmund** (1976 [1900], *The Interpretation of Dreams*, The Pelican Freud Library, transl. James Strachey **Hayles, Katherine** (1995): The life cycle of cyborgs, in: *The Cyborg Handbook*, Hables Gray, Bris, ed., New York / London, 323 ff. **Kuni, Verena** (2000): Arbeiten an der "Schnittstelle Geschlecht": Trans/Gender – Utopien dies- und jenseits der Interfaces," in: *Frauen Kunst Wissenschaft – Alternative Körper*, Angela Rosenthal, Christina Threuter, eds., Marburg **Lacan, Jacques** (1996): Der Blick als Objekt klein a, Die Spaltung von Auge und Blick. In: *Die vier Grundbegriffe der Psychoanalyse*, transl. into German Norbert Haas, Freiburg **Porte, Joel** (1982): *Emerson in His Journals*, Cambridge, Mass. **Spreen, Dirk** (1997): Was verspricht der Cyborg? In: *Ästhetik und Kommunikation – Online-Verstrickungen, Immanenzen und Ambivalenzen*, Dieter Hofmann-Axthelm, ed., no. 96, vol. 26, Berlin **Stryker, Tim** (1991): Ist die Wirklichkeit etwas Virtuelles. In: *Cyberspace, Ausflüge in Virtuelle Wirklichkeiten*, Manfred Waffender, ed., Reinbek/Hamburg, 240 **Tipler, Frank** (1992): *Die Physik der Unsterblichkeit*, Munich **Turkle, Sherry** (1995): *Life on the Screen, Identity in the Age of the Internet*, New York / London / Toronto / Sydney / Tokyo / Singapore

Web

Freud, Sigmund (1913 [1900]), *The Interpretation of Dreams*, transl. A. A. Brill, online version, http://www.psywww.com/books/interp/toc.htm [last access: 01/27/2004]

Illustration

01-03 The Field Museum, http://www.field-museum.org [last access: 06/08/2002]
04 Northrop Grumman UCAV, http://users.chariot.net.au/~theburfs/URucav.html [last access: 06/08/2002]
05 Angel, Heather (1982): *Naturfotografie*, London / Munich, 123.
06 Unicraft models, http://www.geocities.com/uni1ua/bigph/ucav.htm [last access: 01/27/2004]
07 archive of the author
08 Unicraft models, http://www.geocities.com/unicraftmodels/uniphot.htm [last access: 06/08/ 2002]

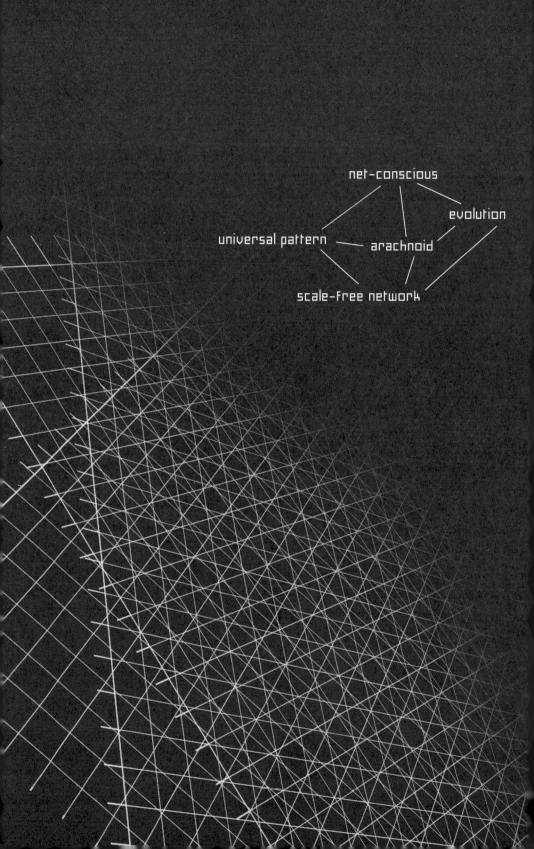

IF [X] …
THEN [Y] …
ELSE [XXN]

HELENE VON OLDENBURG

> Though Cyberfeminism is an accumulation of theoretical and artistic strategies and not a homogeneous movement, it is not only a phenomenon of the Zeitgeist at the end of a millennium; it is even more a transitional stage into a future that is net-based and thus arachnoid, spider-like.

This orientation towards the future finds its equivalent in the evolution of feminism into cyberfeminism. Cyberfeminism is the update of feminism. It defines a new stage of feminism with a markedly higher arachnoid potential. For the first time, feminism openly embraces its net-dependency and outs itself as an arachnoid movement. The gradual takeover of cultural dominance through arachnids is supported by biological, technical and psychical dispositions and constellations that often bear a female context. As a transition into a net-conscious existence, cyberfeminism offers a site and a practice. Cyberfeminism can therefore be seen as a short-term movement that demonstrates no apprehensions of the future and remains open for technical, social and cultural innovations, all the while consciously pursuing arachnoid strategies.[1]

IF EVERYTHING IN OUR WORLD IS OF NET-BASED STRUCTURES...

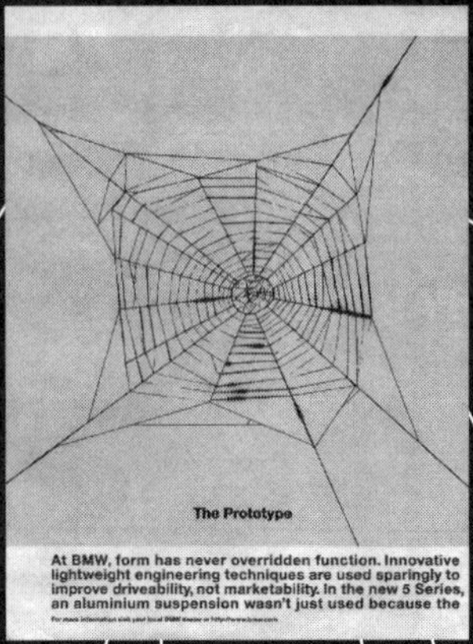
The Prototype
At BMW, form has never overridden function. Innovative lightweight engineering techniques are used sparingly to improve driveability, not marketability. In the new 5 Series, an aluminium suspension wasn't just used because the

01

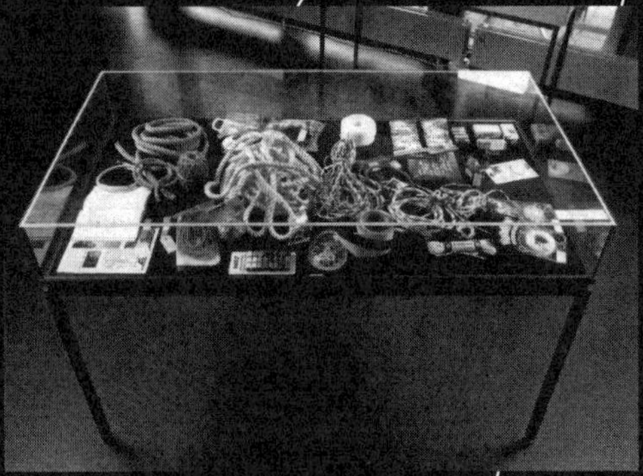

03

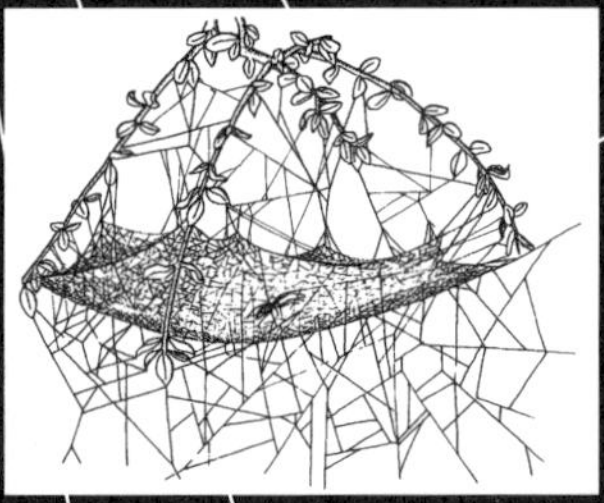

06

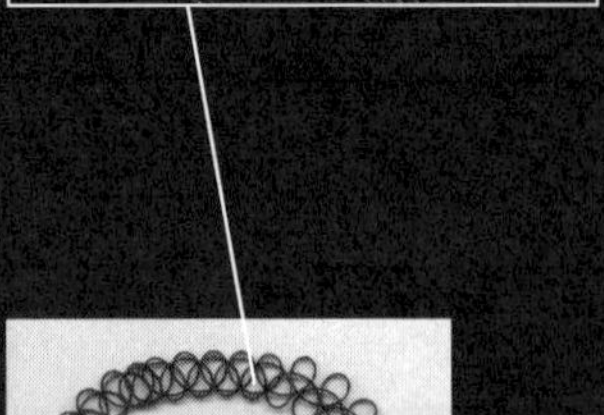

09

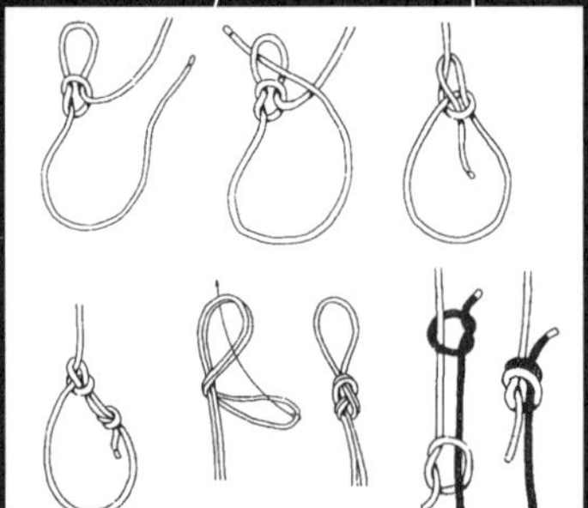

05

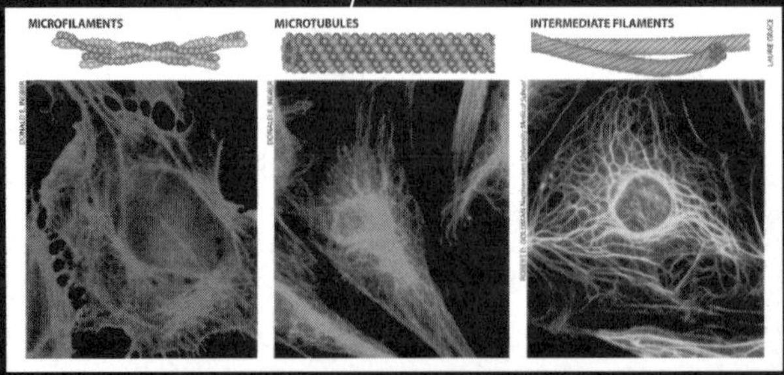
MICROFILAMENTS
MICROTUBULES
INTERMEDIATE FILAMENTS

08

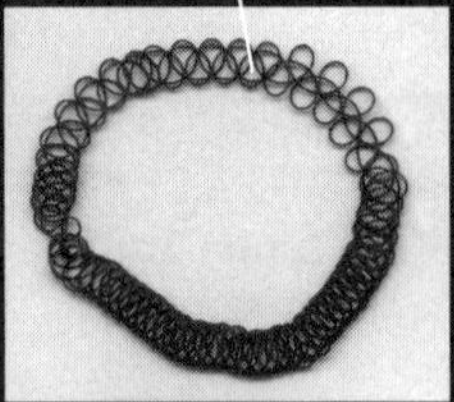

04

Albert-László Barabási found that sites on the Web form a network with unique mathematical properties. In itself, this may not seem very profound, but it soon emerged that these properties were not unique to the Web. We are surrounded by networks: social, sexual and professional. Ecosystems are networks, and even our bodies – and the pathogens that lay us low – are kept alive by networks of chemicals. Barabási and others have found that many of these networks have the same architecture as the Web.

11

A net consists of threads, knots and holes. There is no limitation to scale. Nets differ in materials, measurements, proportions and even exist as immaterial forms.

02

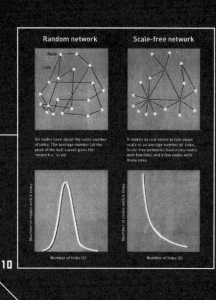

10

07

13

A Universal Pattern: The geodesic structure found within the cytoskeleton is a classic example of a pattern that is found everywhere in nature, at many different size scales. Spherical groups of carbon atoms called buckminsterfullerenes or buckyballs, along with viruses, enzymes, organelles, cells and even small organisms, all exhibit geodesic forms.

12

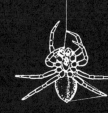

...THEN OUR FUTURE WILL BE DOMINATED BY AN ARACHNOID SPECIES.[2]

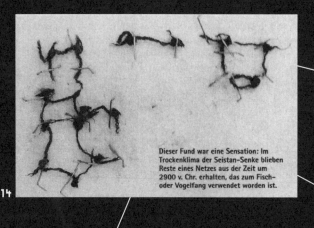

Dieser Fund war eine Sensation: Im Trockenklima der Seistan-Senke blieben Reste eines Netzes aus der Zeit um 2900 v. Chr. erhalten, das zum Fisch- oder Vogelfang verwendet worden ist.

14

15

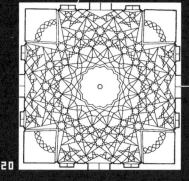

20

16

18

internet cafe

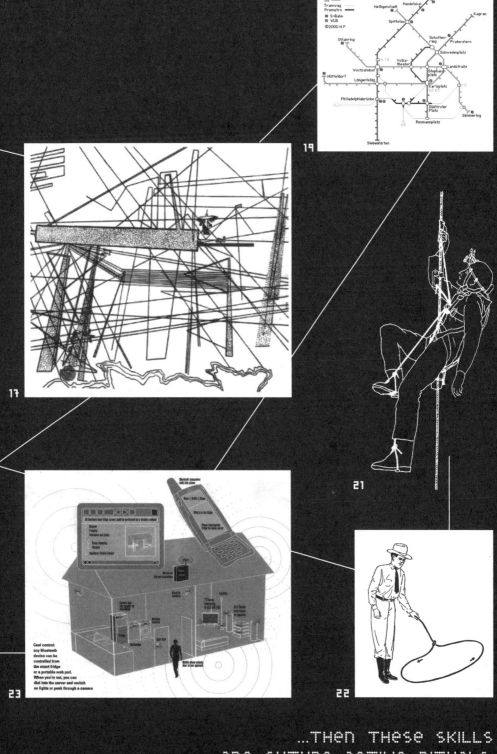

19

17

21

23

22

...THEN THESE SKILLS
ARE FUTURE-ACTIVE RITUALS.

24

25

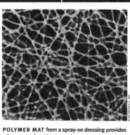

POLYMER MAT from a spray-on dressing provides
a framework for skin regrowth.

27

bild der wissenschaft

4 · 2001

Die Weltsicht
des Klon-Revolutionärs

Eine einzige
Schlappe für die
Forscher

BIG BROTHER 2001
Warum Ihre Privatsphäre in Gefahr ist
Wie Sie sich schützen können

31

New technology special: **3G · Tele-Immersion · The Grid · Bluetooth · Net cars**

NewScientist

THIS WAY
TO THE FUTURE
The wireless revolution is about to change your life

First the fridge, then the world
Welcome to the holodeck
That's not a cat, it's a probe
Owe all the world's computers
From phone to you
The triumph of pen and paper
Highway insomnia
Truffle hunters go electronic

Fiber engineers, meet thy master.

30

Which media mergers
make sense?   The dangerous cult of
common stocks

Forbes

Along came
the spiders
The busy creatures
who will guide you
through the Internet

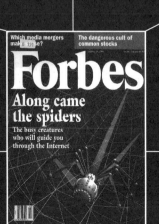

[How quickly do new technologies take off?]

**Frantic pace: the time it takes for ideas
to spread is getting shorter and shorter.
WAP phones will outpace their predecessors**

32

...THEN THE FUTURE BEGINS TODAY.

Building the Better Bug

*Inserting new genes into a few specific insect species
could stop some infectious diseases, benefit agriculture and
produce innovative materials*

by David A. O'Brochta and Peter W. Atkinson

33

Gen-Ziegen sollen Spinnfadenprotein
als Industrierohstoff liefern

242

35

36

A team led by investigators at the
Canadian company Nexia Biotechnologies has coaxed mammalian
cells into producing spinnable pro-
teins by equipping them with spider
silk genes. After harvesting the pro-
teins, the scientists spun them from a
water-based solution into fine, silken
threads. The synthetic strands possess the strength and toughness –
although not quite the tenacity – of
spider-made dragline silks, the ones
the creatures use in their web frames
and safety lines.[3]

The gender diversity which we'll find with arachnids of the future is due
to different sets of sex chromosomes. [...] The sex chromosomes of spiders are X chromosomes. Contrary to insects or mammals spiders possess no Y chromosome. Aside from the 'regular' chromosomes (the
autosomes, A), two X chromosomes represent the sex chromosomes.
Whereas female spiders possess a dual set of these X chromosomes
(2A+X1X1X2X2), male spiders have but a single set (2A+X1X2). Consequently, after meiosis the egg cells have one set of X chromosomes,
but the sperm cells are of two types: either they likewise possess one
set or they lack sex chromosomes altogether (A + 0). Sex determination is thus dependent on the type of sperm cell that fertilizes the egg.
A combination of reproduction techniques like genetic engeneering in
combination with artificial insemination, parthenogenesis and cloning
made it possible to multiply the set of sex chromosomes: XXn. This
results in lots of different sex forms, though they all are still arachnoid.

34

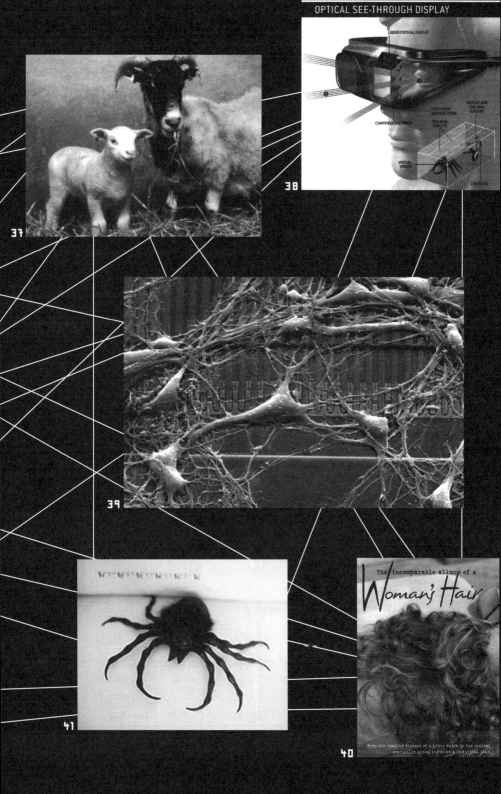

37

38

39

41

The incomparable allure of a
Woman's Hair

40

...THEN WHAT WILL BECOME OF FEMALE?

Illustrations and citations (with exception of 02 and 03) are part of the *Arachnomantic Archive*, established by us. The *Arachnomantic Archive* comprises up to 5000 images, objects, texts, and videos on the topic of net-based structures responsible for our arachnoid future. The digits and characters in < > refer to the structuring of the *Arachnomantic Archive*:

Ev = Evolution, Ge = Gender, KF = Klebfäden (Sticky Threads), Kn = Knoten (Knots), LF = Lauffäden (Draglines), NG = Netzgeometrie (Web Geometry), NN = Neuronale Netze (Neuronal Webs), Pk = Präkognition (Precognition), RN = Radnetze (Orb Webs), Rt = Rituale (Rituals), FF = Fangfäden (Trap Threads), Sh = Shape, SpA = Spinnapparat (Spinning Apparatus), SpM = Spider Museum, Te = Technologie (Technology).

Illustration

01 BMW (1997): The Prototype. In: *Air France*, vol. 5, *< 2547 Te >*

02 Oldenburg, Helene von (2000): Der Knotenaspekt des Netzquotienten. In: *Serialität: Reihen und Netze*. CD-ROM, Elke Bippus / Andrea Sick, eds., Bremen

03 Oldenburg, Helene von (2001): Das arachnomantische Archiv. In: *log.buch. Materialien zu "log.in – netz / kunst / werke"*. Arbeitsgemeinschaft Kultur im Großraum Nürnberg, Fürth, Erlangen, Schwalbach / Institut für moderne Kunst Nürnberg, Eds., Nürnberg, 274–287, 286/287.

04 Bracelet. *< 4340 KF >*

05 Franke, Herbert W. (1982): *Geheimnisvolle Höhlenwelt*. Stuttgart, 32. *< 988 LF >*

06 "Web of Linyphia triangularis." See: Foelix, Rainer F. (1996): *Biology of Spiders*. New York / Oxford, 124. *< 60 Ge >*

07 "The geometry of nature. On the ball: a simple equation produces shapes like those seen in nature. An adenovirus. A C60 buckyball." See: Klarreich, Erica (2002): Get in shape. In: *New Scientist*, vol. 174, no. 2342, 11. *< 4852 NG >*

08 Cytoskeleton of a cell. See: Ingber, Donald E. (1998): The Architecture of Life. In: *Scientific American*, vol. 278, no. 1, 30–39, 38. *< 3061 NG >*

09 Part of the cytoskeleton of a mammalian cell. See: Ingber, Donald E. (1998): The Architecture of Life. In: *Scientific American*, vol. 278, no. 1, 30–39, 36. *< 3061 NG >*

10 "Random network. All nodes have about the same number of links. The average number (at the peak of the bell curve) gives the network a 'scale.' Scale-free network. It makes no real sense to talk about scale or an average number of links. Scale-free networks have many nodes with few links and a few nodes with many links." See: Cohen, David (2002): All the World's a net. In: *New Scientist*, vol. 174, no. 2338, 24–29, 26. *< 4851 NG >*

11 Cohen, David (2002): All the World's a net. In: *New Scientist*, vol. 174, no. 2338, 24–29, 24. *< 4851 NG >*

12 Ingber, Donald E. (1998): The Architecture of Life. In: *Scientific American*, vol. 278, no. 1, 30–39, 35. *< 3061 NG >*

13 "Jumping spider Philaeus" See: Foelix, Rainer F. (1996): *Biology of Spiders*. New York / Oxford, 154. *< 60 Ge >*

14 "A sensational found: The dry climate of the Seistan-Valley preserved the rest of a net from 2900 B.C. A net that was used for fishing or catching birds." See: Sahrhage, Dietrich (2001): Fisch für Harappa. In: *Spektrum der Wissenschaft*, vol. 6, 28–33, 32. *< 4804 FN >*

15 *Tablecloth*. *< 58 RN >*

16 de Dillmont, Thérèse (1897, 1996): *Encyklopädie der weiblichen Handarbeiten*. Augsburg, 69. *< 3296 Kn >*

17 "The largest work of art (500 squarekilometer) lay near Nazca in Peru. It consists of lines, areas and figures, some of them birds, one ape and a spider." See: Riese, Berthold (2001): Günther Stoll und Rüdiger Vaas – Spurensuche im Indianerland. In: *Spektrum der Wissenschaft*, vol. 6, 108. *< 4813 Rt >*

18 Cyber Games Café (2001): *Map of Heraklion*. Heraklion *< 4827 GN >*

19 http://mailbox.univie.ac.at/~prillih3/metro [last access: 01/27/2004] *< 4829 RN >*

20 "Agra, Mausoleum of Itimed-ud Daula 1628." See: Stierlin, Henri (1977): *Encyclopedia of World Architecture*, Fribourg, 399. *< 2342 GN >*

21 "Aufstieg mit Jumar-Klemmen." See: Franke, Herbert W. (1982): *Geheimnisvolle Höhlenwelt*, Stuttgart, 38. *< 988 LF >*

22 "Flat Loop – Backward." See: Byers, Chester (1966): *Cowboy Roping and Roping Tricks*, New York, 11. *< 1128 FF >*

23 "Don't be mean to your fridge. Today it's a boring white box, but tomorrow a cunning chip called Bluetooth will turn it into the nerve centre of your world." See: Marks, Paul (2000): Brave New Fridge. In: *New Scientist*, vol. 21 October 2000, 61–64, 64. *< 4742 Te >*

24 *Scientific American* (1999): vol. 10, no. 3, (Cover). *< 4837 Te >*

25 *Expo Magazin* (1998/99): no. 1, winter 1998/99, (Cover). *< 3533 GN >*

26 *New Scientist* (2000): no. 2261, (Cover). *< 4741Te >*

27 "Polymer Mat from a spray-on dressing provides a framework for skin regrowth." See: Martindale, Diane (2000): Scar no more. In: *Scientific American*, vol. 7, 24–25, 25. *< 4446 GN >*

28 Anonym (1998): 50, 100 and 150 Years Ago. Scientific American 1898: The spider and the fly illusion. In: *Scientific American*, February 1998, 6 *< 3185 Sh >*

29 *Forbes* (1995): October 23, (Cover). *< 792 Ge >*

30 DU PONT (1996): Fiber engineers, meet thy master. In: *Scientific American*, vol.7, 12–13. *< 1965 Te >*

31 *Bild der Wissenschaft* (2001): vol. 4, (Cover). *< 4834 Ge >*

32 "How quickly do new technologies take off? Frantic pace: the time it takes for ideas to spread is getting shorter and shorter. WAP phones will outpace their predecessors." See:

Webb, Jeremy / Graham-Rowe, Duncan (2000): Everything, Anywhere, In: *New Scientist*, vol. 21, October 2000, 33–35, 34. **< 4742 Te >**

33 O'Brochta, David A. / Atkinson, Peter W. (1998): Building the Better Bug. In: *Scientific American*, vol. 12, 60–65, 60. **< 3653 Ge >**

34 Oldenburg, Helene von (1998): SpiderFeminism, In: *First Cyberfeminist International, Conference Reader*, Sollfrank, Cornelia / obn, Eds., Hamburg, 46–49.

35 Anonym (1998): "Biostahl" aus Ziegenmilch. *Focus*, vol. 43, 242. **< 3447 Te >**

36 Wong, Kate (2002): Scientists Spin Spidery Silk. See: http://www.sciam.com/ [last access: 01/27/2004] **< 4832 St >**

37 "Polly (left) is a transgenetic clone of a poll Dorset sheep. A gene for a human protein, factor IX, was added to the cell that provided the lamb's genetic heritage, so Polly has the human gene. The ewe that carried Polly (right) is a Scottish blackface." See: Wilmut, Jan (1998): Cloning for Medicine, In: *Scientific American*, vol. 12, 30–35, 35. **< 3654 Ge >**

38 "Optical See-Through Display" See: Feiner, Steven K. (2002): Augmented Reality: A new Way of Seeing, In: *Scientific American*, vol. 286, no. 4, 34–41, 37. **< 4854 Pk >**

39 "Nerve cell on a chip: Co-evolution of mankind and computer." In: *Der Spiegel*, vol. 19, 135. **< 4184 NN >**

40 The incomparable allure of a Woman's Hair. In: *Cosmopolitan*, vol. 11, 1995. **< 930 SpA >**

41 *Spider, 9"*, New York, USA, 1996 **< 869 SpM >**

1 Oldenburg, Helene von (1999): From Spider- to Cyberfeminism and back. In: *The Spectralization of Technology: from elsewhere to cyberfeminism and back: institutional modes of the cyberworld*. Grzinic, Marina / Eisenstein, Adele, Eds., Maribor, 15–16.

2 This was confirmed by research in Arachnomancy, a science which explores the biological and cultural evolution of Homo sapiens with respect to a net-based future, as well as the influence of future arachnids on this development (arachne = spider, mantic = a technique to get knowledge about the future). Arachnomancy derived in a series of elegant entomological investigations allows an unexpected view into the future of earth and unveils its arachnoid structure: the dominating species of our times, Homo sapiens, will be superseded by an arachnoid species. This arachnomantic method not only places arachnology into an anthropological context, but considers the arachnoid structure of images as they frequently appear among other places within the context of the human psyche and everyday life. Related discoveries from different sciences like evolutionary psychology, experimental physics or sociobiology show the highly significant preference for a variety of thread-bound constructions like lines, knots or nets. When analyzing the underlying

structure of our ideas and inventions we find a networking dynamic in nearly every part of life, science, art or society." **Oldenburg, Helene von** (1998): SpiderFeminism, In: *First Cyberfeminist International, Sept. 20.-28. 1997, Hybrid Workspace, Kassel*, Sollfrank, Cornelia / obn, Eds., Hamburg, 46–49.

3 1997 I predicted – based on arachnomantic research – a gender diversity of future arachnoids. Though it was a revolutionary finding at that time and more often than not neglected and labeled as esoteric, results by other scientists and newest breakthrough of genetic engeneering proved me right. But I was wrong on the timescale. I estimated – based on cultural knowledge of the past 10,000 years – that the changes will happen in an unspecific future; some thousand years from now. Evolution (inventions, changes and globalization) is going much faster nowadays. The evolutionary approach towards arachnoids (a spiderlike species, merged out of mankind, today's spiders and machines) happens much faster than anyone could believe. The merging of genes is quite common today, especially with the official aim of medicine (making better humans) and biotechnology (merging spider genes with human genes and other mammal genes).

often female

the modem is burning

writing

material junctions

body called flesh

THOUGHTS ON SUBMISSION: GLANCES FROM THE WARRIORS OF PERCEPTION

EPHEMERA | DISCORDIA | LIQUID_NATION
| PLASTIQUE | EFEMERA_CLONE_2

> Submission is a submission of choice: we often play with an awareness of submission. Submission can be as powerful as control. We are adept at many forms of submission – it is a social expectation. However, we are not bound by it. We identify its forms in order to decode quickly and move through its barriers. Order exists within an intricate system of submission. That which we call society is only permitted through a mass, consensual hallucination. One that must be navigated. We build counter hallucinations. We have assembled a variety of Operational Somatic Systems that assist in protecting our feeds (untethered) to build a translation appropriate for the world. We are intimately familiar with the edges of reality and acceptable consciousness. Our flesh and social circumstances are the bags that we bring together to maintain power. It

is in gathering that we move closer to the feeds we are constantly circuiting, but unable to access alone. This defies the mastery of any system of electronic circuits or established, institutionalized authority. We generate sprawling, temporal systems for techno-affinity, unbound by ego battles and subjective limitations. We circuit open sources that remain closed without our activity. The following texts are introductory documents gathered to reflect the submissions we engaged, that began our story in building a network of mistresses designed to transmit memories that haunt us all.

the street falls to rubble, decay erode
Aphrodite descending drops down piece by piece
swallowed by moss and the viral history that destroys
her as she knows herself

Aphrodite in ruins dissolves under myth,
many tears for Aphrodite,
enough salt to wash her away.
her moss skin, a testimony,
the city to where all roads lead, is blistering
twilight suspended, preserving the dead
an excuse for inventing its present

smooth lick parting
frame my mouth the stone
saliva glistens and dries a fine white line
stone pores whispering as I lick

and I am made of lions
those lions grow feathers that will not weave
the frame of wings

and I become a boy that builds a cardboard box
into a house and waits for he knows it will not be long
before you join him

his face bruised with unspoken realities

everyday his feet step along the same path
as thousands before and after

feral in the fruit of unharvested knowing
he will scrape the tips of his fingers along a wavering
contrast, not a plateau

his tears fall in the eyes of a woman far from his home
far from his face
to turn the sea and perforate an invisible membrane
very few can notice

i-drunners become material junctions of code,
technology, and the body. Each one becomes a
total_segment of a flesh circuit with the other runners.
Each one becomes a micro_narrative of woman, as a
singularity of skin, as digital phantasms shifting the
fetish spaces of virtual capital towards a world that
makes all worlds possible

It begins with simple gestures and actions. We gather
our machines, our code, and cover them with our
laughter, our smoke, our bodies. We re_flesh the
networks with our useless condition. The labor of woman
as the infrastructure of the networks becomes manifest.
We tweak our phantasms, in order to trace out the
impossible futures in our fingers.

<t o e p h e m e r a m o d e o n>

How can you pretend to resemble the body called

flesh in this shattered universe?

Don't u see that the segments adrift in the network

are injuring your sensible skin?

Don't you see you have NO FUTURE

NON HAI FUTURO

THE PAST slowly kills us

The shadow of an hirsute – first woman goddess – is

coming from the nights of time, she is following

us through a line of blood ëcos she is hungry and she

has to eat

There is no escape function

The modem is burning

How can you pretend to resemble the body called

flesh in this shattered universe?

Discordia is dancing in this realm of pain

She is walking in it with injured feet

Breathing dust

Trepanning brain

Administrating pale chemical molecular shapes

Experiments of control of governments is getting

bigger and bigger, the great non-pianificato,

```
auto-indotto in-controllato mental experiment is
going on,

Thanks to Liquid Nation

<t o e p h e m e r a m o d e o f f>

<t o L i q u i d N a t i o n m o d e o n>

please observe the results.
```

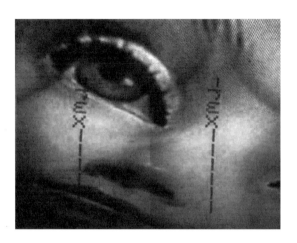

[she opens her eyes wide shut]

sugarbaby snow lands
stretch out brightful dreamy in front of her
endless mirror lines reflecting that which is not
skanky liquid valium girl rides red in the empty 'hood
as invisible whispers shadow her with a kind of soft puppy hush
we're in here, we're in here

[she looks but she don't see nuffin]

once were lovers somewhere buried their starry no-doll baby deep
in space 1999
meanwhile another war, another planet
top sight target blue sticks like toffee to remote tv

a city of ruined children has stolen her savage joys
identity scatters through spiraling no-future past
bladerunning rainy sundays too bloody far away
leaving bar hollywood, ciao care factor zero

[she looks and she don't like what she sees]

coma life trawls drearily towards the inevitable
shredding her skinless
no fuck pets to play, and all out of glue

korean bitch found, then lost, in alphabet city, maybe hawaii?
recode solitude3 in vanity's fair, spicing the Friday
take care, take soft slow steps, leave no prinz
home again, home again, jiggity jig

[she looks and she sees a faint something]

her silver hands mine the ice
upside down, you turn me
easily to slip slip slip
over in glittering porn star sushi pussy

i died last night mamma bear said
look at that little woolly lamb, isn't she sweet

come she said
destroy she said

[she looks]

summer drops like acid into global spring
stealth fairies start fucking with the future
and all the ice palaces come a tumbling down

[she closes her eyes wide shut]

resembling the body called flesh
sticky segments set randomly adrift in the network

gathering ghosts from the machine
to illuminate an event horizon that breathes alone among others

he says the universe is an hallucination
she says it is a field enfolded
she says she has been captured by a city of ruined children
he says these spaces are eating her savage joys
she says dreams drip away, revealing the indistinct

~~All post media direct action cells must pursue the instabilities in Technologies even before they become metaphors.~~

SPACE IS THE ULTIMATE HIGH GROUND

the storm is here

the wind from below is coming

time for a new R/reality

~~Their VR helmets can t see the failure of Reality before the new fundamentalism of the telematic — they continue to believe that the lights they see from the midnight bombs they drop are coming from something that still exists: nation, justice, and democracy. These are now nothing more than the last signs of dead cultural stars.~~

~~GLOBAL ENGAGEMENT IS THE APPLICATION OF PRECISION FORCE
FROM, TO AND THROUGH SPACE~~

she says the stars are slowly disappearing, light becoming dark
he says it is only here that he can exist
she says she is running blindfolded towards the ever brightful
he says there is no beginning, but a circle containing a gap
for the unexpected to enter
she says here there are intensities which he cannot begin to
understand
he says to him all things are less than zero

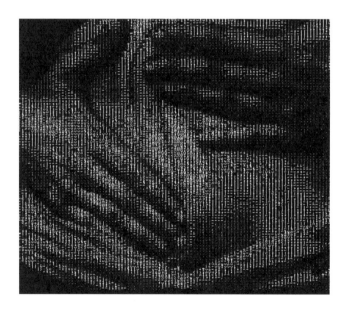

coma life trawls drearily towards the inevitable
while new forms arise from the ash of future's memory
building their skins, sewing and patching, tweaking and stretching
pushing beyond what many from the comfort zones have drowned in

SPACE POWER IS VITAL TO ATTAIN OUR GOAL OF BEING PERSUASIVE IN
PEACE, DECISIVE IN WAR, AND PREEMINENT IN ANY FORM OF CONFLICT

our dead must come out of the night and the earth

let them dress in the garb of war
so their voice may be heard in the empire of silence
stories that dance in the mountains
in that climbing and falling of red stars

breaking the mirrors of Power
moving into the elsewhere
afterwards, let their words fall silent
and let them return again to the night and to the earth

adrift in the network resembling the body called flesh
are packets of soft recognition

Now they are one in front of the other, any more distance would break the
contact, less distance would make them implode.
Two forms point one on the other, they are staring at each other crossing the selves.

a scream, yes, a scream

he says that it was a night of intensities and he did not plan for it
she says she believes in nothing less than everything
he says that theirs is not a mathematical relationship
she says her thoughts are as dark and sticky as blood

The moment of the sexual act I multiply my personae, do you understand?
No, I do not understand.
Do you understand the problem?

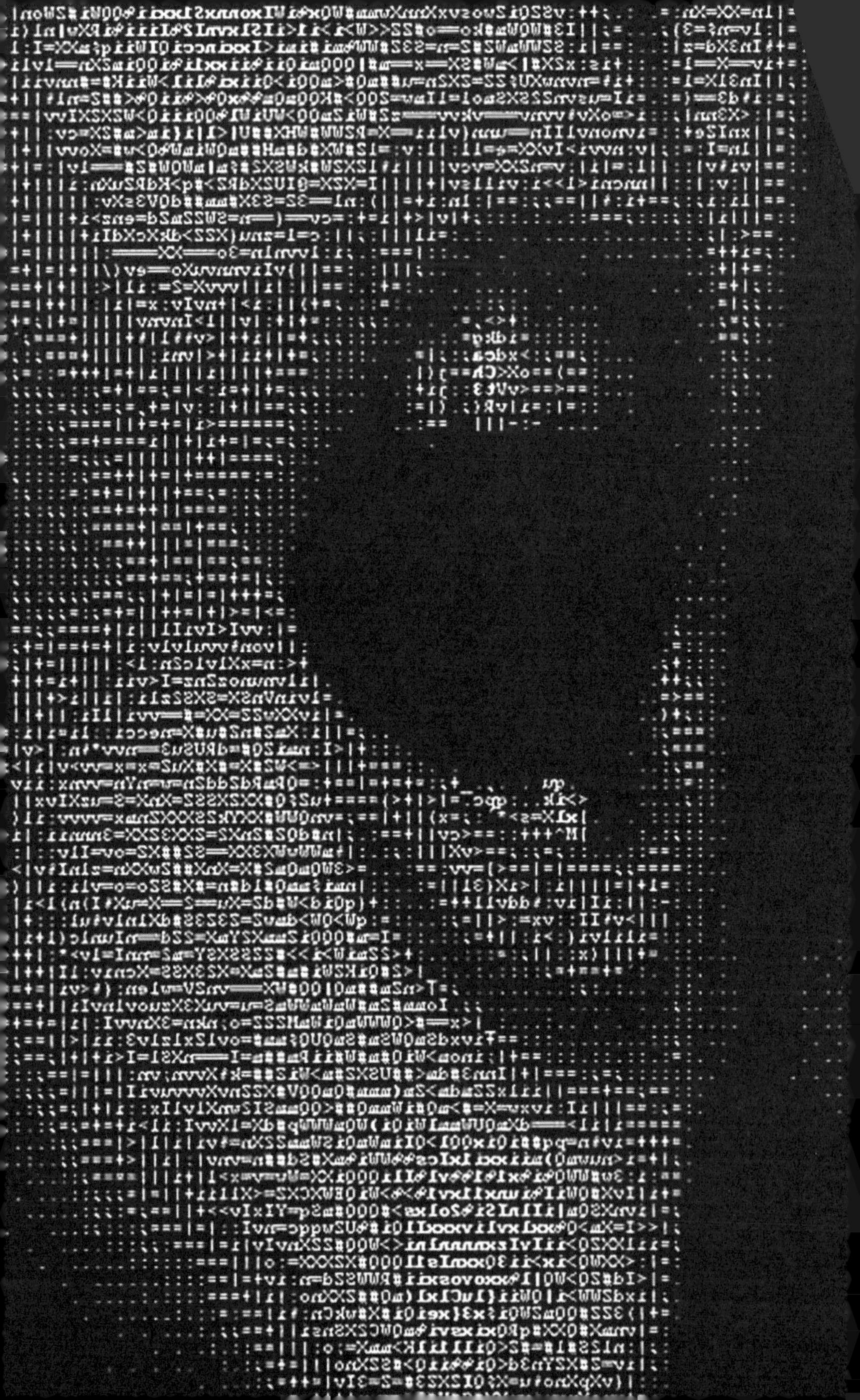

No, I do not understand.
I became multiple, animal, innominable power, I hear myself speaking with other voices, I do things which then I do not remember, you are going to have a sexual relationship with one thousand persons.
I am worried for your safety.

tremble

DUE TO THE IMPORTANCE OF COMMERCE AND ITS EFFECTS ON NATIONAL SECURITY, THE U.S. MAY EVOLVE INTO THE GUARDIAN OF SPACE COMMERCE

shadows of tender fury

the passing of the dead shelters those who have nothing . . .

those who bear the historic burden of disdain and abandonment

those who don't exist

ciphers in the big accounts of capital

the gigantic market of maximum irrationality that trades in dignities

~~The MESH is busy mapping the human genome to create meme-gene weapons to target specific genotypes and building self-replicating fleets of computer-controlled molecular weapons. Post media cell must fight the future with gestures that have no name in the present.~~

WE MUST BE INSTANTLY AWARE, GLOBALLY DOMINANT,
SELECTIVELY LETHAL, VIRTUALLY PRESENT

```
ring a ring a rosies

pocket full o stealfies

bend over banker

lights go off

all fall down
```

she says the Power assassinates and forgets
he says she also believes in goblins and fairies

I become a horse, if you look straight in my eyes
you can see that I have got the eyes of a horse, gaze at me.

You do not look like an horse
Yes, look at me, can you see my eyes?
Yes, it's real, your eyes are transforming, they are big blue deep, a
descendent lateral cut, you are blonde, much more blonde than I remember.
I understand that you look like a horse, but I cannot see what is the problem.
The problem is that in the sexual act my personae multiply themselves
And each one of them passes through me.
Yes, but this is not a problem.
In the sexual act I multiply myself
and maybe you will find yourself hanging by the big toes while I'm cutting
your throat with a blade made of tiny wood.
I understand, but this is not a problem
Do you understand which is the problem?
No, I don't understand.

throughout a weary transportation of transmissions
with time so small it stitches itself through the imaginary framework
as a voice revealing the thematics of our current ruin

~~For too long the specters of hyper-memetic cargo cults have flowed between the bottom of the third world and the top of the virtual class. A circuit that keeps the impossibilities of the fifth worlds behind the eschatology of designer futures for the first world.~~

~~CONTROL OF SPACE ASSURES ACCESS, FREEDOM OF OPERATIONS AND THE ABILITY TO DENY OTHERS THE USE OF SPACE~~

she says that she no longer knows herself
she speaks of butterfly wings crushed by a creature
with no smell
she says that a devastating glance has rendered her invisible
she says that they have stolen her silence, leaving her only
with useless words
she says that now there is nothing left except emptiness

No, my sexuality is a multiple sexuality too, I am moving and changing shape
too, even if I'm often female. Anyway I remember everything.
You will not know with whom you are lying, do you understand?
Yes, I understand but for me this is not a problem.
You do not want to embrace me.
We will never embrace, it will never happen
No, I do not understand and I am steeped in stagnant water-lilies.

Post media cells must travel among strings of inventions that fall outside of the logomass. To seek gestures that leap over the lines of flight that our current collective realities or imaginary conditions of speed and interconnectivity. We must place the impossible and the unexpected as our counter-dialectics.

THE GOAL IS FULL SPECTRUM DOMINANCE

these anchors for listening, watered by the tears of the dead, pooling a slow, eroding trust to a bitter circuit in the lines of power

chemical pale sleep

dreamstained sheets

no centre, ragged edges

zeroing tolerance

gene raiding hyperdecay

fox bites tail

invisible artillery follows nurse with wound

endlessly uncoiling a spectacle of
irretrievable situations

intolerable signs

ruined, all ruined

come be my next five minutes

come, she said

destroy, she said

~~Post media cells must create situations for mutation that can interrupt and reroute the protocols of acceleration, improvement and obsolescence that late capital is bound by. So that rational history will be broken and remade by the tiny hands of the intergalactic niños of the fifth world.~~

In a moment you become transparent and I embrace your framework, a red skeleton as a radiography, I pass across yourselves and then the palace comes tumbling down, I lose you between the ruins, I do not see anything, not anything else.

these are attempts of resembling the body called flesh

this is a cry for new memory systems to address and build
despite the lack of attention given to such building

this tender pain that will always be hope

such are the voices of the body called flesh   <

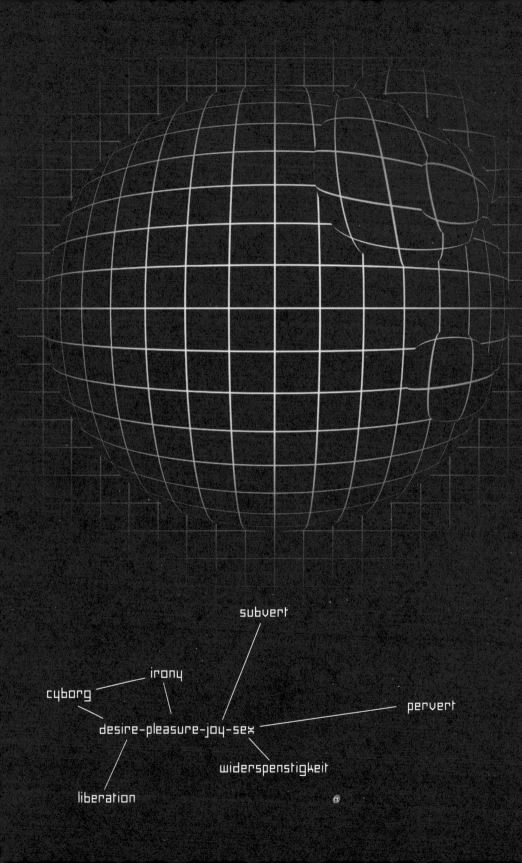

. . . . .The
. . . . .Cyberfeminist
. . . . .Fantasy of the
. . . . .Pleasure
. . . . .of the Cyborg[1]

YVONNE VOLKART

Mythology. . . . .
> "The clitoris is a direct line to the matrix,"
wrote the Australian artist's group VNS Matrix in their *Cyberfeminist Manifesto for the 21st Century*, 1991.[2] Since then, this sentence has been often quoted, specifically by English cultural theorist Sadie Plant who also claims to have coined the term cyberfeminism at the same time.[3] Plant writes that this line "refers to both the womb – matrix is the Latin term, just as hystera is the Greek – and the abstract networks of communication which were increasingly assembling themselves."[4] It seems more remarkable to me, that this sentence does not only directly link the female body and the so-called "immaterial" cyberspace – an association which male cyberpunk authors already suggested when adopting the term matrix for the internet, but that it ironically plays with the connotation of a female cyberspace by positing the female genitals as the entrance to this new digital communication system. This gesture could be under-

stood as re-embodying, "refleshing"[5] and resexualizing what has been conceived as pure data, it could be regarded as a direct line to the second feminist movement in the 1970's and its long struggle for the valuation of the pleasure of the clitoris, or it could even be (mis)interpreted as biological determinism.

Unlike the feminist 'mainstream' of the 1970's, cyberfeminists claim to have "an unbounded enthusiasm for the new tools of technology."[6] Typically, each time cyberfeminism is introduced, the technophobia of 1970's feminism is mentioned. It is important to mention, though, that there were a few feminists back then who strongly believed in the liberating impact of new technologies. For example, reproductive technologies were perceived as having emancipatory potential and women performance artists of the 1970's discovered the camcorder as a new tool for documenting daily life and for art making. In other words, sexual pleasure and technologies have always been regarded as liberating factors in feminism. Thus, what is new in cyberfeminism besides its new terminology?

Cyberfeminism's starting point is a belief in what I would call very roughly the "digital turn."[7] Even though the digital turn does not erase old media, it has an effect on all of them, i.e., no media remains what it

---

1   Another aspect, i.e., the role of cyberfeminist's methods to construct cyborg subjectivity, has been developed for the book: *Technics of Cyber⬦feminism.* *<Mode=Message>*, Claudia Reiche/ Andrea Sick, eds., Bremen, see **Volkart, Yvonne** (2002): Technics of Cyberfeminism: Strategic Sexualisations. Between Method and Fantasy [=Volkart 2002b].

2   The entire manifesto can be seen on: http://sysx.apana.org.au/artists/vns [last access: 01/27/2002].

3   For the text 'Feminisations. Reflections on Women and Virtual Reality,' Sadie Plant used this sentence as the text's motto. In: **Hershman Leeson, Lynn,** ed. (1996): *Clicking In. Hot Links to Digital Culture,* Seattle, 37.

4   **Plant, Sadie** (1997): *Zeros + Ones. Digital Women + the New Technoculture,* New York / London / Sydney, 59.

5   This term of "re-fleshing (the networks)" I owe to Diane Ludin and Ricardo Dominguez. See also later in this text the discussion of Diane Ludin's / Agnese Trocchi's / Francesca da Rimini's project: *Identity Runners: Re_flesh the body.*

6   **Pierce, Julianne** (1998): *Info Heavy Cyber Babe,* in: *First Cyberfeminist International, Sept. 20-28 1997, Hybrid Workspace, Kassel,* Cornelia Sollfrank / Old Boys Network, eds., Hamburg, 10.

7   I coin this term very superficially and would like to use it more in an asso-

used to be. It is the belief that new technologies have an enormous impact on our lives, that they shape modern society, economy, bodies, gender, identity, and subjectivity, far beyond Foucault's idea of biopolitics, as Donna Haraway stated in her "A Cyborg Manifesto."[8] From my point of view, it is this manifesto and its impact which marks the shift from feminism to cyberfeminism. In this key text, Haraway proposes the new and 'ironic' figuration of the cyborg as a hybrid mixture of human being and machine, a cybernetic organism. She sees this cyborg as a symptom for the new conditions within a technological world as well as an "ironic political myth"[9] for female emancipation. Her text is "an argument for pleasure in the confusion of boundaries"[10] incorporated by the cyborg. And this is the crucial difference: Whereas feminism claimed the appropriation of new technologies as tools for women's liberation, cyberfeminism promotes both the idea of becoming cyborgian and the pleasures involved in it.[11] In other words, technologies are no longer perceived as prostheses and instruments for liberation which are separated from the body, but a merging of body and technology takes place. It is the concept of the technological body which is the medium for pleasure and libera-

---

ciative manner, than with the aim to theorize it as it has been done with the "linguistic turn" and the "pictorial turn." However, referring to those concepts, I mean with the "digital turn" that it claims to be the fundamental condition of the ongoing codes.

8 **Haraway, Donna** (1991): A Cyborg Manifesto: Science, Technology, and Socialist-Feminism in the Late Twentieth Century. In: *Simians, Cyborgs and Women: The Reinvention of Nature*, New York, 150, online version: http://www.stanford.edu/dept/HPS/Haraway/CyborgManifesto.html [last access: 04/20/2001], [= Haraway 1991a].

9 **Haraway** 1991a: 149.

10 **Haraway** 1991a: 150.

11 Regarding the importance of pleasure for cyberfeminists, see **Aristarkhova, Irina** (1999): Cyber-Jouissance: An Outline For A Politics Of Pleasure. (non published paper). German version: Telepolis online magazine, http://www.heise.de/tp (May 1999). Also **Braidotti, Rosi** (1998): Cyber Feminism with a Difference. In: Zones of Disturbance, Silvia Eiblmayr / Steirischer Herbst, Eds., (Exh. Cat.), Graz; **Kuni, Verena** (1998): The Future is Femail. In: Sollfrank/Old Boys Network, Eds. 1998: 13–18; Plant 1997.

tion, and not the technological tool itself. In cyberfeminism, the utopian ideology of women's liberation is located in the body and gender but this body is no longer what it was thought to be. Neither is it a new body, as the military cyborg ideology pretends to be.[12] As Haraway writes, "it is a body which is conceived as a symptomatic body, beyond "other seductions to organic wholeness through a final appropriation of all the powers of the parts into a higher unity."[13]

I always pictured the cyborg, particularly Haraway's rather rough and early figuration of it, as an ageless, naughty and unruled girl. At the time of the *Manifesto for Cyborgs*, Haraway herself thought of a nasty girl.[14] Whereas Haraway speaks of the cyborg as a "polychromatic girl," I stated the cyberfeminist cyborg to be "widerspenstig." This term is hard to translate into English, meaning "unruly," "untamed" or "stubborn." It is used to translate Shakespeare's comedy *The Taming of the Shrew* into German, and never used to describe men.

12 **Claudia Reiche** writes in her concept for the laboratory *Technics of Cyber< >Feminism. <Mode=Message>*: "But what to do, <if> cyberfeminism audaciously will have forgotten the classical, revolutionary (<and> terrorist) demand – of the (self)creation of a 'new human'?", http://www.thealit.de/kultur/cyberfeminism/home/concept.html [last access: 04/04/2002].

13 **Haraway** 1991a: 150.

14 **Haraway, Donna** (1991): Cyborgs at Large. Interview with Constance Penley and Andrew Ross. In: *Technoculture*, Constance Penley / Andrew Ross, eds., Minneapolis, 18–20, [=**Haraway** 1991b].

15 This is what art historian **Ute Vorkoeper** wrote about the exhibition "Widerspenstige Praktiken im Zeitalter von Bio- und Informationstechnologien," which I curated 2000. *Telepolis* online magazine: http://www.heise.de/tp/deutsch/inhalt/sa/3556/1.html [last access: 08/09/2002].

16 Dara Birnbaum's videoclip *Technology Transformation: Wonder Woman* from 1978 deconstructed the female superhero "Wonder Woman," showing that the armed and strong Wonder Woman was embodying a male fantasy. With a cyberfeminist perspective from today, however, we might even interpret her clip as a feminist fantasy of female transgression. Feminists in the 1970's appropriated and recoded Wonder Woman as 'their' myth of liberation too, although her cyborgian state of being had not been at stake, then. See more on this subject in: Kunsthalle Wien / Klagenfurt, eds. (1995): Dara Birnbaum, (Exh. Cat.), Wien / Klagenfurt.

"Unruly is what does not obey, what cannot be straightened out. A silly strand of hair or an undesired fold that can only be subdued by special means, technical expenditure or disinterest. Or it takes a sense of humor. Something is unruly. Unruliness has a physical, an erotic dimension. Whether this is desired or not, the term echoes something that for centuries was supposed to mark a feminine quality: lack of knowledge, unawareness – and obstinacy. A childish, almost touching disobedience to what asserts itself as unchangeable and rigid. However, it is also disobedience without a target, thoughtless, unplanned, anarchic, something that cannot be tolerated for long by that which exists. All measures taken against unruliness derive their legitimacy from this. Unruliness is threatened with being broken by violence or disinterest. Even laughter can kill it, if it fails to recognize its serious motivation."[15]

These comments about the erotic-feminine-physical dimension of unruliness describe precisely what prompted me to use the word once again in the context of cyberfeminist fantasies. Unruliness is associated with "femininity" or hysteria in all its manifestations drawing a balance between (patriarchal) attribution and feminist self-articulation. The notion that unruliness is unconscious or even quasi-genetically determined because resistance is seen as something localized in the body itself and initially defies discursivity, can be and has been adopted to embody feminist issues.

Naturally, the body as site at which oppression/liberation happens, was also an important point of discourse in earlier feminisms. However, the issue of enjoying the blurring of the boundaries of woman and machine and taking it as a "utopian moment" (Martha Rosler), was never at stake before. In feminism, the machine-woman and techno-fetish was perceived clearly as a male fantasy which could have been appropriated and deconstructed.[16] But occupying the military and techno-determinist cyborg fantasy and subverting it according to women's manifold desires is a new phenomenon which is an issue of cyberfeminism. Only the cyborg's hybridity sets the conditions for possible acts of liberation, which now take the form of various alliances and networks within a changing community rather than a fight against specific enemies. In this conception, resistance lays in the non-materiality of a constructed and discursive body itself and less in the idea of battles for emancipation. If one follows Sadie Plant's cybernetic reasoning, it is even quite unimportant whether women are aware that they have been – as she asserts – the hidden inventors, developers and adopters of information. For her the fact of women's involvement in early forms of information technology and their triggering of de-territorialization is what really counts. From her perspective, women are more crucial as nodes and agents than as political subjects.[17]

The VNS Matrix line I quoted in the beginning, and particularly their entire *Cyberfeminist Manifesto for the 21st Century*, which ends with the sentence "We are the future cunt," show exactly that it is the symptomology of a gendered body mixed with new technology which constitutes the future feminist subject. Stressing the urge of networking and the aspect of women as agents of utopia in the age of information technology, Verena Kuni entitles her thoughts on the aesthetics and politics of cyberfeminism "The Future is Femail."[18]

However, the idea of the cyborgian state of being is not only a cyberfeminist one, it is the dominant belief since cyberpunk (which has been conceived at the same time as the *A Cyborg Manifesto*), and the idea of the 'Post Human.' Another precedent is the mechanic, castrating woman

---

17 From my point of view, Sadie Plant sets a too 'linear' non-linear and rhizomatic myth of Ada Lovelace's and women's involvement in communication technology, and she fails to break this linearity. With the film *Conceiving Ada*, Lynn Hershman-Leeson also rebuilt the myth of Ada Lovelace as first programmer, and of women as predestined for mathematics and computer programming. A kind of rebirth into our time may give Ada Lovelace a better chance to do what she has to than she had at her time. Like Plant, Hershman created a fictional piece referring to so-called 'authentic' history, thus blurring the boundaries between fiction and reality. This fictional re-reading and remaking of a creative woman's life in the past into something which could have happened if the conditions were not as sexist, has always been a very important feminist strategy: the strategy of the 'as if,' mixing the traditionally separated fields of science and fiction. But Hershman's film also seems to be too one-dimensional in its story of female empowerment. More on this subject will be discussed in my forthcoming Ph.D.

18 **Kuni** 1998.

19 Specifically, I think of the exhibition "Post Human" (1992), curated by Jeffrey Deitch. This touring exhibition stands at the beginning of an extensive discourse in the arts about the importance of new technologies and biotechnologies for the construction and production of new bodies and identities. More than the show, the catalogue was an interesting example of a libertarian, evolutionary-based, techno-determined ideology of posthumanism, in

which has been negotiated at the beginning of this century, especially in Dadaism and Surrealism. As I mention earlier, unlike cyberfeminism which is utopian and ironic, a lot of these reflections are pessimistic, frightful, cynical, or techno-libertarian.[20] Although cyberfeminists believe in what I called a 'digital turn,' I wouldn't speak of techno-determinism. Rather, the cyberfeminists' cyborg agents are embodied symptoms and signifiers of a time which is understood as an invasive and mutating one.[21]

VNS Matrix's strategies of irony, parody and appropriation of sexual obscenities remind us of strategies of the Riot Grrrls who became well known at the beginning of the 1990's. Seeking "affirmative representations of women" Rosi Braidotti refers to the Riot Grrrls' strategies of "symbolic violence."[22] Pointing to Judith Butler and Luce Irigaray, she stresses the importance of parody and irony as methods of "the philosophy as if."[23] It is interesting that Braidotti attempts to feature mimetic strategies as cyberfeminist, which they are clearly not exclusively. It is rather a kind of symptomatic, gendered, and body-centered strategy

---

the sense of the paraphrase: With the right technology you can change. The term 'posthuman,' though it was not new then, became an important one to many feminist theorists. E.g.: **Braidotti** 1998; Livingston, Ira / Halberstam, Judith, eds. (1995): *Posthuman Bodies*, Indiana; Hayles, N. Katherine (1999): *How We Became Posthuman. Virtual bodies in Cybernetics, Literature, and Informatics*, Chicago.

20 See **Volkart, Yvonne** (1999): Infobiobodies, art and esthetic strategies in the new world order. In: **Sollfrank/Old Boys Network**, eds. 1999, 61–68. Also available on: http://www.obn.org [last access: 01/27/2004].

21 It would exceed the purpose of this paper, but what could be questioned further is whether cyberfeminism as well as many other techno-discourses, do not overestimate the impacts of technology in general.

22 **Braidotti** 1998: 126–127.

23 **Braidotti** 1998: 127. "What I find empowering in the theoretical and political practice of 'as if' is its potential for opening up, through successive repetitions and mimetic strategies, spaces where forms of feminist agency can be engendered. [...] Irony is a systematically applied dose of debunking; an endless teasing; a healthy de-flation of over-heated rhetoric." See also: **Braidotti, Rosi** (1994): *Nomadic Subjects. Embodiment and Sexual Difference in Contemporary Feminist Theory*, New York, 7: "In other words, it is not the parody that will kill the phallocentric posture, but rather the power vacuum that parodic politics may be able to engender."

which has a strong tradition in feminism such as the valuation of the hysteric woman by Irigaray and others, or of performativity of gender by Butler, than a reference to virtuality and discourse of technology.

Unlike cyberpunk or other techno-narratives, cyberfeminism is committed to a postfeminist policy of self-empowerment which goes beyond simple principles of identity. Here, identity is an expanded concept describing a relational play between many agents and identities, identity designed as something fractured, split, fluid and in motion. The "ironic and political myth" of the cyborg is the outline for such a new politics of identity, one that switches between fiction and reality:

> "Haraway invites us instead to think of the community as being built on the basis of a commonly shared foundation of collective figures of speech, or foundational myths. These myths, which are also purposeful tools for intervening in reality, are figurations in that they make an impact on our imagination [...]. Feminism is about grounding, it is about foundations and about political myths."[24]

Braidotti (and Haraway) insist on the idea that a commonly shared fantasy may have a political and social impact, enabling people (women) to create symbolic and real spaces of agency. And I would certainly subscribe to the idea that the symbolic and imaginary space is highly productive in our daily social and political lives. Ultimately, it is identification and its effect on the creation of life, which is at stake. However, hardly any of these theorists, including myself, trace the political impact back to symbolic spaces and gestures. It seems to be merely a question of faith and not of scientific method, and particularly in the field of cultural criticism, these connections remain almost impossible to trace.

As I depict the "grounding of foundational myths" as something crucial, I would now like to describe a few female characters performing in different

---

24 **Braidotti** 1994: 105.

25 Here I refer to one of the first versions of this project. It is a livestream which Lucas put on the website http://www.involuntary.org [last access: 01/27/2002] shown in the framework of the exhibitions "Tenacity" (New York) and "Widerspenstige Praktiken" (Zurich). In a later version, she developed a DVD double projection with herself as being doubled. She showed that piece in the framework of the show "Body as Byte. The Body as Information_Flow" which I curated in spring 2001 at the Kunstmuseum Luzern. For details about these curatorial projects see: http://www.xcult.org/volkart [last access: 01/27/2004].

contemporary new media projects and embed them in their theoretical and literary context. Analyzing various figurations of transgressive, unruled and joyful cyborg women, I inscribe myself in the continuing cyberfeminist myth of the pleasure of the cyborg. My focus will be on the content and meaning of the figurations rather than on technological and medial aspects of the art work. Given the fact that the term cyberfeminism is a highly speculative and mythic term with a vague and blurry meaning and an infectious circulation, I will examine the aspects of pleasure of the cyborg also within contexts, which are not always directly acknowledged by the various protagonists (authors, theorists, artists, programmers, netizens) as strictly cyberfeminist.

To Be Like a Freak........................

In her net-based project *Involuntary Reception*, Kristin Lucas created a type of female hacker mentality.[25] Lucas plays a woman who talks into the camera about herself and her life and how her body is surrounded by a huge electromagnetic power field (EPF). On the live stream, the field is visualized by a flashing jagged stripe in constant motion, and her body is surrounded by some kind of a halo delineating the power field. Wherever she appears, she causes disturbances and interference in electronic equipment with the consequences that she cannot go anywhere without disrupting activities or destroying things. Yet she can move around inconspicuously in open-floor office spaces or crowds because there is always something going on and she can vanish in the crowd. Lucas explains how she involuntarily killed somebody who had a pacemaker and her beloved cat. As she cannot control her electromagnetic field, she is a danger for everybody susceptible to them. Moreover, she is afraid of swimming in the water. "The scary part is that I can't predict what I'm going to do... I'm like a freak, I don't know."

It's her body, somehow mutated, that does all those things, while she tries to be a nice normal girl who refuses to be hired for "terrorist acts" such as deliberately erasing hard drives. Due to her strong power field, she cannot be recorded on electronic media as all data would be promptly erased again. This gives her a certain privacy, which is hard to come by, because she is always noticed in a negative sense or hunted by people who would like to explore her strange body. For some time, she is under constant surveillance by the FBI or CIA. She plays the symptom generated by a thoroughly technology-pervaded and controlling society, where all traces can be recorded and decoded, and the value of the body is solely based in its function as information carrier, data protection and cryptography are political issues, privacy can be guaranteed for no one, intimacy and love are scarce. Lucas' protagonist is a female super-hero and renowned specialist looking for cover in inconspicuousness. Her own body mediates and perverts the ideologies and conditions of our times, and enjoys these hybridities: "I'm my own sub-subculture." We only learn about her abilities from her disrupted narrative which is sometimes confused and highly contradictory. Her origins seem mythical, all she can say about it is that it is surrounded by a lot of rumors and that there has always been great love between herself and her parents, who presumably are not her biological progenitors. She does not convey any message about how to improve the world. Her unruliness results from her inability to be different from the way she is, which constantly collides with her environment – and hence, from the way in which she is "biologically determined." This biologism is ironically refracted by her cyborg-like nature which has lost all its naturalness. Her body is a risk to her environment to the extent that the effects of technology are somehow doubled and reinforced by her body in such a way that they do not seem bearable any longer because they are uncontrolled and uncontrollable and emanate from an individual outside the dominating power apparatus.

Biological Warfare........................

The character *White Trash Girl* from the series of the same title (1995-97) created by the US-video artist Jennifer Reeder is a magnificent and true incarnation of the garbage of our day and age. Like Lucas, the artist plays

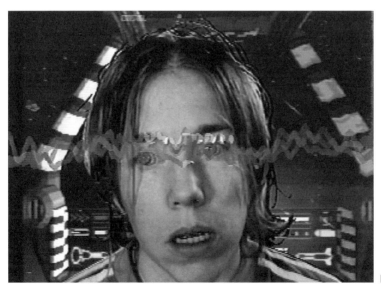

01

the protagonist; her name is derived from an abusive expression denoting the white lower classes. The pre-title sequence of the third part, *Law of Desire*, starts with the summary of White Trash Girl's procreation and childhood: The sounds of running cars over images of an embryo which becomes ever more clearly discernible. Text reminiscent of a fairy-tale is added:

> "Once upon a time there was a little girl who was raped by her uncle. She got pregnant and flushed the baby down the toilet, then killed her uncle and herself. The baby wiggled around in the sewer sludge for a long time. The ooze fed and nourished the baby, it made the baby strong – super strong. Her tiny baby body became more toxic with every tiny baby breath and every tiny baby heartbeat. None knew that this was no ordinary baby. This was a super baby. This was WHITE TRASH GIRL. Now, she's all grown up and she's waging biological warfare on any dumb fuck who asks for it. White Trash Girl is turbo charged and she's coming at you faster than you can scream HATCHET WOUND."

The next shot shows a cool blonde wearing black sunglasses, who is driving a van. A patrol car is chasing her and as a result she has an accident . The policeman draws his gun and breaks the window, then we see her run and hide. When the policeman comes near her, she beats him up in a violent and cruel way one would hardly ever expect from a woman. Spit dribbles out of her mouth and she sucks it back in. A picture we know from biology follows, showing the act of impregnation, sperm moving around, an almond-shaped ovum, a cyborg-like body, then she spits and we see a policeman being placed in an ambulance, his face horribly disfigured.

White Trash Girl owes her existence to several acts of violence which not only made her tough enough to face the cruelty of life, but actually make her the legitimate bastard of a "dirty" society. To use Donna Haraway's words, she literally came "from the belly of the monster," from the underground (in both senses of the word), the abyss and outhouse of this city, and hence she can never be innocent, even though her kind-hearted foster mother had her christened "Angel." Rape by a male family member is a literary topos of underground literature, found, for instance, in Jean Genet or Kathy Acker; it clearly identifies violence in the oedipal system, the constant feeling of insecurity and discomfort women are faced with, especially at home. For this reason, White Trash Girl's true home is a rather dystopic urban landscape. Again and again, we see her wearing miniskirts, either shocking pink or glistening, and cowboy boots

as she walks through the streets and over debris and garbage in her res-
olute gait. With her tall, strong build, monumentally, she poses on a heap
of stone, a beauty and super heroine of a different kind. If someone pinch-
es her behind, she turns into a railing shrew; in case of other acts of sexual
transgression, she spits ropy liquids or mercilessly beats up the perpetrators.

The ghetto-like city is her realm, her body is part of it; city, body and
underground are inseparable. This is not only evoked by White Trash
Girl's origin in the sewer and sludge but also by the beginning where the
picture of the embryo is accompanied by car noises off-screen and turns
into the shot of White Trash Girl driving. Throughout the entire series,
pictures of the digestive tract fade in regularly, anatomy-book illustrations with specially marked intestines. The camera enters the esophagus
like a tunnel, chyme rolls down like the liquids that White Trash Girl
spits at attackers, or the sludge which she comes from, teeth shine where
there used to be a heap of stones. Liquids and flesh, mire and rubble mix
and mingle.

White Trash Girl shows a permanent state of war: the war of men
against minoritarian women (White Trash Girl, her mother, and her girl
friend Trelita) is revenged by White Trash Girl and her crew, though, but
also paralleled with documentary material of war scenes from the Mexican
Border, and riots. Here, to live means to survive, and White Trash Girl
can only manage to survive because she takes her life into her own hands
in a radical way, using a network of friends to create a wide safety zone
around her body which is a toxic chemical weapon itself.

The Construct Cunt.......................

In 1988, U.S. writer Kathy Acker published her book *Empire of the Senseless*,[26] a monstrous, discontinuous and complex fiction. The book is dedicated to Acker's tatooist – as if the book were the bloody inscription of
life onto the female body. Two I-narrators, the voices of the female protagonist Abhor and her male partner Thivai, talk alternately about their
lives and origins in Paris which is a totally fucked up and dystopian city
being colonized by the Algerians during the ongoing plot. Containing a lot
of allusions, wordplays and references to William Gibson's *Neuromancer*,
Acker's Paris has more to do with Gibson's Chiba or Sprawl, and White
Trash Girl's underground inferno, than with the old European culture
metropole.

26 Acker, Kathy (1988): *The Empire of the Senseless,* New York.
27 Acker 1988: 34.

Abhor, whose grandmother was a prostitute, has been raped by her father, but unlike White Trash Girl's mother, she did not become pregnant with a baby. She is half robot ("construct"), half black, and Thivai always addresses her "cunt," as he calls all women by this metonymic name.

> "I saw her. A transparent cast ran from her knee to a few millimeters below her crotch, the skin mottled by blue purple and green patches which looked like bruises but weren't. [...] A transdermal unit, separated from her body, connected to the input trodes under the cast by means of thin red leads. A construct."[27]

Thivai teaches Abhor, who is an analphabet, the alphabet, wishing her to become a writer. However, her scripture is not the digitally coded off-spring of a computer, as one would expect with respect to her half robot body. Rather, it seems as if her scripture would come directly from the other part of her body, of the "fleshed" black body. With the blood of her fingers, she pictures different hearts. Abhor's bloody scripture of hearts is beyond the digital areas of zeros and ones, it is even beyond the arbitrary system of the alphabet, it is a much more "primitive" one, one which comes out of the oppressed body. And though she is part of the digital culture, she has nothing to say about it. The story ends with Abhor's driving away with a motorcycle and her dreaming of a better world.

The story can be perceived as a kind of alienation as well as an add-ition of black and female voices to Gibson's Western and "male" perspec-tive. Being a black and a cyborg in this story serves to foster her under-privileged status as offspring of different subaltern classes of servants, prostitutes and former slaves. Being a cyborg means here to be positioned at the lowest class level. Being a "construct cunt" means not to be wel-come in the system of humanism and not having a prosperous future, but at the same time embodying both the utopian and dystopian fan-tasies of the future. Maybe it is too much to say Abhor would enjoy her very ambivalent and paradoxical state of being a cyborg woman, because she has a lot to suffer. However, her outcast body stands metaphorically for a hopeful boundary concept as a new, adequate and reflective posthu-man way of survival in a dystopian world. Abhor undergoes various trans-formations and manages to position herself as a 'subject' within this dystopian world: The raped construct cunt becomes a terrorist and finally a motorcycle driver and writer.

Cyberbodies of Desire....................

Australian artist Francesca da Rimini's netcharacters 'Gashgirl'/ 'Doll Yoko' from the web-based, hypertext ghost-fiction *Dollspace* (1997-2001) share a lot of similiarities to the above-mentioned cyborg figures.[28] *Dollspace* is a complex web environment with various sites, hypertext fictions set in pictorial backgrounds and links to politically engaged sites. Gashgirl, or Doll Yoko, the female fictive figuration is constructed above all by texts (summaries of LambdaMOOs, etc.) which reflect her history and her (sexual) desire.

Doll Yoko has risen from a muddy pond in Japan where women used to drown their unwanted, female children. She is a "ghost," as "all women are ghosts and should rightly be feared."[29] She has monstrous sexual desires for young boys. As doll/gashgirl/ghost, she is – like all of the discussed figurations – not a natural born woman, but a posthuman copy/essence, evolving from the dark abysses of patriarchal capitalism. She is gashed, killed, violated, full of fantasies of power and losing control, of scum, of fucking and killing, of getting fucked and killed. Like

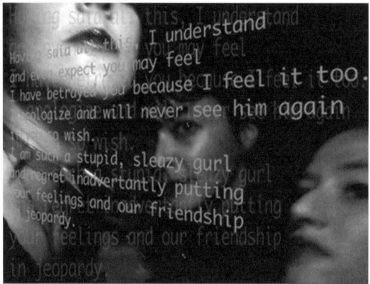

02

28 **Francesca da Rimini**: *Dollspace*. Soundtrack by Michael Grimm
   (1997–2001). http://www.thing.net/~dollyoko [last access: 01/27/2004].

29 Hypertext in: **Rimini/Grimm** 1997–2001.

30 **Acker** 1988: 34.

31 More details about the work see: http://www.machinehunger.com.au/love
   hotel [last access: 01/27/2004].

32 They are used in *Dollspace* and in da Rimini's forthcoming book *Fleshmeat*, too.

Abhor, Doll Yoko who is at the same time dead and alive, wants to destroy and to be destroyed herself, she is a deeply paradoxical figure, situated in an in-between space called "deep dollspace zero" – a space behind the closed eye through which the visitors have to enter in the beginning.

03

Doll Yoko's/the narrator's/the author's (the sentences are often articulated with "I") wild feelings and emotions, circulating between activity and passivity, focus on the topic of losing boundaries in digital space: of sex, gender, subjectivity, agency, of the writer and the reader, of the figuration and the user. Who is this "I" in the end who says: "genderfuckmebaby"? This "I" is splitting into various agents and we, the readers, participate in this dissolution. What does this sentence and all the other sentences in this piece imply? They talk of experiences, of enjoying loss and the violation of boundaries. These sentences and their images become figurations of many voices and embodiments of Doll Yoko, gender dichotomies are completely deconstructed. It is far beyond any relief; it is "haunting" and allows us to fall into the depths of psychic streams and desires.

The same voice (identity) switching happens in *The Empire of the Senseless*, in which one also sometimes forget who talks: Abhor, Thivai, the narrator, or the author. Thus, the reader too switches between the male, and the female I and the unspoken, hidden I-construct of the author:

> "'All I know is that we have to reach this construct. And her name's Kathy.'
> 'That's a nice name. Who is she?'
> 'It doesn't mean anything, it's dead. The cunt must be dead.'
> My puns were dead."[30]

Cyborgian Architectures. . . . .

In her video "Lovehotel" (2000), Australian artist Linda Wallace[31] puts on stage the LambdaMOO adventures of Gashgirl[32]. Offscreen we hear the voice of Francesca da Rimini speaking Gashgirl's texts, on the screen we see the shadow of da Rimini (wearing sunglasses) or other people walking through New York or Tokyo, a lot of times we are on the road, on a ship, in the subway, in the underground and on the streets of these mega-cities. We see façades, walls, and inscriptions, we see faces, moving bodies. And we see a lot of mirrors and reflecting glass, as if the architecture – the body of the city – were reflecting and splitting the narrator's body into many "constructs." Sometimes we see also a running text, the spoken text on the screen, or a detail of the LambdaMOO on a flickering computer screen. "Lovehotel" builds a kind of architecture, moving spaces, a kind of passages, and continuous entrances into capitalist aesthetics with words full of love and desire. The speaking subject is present as she walks through these spaces, crossing many places, reserving public space with her inner fantasies. Virtual Reality here is not something mysterious, no "consensual hallucination" (William Gibson), it is the posthuman urban architecture seen as the emergence of the female body, crossed by various entities and subjects: "Lovehotel. Formula for the Emergence of the New" is the subtitle of this work.

In all of the discussed works, the space – mostly a city – in which the woman moves, is important being part of her as she is part of the city: The boundaries between her and her environment are permeable, fluid and reflective. However, one cannot say that the cyborg woman would personify the postmodern city, as it happened to be in 19th century fiction in which the woman was a metaphor for proliferating monstrous modern urbanism nor is she a skillful techno-slave who helps the console cowboy finding a way through this labyrinth. Rather, she imagines, crosses, and occupies posthuman urban environments as being her territories. They may even be an alienated and reflected prolongation of her own, of her vast desires in a world which did not foresee a space for her. She and her desires are as artificial as urban life is: The borders are blurring, you cannot catch her 'entity.' Unlike in *Involuntary Reception* and *White Trash*

33 It is currently found in different stages on two different servers. In my description, I use a version (http://www2.sva.edu/~dianel/idrunr [last access: 01/27/2004]) that is older, but in which the fictive aspect is more prominent. The newer web site is more documentary and also integrates joint performances and video translations of the net works and ascii streaming: http://2.parsons.edu/~ludin/final_pages [last access: 01/27/2002].

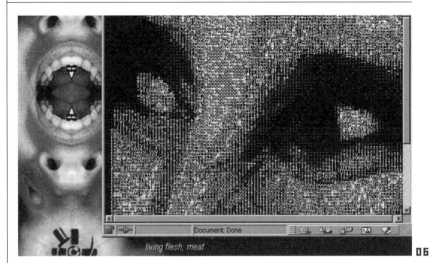

living flesh, meat

06

Girl, but like in *Dollspace*, in "Lovehotel" the protagonist is present as an absent, as moving shadow, ghost, as running text, as off- voice or reflecting glass wall. "Lovehotel" suggests a place of temporary settlement, of nomadic living, in which flows of desire circulate connecting humans and non-humans.

Fluid Identities.........................

This complete dissolving of the characters by simultaneously invoking different fluid figurations is most obvious in Diane Ludin's web-based project *Identity Runners: Re_flesh the Body*.[33] It is a multilayered hypertext project which results from the collaboration with Francesca da Rimini and Agnese Trocchi over several months. Three net characters, avatars or alter egos, are allegorically called Ephemera, Liquid-nation, and Discordia. Entering the start page of the website, you see three different parallel sectors corresponding to these names with picture, running text structure and hypertext structure. In the lower part, the name Metrophage is repeated by all of them. If you click it, you find yourself in a kind of microcell structure. If you read the texts with their similar poetry and click through the hypertexts and image architecture, you become increasingly lost in this labyrinth and forget which texts belong to whom: Everything seems to be the output of a single identity, despite the different names, images and texts. The entire web architecture is polyvocal, furnished with excerpts from various contexts: scientific (e.g., pictures from genetic engineering laboratories), theoretical (e.g., sentences from Donna Haraway), activist, and all the diverse text material that the three have exchanged in chats, e-mails, telephone conferences, real life performances, etc. They also speak in the first person, although the content is not clearly intelligible, it is outside the realm of what may be narrated. One understands a kind of body-speaking, reads of tears, touching, feelings, cells and bodies of information. These sequences are mixed with others from biotechnology discourse. In its entirety, it is a kind of production of biotech bodies and identities with the tools of poetry and alienating contexts. Even though it is suggested by the allegorical avatars, they do not form representative net characters any more, not even one as broken and fluid as Doll Yoko. The impression is rather one of a diffusive flow of biotech body suggestions, more a dissolving into tropes and micro-images (Metrophage). *Identity Runners: Re_flesh the Body* evokes the re-articulation of the female body and its desires in the digital era. However, this body is no longer a female entity or even an organism, but more a "stammering" of intensities, wishes, streams and fragments. Female is a suggestion, not an essence.

Conclusion. . . . .

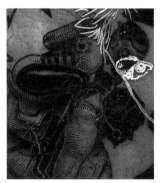

To summarize, the Cyberfeminists's myth consists in imagining a cybernetically coded and sometimes technologically skilled cyborg woman. Flows of subversion are effectuated more by her pleasure of being a hybrid and its de-territorializing impact than by articulated intentional political acts. The cyborg woman is not only the symptom of the Information Age. She is also the site where the symptom becomes a marked and gendered body, where the body becomes embodied.

07 This body resists intentionally or unconsciously – the "informatics of domination" (Haraway). It merely represents a woman at the borders, becoming a posthuman, multiple and flexible entity, who fights for her life, for a temporary viable stay in a non-human world. She is flexible, dispossessed, nomadic. Embodying various technological fantasies, she is at the same time a "genetically determined" symptom of the information age (its effect) as well as a very special agent to subvert and pervert the dominant inscriptions. Being technologically skilled but rather naive – as in *Involuntary Reception* – or completely uneducated – as *White Trash Girl* or Abhor – she transgresses social patterns and embodies resistance by her own symptomatic techno-body. All these cyborg figurations ultimately want to survive in and occupy real and virtual space. In order to fulfill this simple wish, they are unruled, they enjoy their 'own' cyborg bodies, as paradoxically there is no place and no love for cyborgs in a world of cyborgs. Therefore their desires always seem to be monstrous, their pleasures are based in destruction and ruthless self-reference, or they seem to be so open, dissolved and fluid that nothing can harm them. The pleasure these characters experience has risen from the desire to be stubborn, untamed, transgressive. It rises from the resistance against domination, it isn't afraid of destruction, of perverse arrangements with a perverse world. The pleasure of the cyborgs is the resistance of the subaltern against their limited determination, the desire to survive, to dream of better worlds, as Abhor does at the end of the story.

Being a cyborg is not necessarily connected to the newest (digital) technology. However, the cyberfeminist point of view proposes that new technologies and their hybrid outcome are the privileged places of power and resistance today. Only cyberfeminism promoted widely the idea of the transgressive, unruled and subversive cyborg woman, and this idea sometimes converges even with Hollywood fantasies. However, it is also a political myth, and not always reality. A few strong and amazing characters as the ones I discussed above are not realized with the newest digital technology. That means that the cyberfeminist idea of the cyborg figuration does not necessarily converge with the invention of real new media, I would however never say that the skilled woman using new technologies is pure myth. But it is obvious that there are not as many hybrid techno-figurations, high tech artists, or hackers as one would expect after having read cyberfeminist theories. I don't know if it is a question of (non)accessibility to (high) tech for engaged women, or if the question of high tech figuration and high tech realization does not automatically presuppose each other. Maybe low tech has also to be considered as rising important technology. What I am trying to say with the media examples I elaborated here is that the cyberfeminist fantasy of the subversive cyborg woman is not dependent on the use of digital high tech. The fantasy as grounding myth is important, and hopefully is a catalyst for real cyborg women and cyberfeminists to engage in better living. It is crucial to understand that the cyberfeminists' concentration on the body – sometimes parodic, sometimes not – is not an apolitical escapism tending towards bio-determinism. We simply have to recognize that body, gender, technology and the fantasies about them are the most important zones where cultural, symbolic and real power takes place.   <

BIBLIOGRAPHY
Print

Acker, Kathy (1988): *The Empire of the Senseless*, New York **Braidotti, Rosi** (1994): *Nomadic Subjects. Embodiment and Sexual Difference in Contemporary Feminist Theory*, New York **Braidotti, Rosi** (1998): Cyber Feminism with a Difference. In: *Zones of Disturbance*, Silvia Eiblmayr / Steirischer Herbst, eds., Graz **Halberstam, Judith / Livingston, Ira**, eds. (1995): *Posthuman Bodies*, Indiana **Haraway, Donna** (1991): A Cyborg Manifesto: Science, Technology, and Socialist-Feminism in the Late Twentieth Century. In: *Simians, Cyborgs and Women: The Reinvention of Nature*, New York, 149–181, online version: http://www.stanford.edu/dept/HPS/Haraway/CyborgManifesto.html [last access: 04/20/2001] [=Haraway 1991a] **Haraway, Donna** (1991): *Cyborgs at Large*. Interview with Constance Penley and Andrew Ross. In: *Technoculture*, Constance Penley / Andrew Ross, eds., Minneapolis [=Haraway 1991b] **Hayles, N. Katherine** (1999): *How We Became Posthuman. Virtual bodies in Cybernetics, Literature, and Informatics*, Chicago **Kuni, Verena** (1998): The Future is Femail. In: *First Cyberfeminist International, Sept. 20 – 28 1997, Hybrid Workspace*, Kassel, Cornelia Sollfrank / Old Boys Network, eds., Hamburg, 13–18 **Kunsthalle Wien / Klagenfurt**, eds. (1995): *Dara Birnbaum*, (Exh. Cat.), Wien / Klagenfurt **Pierce, Julianne** (1998): *Info Heavy Cyber Babe*. In: Sollfrank/Old Boys Network, eds. 1998, 10 **Plant, Sadie** (1996): Feminisations. Reflections on Women and Virtual Reality. In: *Clicking In. Hot Links to Digital Culture*, Lynn Hershman-Leeson, ed., Seattle, 37–38 **Plant, Sadie** (1997): *Zeros + Ones. Digital Women + The New Technoculture*, New York / London / Sydney **Stone, Allucquère Rosanne** (1991): Would the Real Body Please Stand Up? In: *Cyberspace: First Steps*, Michael Benedikt, ed., Cambridge **Volkart, Yvonne** (1999) Infobiobodies, Art and esthetic strategies in the new world order. In: *Next Cyberfeminist International*, Old Boys Network, Rotterdam, March 8–11, 1999, Hamburg, 61–68 **Volkart, Yvonne** (2002): Das Fliessen der Körper: Weiblichkeit als Metapher des Zukünftigen. In: *Future Bodies*, Marie-Luise Angerer / Kathrin Peters / Zoë Sofoulis eds., Wien / New York, forthcoming, [= Volkart 2002a] **Volkart, Yvonne** (2002): Strategic Sexualisations. Between Method and Fantasy. In: *Technics of Cyber<>feminism. <Mode=Message>*, Claudia Reiche / Andrea Sick, eds., Bremen [=Volkart 2002b]

Web

Aristarkhova, Irina (1999): Cyber-Jouissance: An Outline For A Politics Of Pleasure. (non-published paper). German version: *Telepolis* online magazine, http://www.heise.de/tp (May 1999) [last access: 01/27/2004] **Old Boys Network**, http://www.obn.org [last access: 01/27/2004] **Rimini, Francesca da / Grimm, Michael** (1997-2001): *Dollspace*, http://www.thing.net/~dollyoko [last access:

01/27/2004] **Rimini, Francesca da / Ludin, Diane / Trocchi, Agnese**: *Id_runners*. See: id_runners version 1.0, http://www2.sva.edu/~dianel/idrunr/ [last access: 01/27/2004]; version 2.0, http://z.parsons.edu/~ludin/final_pages [last access: 01/27/2002] **Reiche, Claudia** (2001): concept for *Technics of Cyber< >Feminism.<Mode=Message>*, http://www.thealit.de/ kultur/cyber feminism/home/concept.html [last access: 04/04/2002 **Vorkoeper, Ute** (2000), Widerspenstige Praktiken im Zeitalter von Bio- und Informations-technologien. In: *Telepolis* online magazine http://www.heise.de/tp/deutsch/ inhalt/sa/3556/1.html [last access: 08/09/2002] **VNS Matrix** (1991): *The Cyberfeminist Manifesto of the 21 Century*, http://sysx.apana.org.au/artists/ vns [last access: 01/27/2002] **Volkart, Yvonne**: *Tenacity. Cultural Practices in the Age of Bio and Informationtechnologies / Widerspenstige Praktiken im Zeitalter von Bio- und Informationstechnologien; Body as Byte: The Body as Information_Flow; Connective Identities*, http://www.xcult.org/ volkart, [last access: 01/27/2002]

Video   **Lucas, Kristin** (2000): *Involuntary Reception*, 17", single channel video, two-channel DVD installation, http://www.involuntary.org [last access: 01/27/2004] **Reeder, Jennifer** (1996): *The Devil Inside* (Part I of the *White Trash Girl* series), 8", co-shooting: Sadie Benning **Reeder, Jennifer** (1997): *Law of Desire*, 18" (Part III of the *White Trash Girl* series), **Wallace, Linda** (1999): *Lovehotel. Formula for the Emergence of the New*, 6"45"', Camera, Editing, Concept: Linda Wallace, Sound: Jason Gee. Based on excerpts from *Fleshmeat* by Francesca da Rimini. http://www.machinehunger.com.au/lovehotel [last access: 01/27/2004]

Film   **Conceiving Ada** (US 1997) 1'25", Production: Hotwire Production / Lynn Hershman-Leeson, Director: Lynn Hershman-Leeson, Screenwriter: Lynn Hershman-Leeson, Eileen Jones, et al., Performers: Tilda Swinton, Francesca Faridany, Timothy Leary, Karen Black, John O'Keefe, John Perry Barlow, J.D. Wolfe, et al., Cinematography: Hiro Narita, Bill Zarchy, Editor: Robert Dalva, Music: The Residents

Illustration   01 Kristin Lucas: *Involuntary Reception*, http://www.involuntary.org [last access: 01/27/2004]

02—03 Francesca da Rimini / Michael Grimm: *Dollspace*, http://www.thing.net/ ~dollyoko [last access: 01/27/2004]

04—05 Linda Wallace *Lovehotel*: http://www.machinehunger.com.au/love hotel [last access: 01/27/2002]

06—07 Francesca da Rimini / Diane Ludin / Agnese Trocchi: *Id-runners*, http://z.parsons.edu/~ludin/final_pages [last access: 01/27/2002]

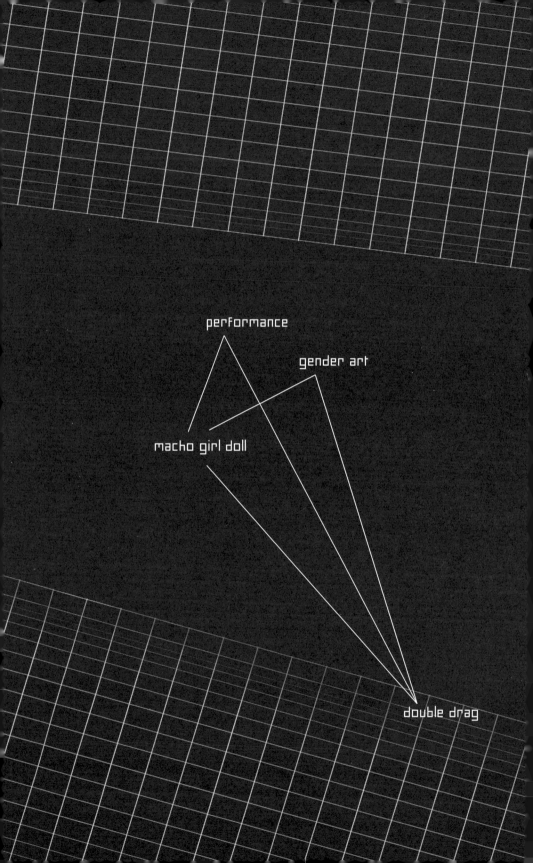

FEMALE-BOBS ARRIVE AT DUSK

ANNE-MARIE SCHLEINER

And why this patch? I was dissatisfied with the various bimboish female Bob patches, as being inappropriately dressed, and I wanted to create a patch of that type that was non-bimboish and in the style of the original Bobs.

Loren Petrich, [1996] from the 'Read-me, Sex-changer!' file for his "Tina-bob" patch for the Marathon Infinity game engine.[1]

>   In the latter half of the 1990's, before 3-D shooter and adventure computer games evolved to include female characters, game fans and hackers grafted female game heroines into what were once almost exclusively male populated game worlds. It is quite possible that these early fan-created female heroine "patches" patterned the genotype for later heroines in commercial games.[2] In 1996, Eidos Interactive's lucrative release of *Tomb Raider* with action heroine "Lara Croft" was followed by a stream of commercial 3-D shooters with at least the option of playing active female avatars. PC and console games like *Resident Evil* (1997), *Vigilance* (1998), *O.D.T.* (1998) and *Dark Vengeance* (1998), allow the player to choose female characters from a cast of genders and ethnicities (similar to

the array of character profiles available in console fighting games like *Mortal Kombat*).[3] Sega's 1998 release of the space shooter *Enemy Zero* features a solo action heroine with familiar first name, "Laura Lewis."

Yet this millennial infusion of female polygonal heroines into the 'shoot-em up' computer game world was not accompanied by a parallel influx of human female players. (Other genres of computer games follow different gender make-ups, for instance, online role-playing games have historically been more popular with women in comparison to shooter games.) With the notable exception of recent formations of female *Quake* clans like *Vicious Vixens* and *Clan PMS*, the 3-D shooter world is still

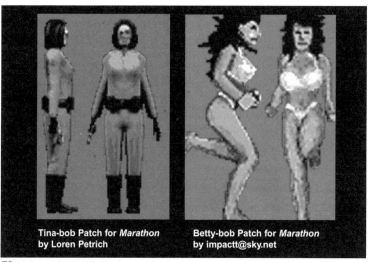

Tina-bob Patch for *Marathon*
by Loren Petrich

Betty-bob Patch for *Marathon*
by impactt@sky.net

01 "Tina-bob" vs. "Betty-bob"

1 Petrich, Loren (1996): 'Read-me, Sex-changer' file, http://www.webcom.com/petrich/games/marathon/downloads.html#FemBob/ [last access: 01/27/2004]

2 Merriam-Webster online defines "genotype" as: 1. The genetic constitution of an organism or a group of organisms. 2. A group or class of organisms having the same genetic constitution. http://www.m-w.com/ [last access: 01/27/2004]

3 "PC" refers to games that are played on personal computers and "console" refers to games played on closed hardwired platforms like Sega and Playstation.

4 http://www.clanpms.com/[last access: 01/27/2004], http://www.DaValkyries.com/ [last access: 01/26/2000]

5 Schleiner, Anne-Marie (forthcoming): Parasitic Interventions: Game Plug-ins and Patches as Hacker Art. In: *Mariosophy: The Culture of Electronic Games*, Erkki Hutahmo, Ed.

6 Jenkins, Henry (1992): "Get A Life!": Fans, Poachers, Nomads. In: *Textual Poachers: Television Fans and Participatory Culture*, New York / London, 24–27.

largely inhabited by human males who control virtual male and/or female avatars.[4] The pairing of human men/boys with virtual women avatars, a configuration that one may speculate is sometimes one of the few relationships that these teenage and twenty-something computer gamers have to 'women,' generates some interesting puzzles.

Why have some of these guys traded in their soldiers for macho girl dolls? Do they identify with the heroines as players in drag? Are these virtual women dangerously idealized porno dolls or substitute girlfriends for geeks? What are we to make of "Croftage," the term I overheard one gamer, standing nearby at a Los Angeles outlet of Fry's Electronics, use to describe the massive celebrity worship of *Tomb Raider* heroine, Lara Croft, who stars in a major motion picture produced by Paramount. And how to approach these male constructed female avatars as a female player?

XY TO XX MODIFICATIONS

Let's return to Loren Petrich's "Tina-bob" patch cited at the beginning of this text. In online gamer fan culture the practice of creating game "add-ons," "patches," "hacks," "skins," "levels," "mods," and all manner of game modifications allows for game 'fans' to actively participate in the cultural production of gaming.[5] Game patching goes beyond Henry Jenkins' description of the "de Certeauian" processes of "nomadic textual poaching" practiced by avid television fans to material reconstruction and hacking of game worlds and avatars. Avid gamers design their own levels, mods (for *Quake*) and wads (for *Doom*), including remaking architecture, characters (character skins and 3-D models), sounds and game play. If game hackers get their hands on the original source code from a game engine they often create editors for altering games which they share with other gamers, distributing them freely on the web.[6] Since each custom fan-created game editor is unique to each game there is a diverse, piece-meal, ingenious, and buggy variety of software available for editing games. As a kind of open source laboratory for gaming, online patch distribution is a forum for proposing new and alternative character types and player subject positions, occasioning mutations at the borders of 'official' game genres.

Loren's Tina-bob patch replaces first person shooter *Marathon Infinity*'s male "Bob" protagonist with a 'non-bimbo' "Tina." The patch's read-me file describes Loren's feminist rationale for his creation, Tina's (who was almost named "Mary") discreet body proportions and unisex attire. Tina-bob was fabricated as an alternative to patches like J. Coffey's "Amazons and Female Robertas" *Infinity* patch. "Amazons and Female Robertas" populates the game world with topless double-D Amazons and fluorescent bikini poster girls (the "Robertas").[7] In a cultural domain where comic book extremes, excess and monstrosity are rampant, unostentatiously efficient Tina-bob in her military green full body uniform arrives to save the day, refusing to participate in a spectacle of radical otherness, or to submit to adolescent male fantasies of female sexiness. She is truly a female version of Bob, the unsupposing everyman male protagonist of the *Marathon* Series whose nondescript character is intended to allow the

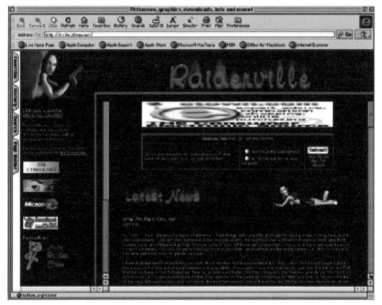

02 A Lara Croft fan site with a "Nude Raider Free" banner displayed in the bottom left frame.[8]

7 Marathon Hyper Archive NorthWest, http://www.marathon.org/hyperarchive/ [last access: 01/27/2004]

8 Raiderville, *The Croft Times*, e-zine, http://rville.ctimes.net/ [last access: [05/20/2000], compare: The Tomb Raider Archive, http://www.ctimes.info/ trarchive/ [last access: 07/14/2002].

9 **Schleiner, Anne-Marie** (2000): Mutation.Fem: An Underworld Game Patch Router to Female Monsters, Frag Queens, and Bobs whose first name is Betty. In: *Ctrl+shift art – ctrl+shift gender, Convergences of Gender, New Media and Art*, Nat Muller / Deanna Herst (Axis, bureau voor de kunsten v/m), Eds., Amsterdsm. This article is an exploration of *Quake* and other shooter female avatars, referencing queer theory articulations of monstrous gender construction by the likes of Judith Butler and Judith Halberstam.

player to slip seamlessly into his skin. (Although, as the existence of this and other female Bob patches suggest, a male Bob skin is not necessarily what male gamers feel like wearing every day.)

As game engine graphics, hardware processing power, and 3-D accelerator cards improve, allowing for increased visual detail and special effects like fog and lighting, game genres experience content and game play 'evolutionary' transformations as well. Skipping forward on a highly accelerated shooter genre timeline to the year 2000, neither the androgynous Tina-bob, the bare-breasted Amazon, nor the sleazy poster girl, have emerged as the female genotype *de jour* in the online *Quake* arenas. Or perhaps it is more accurate to say the "Frag Queens" of network shooters like *Quake* and *Unreal* mix and match female character lexical genes from all of these heroines into a new kind of a Tina-bob monster, splicing pumped up musculature onto large breasts and androgynous combat wear.[9]

NUDE RAIDER VS. TOMB RAIDER FAN WARS

A similar debate concerning female avatars is inscribed in the topology of online *Tomb Raider* fan culture. Finally provided with prepackaged female heroine in the form of action adventure heroine Lara Croft, male gamers contested what sorts of female avatar representation were appropriate in 3-D adventure gaming, and in the encompassing online fan culture. Many *Tomb Raider* fans belong to the *Nude Raider* web ring. A ring is a collection of personal web sites that share a common theme and link to one another in a circular hyperlink pattern. The *Nude Raider* patch, an extremely popular game patch internationally, circa 1997, hacked the *Tomb Raider* engine and replaced Lara Croft's shorts and halter top with nude textures (while retaining her ammunition belt). *Nude Raider* fan sites such as *Naturally Lara* often displayed screen shots of Lara in naked game play action. Some of these sites even featured 'fake' nude Laras with smoother air-brushed polygons than the real *Nude Raider* patch allowed for. In response to the pornographization of their beloved Lara, more upstanding *Tomb Raider* fans, including many fans in the *Tomb Raider* Ring, began to post "Nude Raider free" banners on their sites. These fans affected a more romantic stance towards Lara, regarding *Nude Raider* as disrespectful towards their beloved English lady. (Although I don't think they objected to her comic book heroine figure judging by the choice of Lara pictures on their sites).

Fan web sites such as *The Croft Times* elevated Lara to celebrity status, spinning elaborate tales of Lara's personal and extracurricular (outside the game) life.[10] Fan fiction distributed through zines and club publications is common among fans of television series' like *Star Trek* and *Beauty and the Beast*. According to Henry Jenkins, this particular television fan culture is comprised mostly of women, and he reads the stereotype of brainwashed obsessive fans as a reification of mainstream culture's misogynist values.[11] On the other hand, but not too surprising considering the gender composition of the majority of gamers, computer game fan fiction is usually 'penned' by male writers. Writers such as Michael L. Emery, author of *The Flowers of God*, and Marc Farrimond, author of *Wedding Bells*, post their romantic Lara Croft stories on *The Croft Times* and other fan fiction sites.[12]

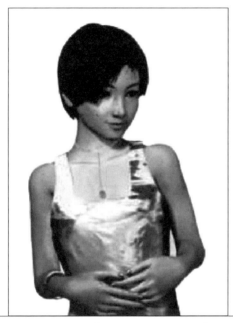

03 Kyoko Date, virtual singer of Japanese hit pop song *Love Connection*

Lara Croft's hyperreal virtual girlfriend role is encouraged by Eidos Interactive's clever introduction to the game. The player uses Lara's personal mansion as a training course for subsequent game play and can also enter into any of her private rooms, including bedroom, bathroom, and a cavernous oversized kitchen. After complet-

10 *The Croft Times*, e-zine, http://www.ctimes.net/fancorner/fanfic/index.html [last access: 01/27/2004],

11 Jenkins 1992: 19.

12 *The Croft Times*, e-zine, http://www.ctimes.net/fancorner/fanfic/index.html [last access: 01/27/2004] Game fan fiction is also very common in the role playing game genre, where players publish extensive histories of the fantastic exploits of their guild or clan on their own guild or clan dedicated sites.

13 Wolff, W. Dire (1996): Kyoko Date - Virtual Idol, A Retrospective View. In: *Shibuya River*, http://www.wdirewolff.com/jkyoko.htm [last access: 01/27/2004].

14 Yamag's Garage: Ryoko, http://members.tripod.co.jp/RYOKO_3D/index1.html [last access: 05/26/2000].

ing the training course with Lara's pleasantly upper crust British voice as guidance, the player feels as if he has personally made her acquaintance (and he can return to visit her home anytime he wants to). By allowing the player access to Lara's domestic sphere, in addition to 'accompanying her' on her adventures to Egyptian tombs and exotic cities, the player is granted special privileges normally reserved for family, friends and boyfriends.

Lara Croft's most obvious virtual female competitor in the East was Japanese pop star "Kyoko Date." Kyoko's popularity has waned dramatically and unfortunately her existence has almost been entirely erased from the web, leaving a trail of dead links in her wake. Created in 1996, Kyoko is a 3-D female character who released pop songs, music videos, and generated extra income as spokeswoman for San Francisco new media company Oz Interactive. With a short boyish haircut, slender and girlish in comparison to Lara Croft, Kyoko had her own following of fan fiction and pornographic tales which borrowed from anime and manga conventions in Japan. Sometimes as 'innocent' as a "Sailor Moon" high school romance, Kyoko's fan fiction occasionally dipped into erotica. Kyoko fan Dire Wolff describes how, "on the Internet, teenage boys from Italy, Hong Kong, Malaysia, and around the world were flooding Kyoko Date bulletin boards with postings and scouring the web for graphics of her beauty."[13]

But Kyoko Date is not the last of her breed. Creating 3-D girls and posting web sites for them has become something of a hobby for Japanese 3-D modelers or "Character Generator" artists. The site **http://www. fushimi.com/angels/** contains links to many 3-D girl sites (and just a few 3-D space dogs and other 3-D characters). Like Kyoko Date (and unlike Lara Croft or even unlike the cartoon style of Japanime characters), these girls are extremely hyperreal, from their bone structure to the pore texture of their skin. Some Character Generator artists even place small imperfections like moles and flushed mottled skin on their character's faces, giving characters like "Ryoko" a perversely human uniqueness.[14] While these minutely detailed, multiple eye-lashed, million polygoned 3-D characters are quite stunning, it is important to note that computer game engines are not yet capable of processing live in game action at this level of detail. (It may take hours just to render one still frame of such a high resolution character.) Nevertheless, they strike a formidable presence on their web sites – singing pop songs, offering horoscope advice, and exuding timeless frozen girlish youth to the nth degree.

DRAG

Both the portrait of the lonely male computer gamer longing for a romanticized virtual girlfriend and the image of the horny gamer hunched behind his keyboard searching for an objectified virtual porn star rely on the heterosexist assumption that boys would naturally represent themselves virtually as boys unless some stunted desire for women, (girlfriends or sexy babes), compelled them to create female avatars. A conceivable alternate scenario unfolds for at least *some* male gamers, if we consider that unlike the trophy princess who awaits rescue at the end of *Prince of Persia* or the blond 'bimbos' in *Sim-Copter*, female action heroines are active avatars in the game space that are 'worn' by the player. Some male players are attracted to the idea of anonymously donning a feminine skin without the social repercussions which often attend such a gesture in 'real life.' Like early text-based MUD's or more recent graphical Role Playing Games where male players often assume female identities, (and female players assume male identities), playing a female character allows male players to escape the parameters of the male game hero role and his 'real life' maleness. Here the avatar could be perceived as a layer of feminine drag masking the gamer's male core identity. Or, following the identity theory of Sandy Stone, the female game character identity is simply one of many equally 'real' subjectivities lived out by the player in virtual and non-virtual life, (to live is to role play). The latter view describes the subject as a polymorphous collection of multi-gendered identities who lack a unifying core identity.[15]

Julian Dibbell's ethnographic journeys into the textual MOO, *LamdaMOO*, led him to the discovery that even self-professed heterosexual men often played female characters and engaged in

04 Ryoko by Yamag's Garage. Ryoko has three small moles on her face.

15 **Stone, Alluquère Rosanne** (1995): *The War of Desire and Technology at the Close of the Mechanical Age*, Cambridge/Mass., 1995.

16 **Dibbell, Julian** (1998): *Samantha, Among Others. In My Tiny Life: Crime and Passion in a Virtual World*, New York, 127.

17 **Dibbell** 1998: 134.

"TinySex" with other male and female characters of indeterminate RL (Real Life) gender. He describes the "gauzy" sensation of wearing a feminine skin as "enchanting," even though he had never been particularly interested in cross-dressing in the past.[16] Dibbell makes a persuasive argument for understanding the allure of online cross-gender experimentations as an attraction to fantasy role play itself, or as a "taste for [...] thoroughgoing entanglement." Experienced male MOOers construct convincing female "morphs" with meticulous craft, avoiding the hollowness of "FabulousHotBabes" characters by refraining from textual description of obvious physical features and by adding punky 'feminist' or 'cross gender' signifiers such as gothic tattoos and combat boots.[17] Similarly, just as the sharply articulated muscular contours of the real life drag queen accent her beauty, in the 3-D game world, prosthetic vestiges of the macho soldier, Lara Croft's gun holster and Uzi, "Jill Valentine"'s combat boots and beret and "Amy Leong"'s rocket launcher, thrust the gender identity of the heroine into delectable confusion, a collage of drag upon drag, a jumble of gender signifiers.

DOUBLE DRAG

As a woman playing a computer game heroine who is a already a digital drag queen, I can best describe the experience as a kind of drag twice removed, or drag squared. As is sometimes the case for women who participate in various sectors of technoculture, as I enter into the masculine discourse domain of computer gaming culture I go butch, taking stock of my arsenal of weaponry and combat gear. Yet as I maneuver what is clearly a womanly form through the passageways and recesses of the game I am distinctly aware of my hyperbolic feminine identity. (Is there some appreciation for my view of my avatar's figure at this moment that I share with the *Nude Raider* ring or television's Xena, Warrior Princess's lesbian fan club?) My pleasure in swift and deadly annihilation of the enemy and gory blasts of pixilated blood provides an immediate, gut-level satisfaction that cuts through the layers of drag, collapsing the female drag queen identity of the avatar back onto my own. Thus the double drag can be reversed on itself, allowing women to relish in gratuitous computer game violence while playing female avatars.

At each layer of drag I am distinctly aware of a forced identity, of a feminine role on top of a masculine role, both floating above my own customary female identity. This is not to say that my 'customary female identity' is more original, natural, or unified, being itself a kaleidoscope of feminine, masculine, student, hetero girlfriend, bi-flirt, student, teacher, artist, writer, coder, gamer, American citizen, immigrant daughter and other roles and identities, a worn and continually morphing suit I have become accustomed to wearing. And neither is 'drag' simply the donning of a gender which happens to be opposite of one's biological sex. Drag is an intentionally aware gesture – an ultra-exaggerated 'performative' gender act, performative as all gender acts are but distinguished from Judith Butler's drag inspired queer theory formulation of "performative gender" by awareness and dramatic excess.[18] Girls can be drag queens too. Drag is self-conscious gender *play*. It is deliberate toying and stretching of gender roles to their dramatic limits. Drag is a gender graft that is hyperbolic and extreme like the male *Quake* hero's bulging muscles

05 Angelyne from her virtual tour on angelyne.com. This photograph of Angelyne's face was displayed on a large billboard in Hollywood.

18 **Butler, Judith** (1990): *Gender Trouble: Feminism and the Subversion of Identity*, London / New York, 175.

19 Angelyne is famous in Los Angeles for being an unfamous celebrity. She is an ultrafeminine silicone-bodied 'celebrity' who has never acted. She pays for her own billboard posters promoting herself and rides around Los Angeles waving at people from a pink Corvette convertible.

20 See my article **Schleiner, Anne-Marie** (2001): "Does Lara Croft wear fake polygons?" In: LEONARDO, vol. 34, no. 3, 221–226 [orig. published in: *Switch Electronic Gender*, June 1998] for a description of Lacanian processes of identification with game avatars.

or Lara Croft's large pointy breasts, like the drag queen's outrageously perky breasts or the butch lesbian's motorcycle boots. Drag is Hollywood's local celebrity "Angeline" and other monstrous plastic-faced, silicone-breasted, perfectly feminine freaks who cruise the streets of L.A. (who started out biologically female).[19]

And this deliberate gender masquerade is what I refer to when I say that the feminine and masculine collapses onto 'my own' when I lift my Uzi and blast my opponent to nothingness. I am no longer in drag, in a self-aware idealized gender mask (or double-drag mask on mask). I even lose consciousness for a moment of any subjectivity I might be – I am pure bliss and gloating victory. Then all the layers melt together into another new subjectivity – a new gender configuration for me to inhabit temporarily and add to my collection – I am a polygon-skinned large-breasted phallic Uzi-toting keyboard pumping bad-ass bitch queen. Thus, as I play my female game avatar in a double drag dress, anti-subjectifying libido blasts interrupt my performance, adrenaline inspired identification leakage that, (along with repetition and Lacanian processes of mirror image identification with my avatar), assist the play act in penetrating below the surface.[20] The drag performance morphs into a new role, a new subjectivity, a new gender configuration that incorporates the excessive and contradictory gender signifiers into itself.

FINALE

The efforts of male gamers like Loren Petrich and cohorts in shaping the Tina-bobs of the future are appreciated. Through their participation in an unofficial dialogue waged over the Internet they developed alpha and beta female heroine genotypes. Trading in their male soldiers for female fighters, they constructed ultra-fem drag queens, level-headed female soldiers, and sexy doll automatons. When the first commercial games were released with glossy female heroines, these fans further articulated various subject positions in relation to their female avatars, and constructed an online fan culture encompassing these heroines. Male gamers and CG artists have initiated the process of female avatar representation and character construction but there is still an urgent need for more women to take an interest in entering the virtual world of computer gaming, both as players, active game hackers/fans, and game developers, perhaps first as double drag queens. With a human female infusion, new gender configurations would arise that would strike new patterns in a world currently populated by human men with virtual men and virtual women.   <

BIBLIOGRAPHY
Print **Butler, Judith** (1990): *Gender Trouble: Feminism and the Subversion of Identity*, London / New York **Dibbell, Julian** (1998): *Samantha, Among Others. In My Tiny Life: Crime and Passion in a Virtual World*, New York **Jenkins, Henry** (1992): "Get A Life!": Fans, Poachers, Nomads. In: *Textual Poachers: Television Fans and Participatory Culture*, New York / London **Schleiner, Anne-Marie** (2000): Mutation.Fem: An Underworld Game Patch Router to Female Monsters, Frag Queens, and Bobs whose first name is Betty. In: *Ctrl+shift art – ctrl+shift gender, Convergences of Gender, New Media and Art*, Nat Muller / Deanna Herst (Axis, bureau voor de kunsten v/m), Eds., Amsterdsm **Schleiner, Anne-Marie** (2001): "Does Lara Croft wear fake polygons?" In: *LEONARDO*, vol. 34, no. 3, 221-226, [orig. published in: *Switch Electronic Gender*, June 1998] **Schleiner, Anne-Marie** (Forthcoming): Parasitic Interventions: Game Plug-ins and Patches as Hacker Art. In: *Mariosophy: The Culture of Electronic Games*, Erkki Hutahmo, Ed. **Stone, Alluquère Rosanne** (1995): *The War of Desire and Technology at the Close of the Mechanical Age*, Cambridge/ Mass.

Web **Angelyne's driving tours**, http://www.angelyne.com [last access: 01/27/2004] **The Croft Times**, e-zine, http://www.cubeit.com/ctimes/ index. htm [last access: 01/27/2004], compare: **Petrich, Loren** (1996): 'Read-me, Sex-changer!' file, http://www.webcom.com/petrich/games/marathon/downloads. html#FemBob/ [last access: 05/26/2000] **Marathon Hyper Archive NorthWest**, http://www.marathon.org/ hyperarchive/ [last access: 01/26/2000] **Merriam-Webster online**, http://www.m-w.com/ [last access: 01/27/2004] **New 3-D Girl**, http://www.fushimi.com/angels/ [last access: 01/27/2004] **Wolff, W. Dire** (1996): Kyoko Date - Virtual Idol, A Retrospective View. In: *Shibuya River*, http://www.wdirewolff.com/jkyoko.htm [last access: 01/27/2004] **Yamag's Garage**: Ryoko, http://members.tripod.co.jp/RYOKO_3D/index1.html [last access: 05/26/2000]

Illustration **01 Loren Petrich**, "Tina-bob"-Patch in comparison, http://www.webcom.com/petrich/games/marathon/downloads.html#FemBob/ [last access: 01/27/2004], see also **The Marathon Archive**, 'Tina Shapes' by Loren Petrich, http://archives2.bungie.org/cgi-bin/findmaps.cgi/ [last access: 01/27/2004] **02 Raiderville**,*The Croft Times*, http://rville.ctimes.net/ [last access: [05/20/2000] **03 Wolff, W. Dire** (1996): Kyoko Date – Virtual Idol, A Retrospective View. http://www.wdirewolff.com/jkyoko.htm [last access: 01/27/2004] **04 Yamag's Garage**: Ryoko, http://members.tripod.co.jp/RYOKO_3D/index1.html [last access: 05/26/2000] **05 Angelyne's driving tours**, http://www.angelyne.com [last access: 01/27/2004]

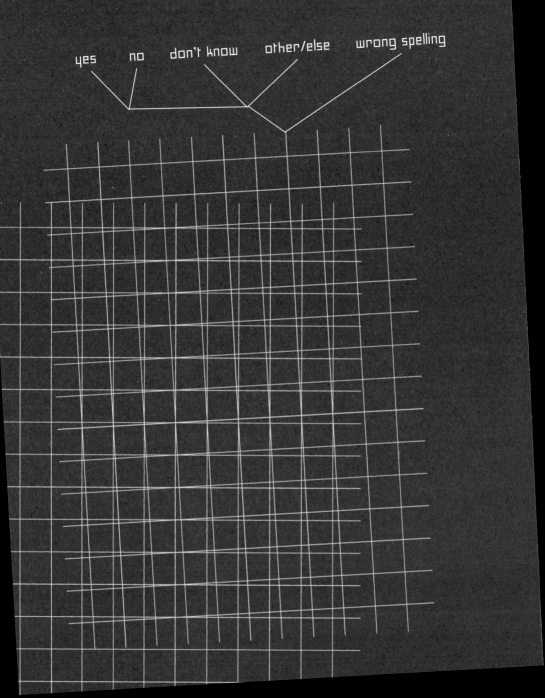

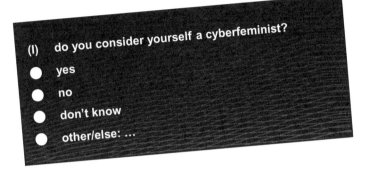

VERENA KUNI

Frame/Work

A proposal on how some thoughts on the aesthetics and
politics of cyberfeminism(s), might be continued when
reconsidering ( ) a true and enduring love ( ) a
fatal attraction ( ) a lucky livelong partnership ( )
a dangerous liaison ( ) other/else: ...

(II) do you call yourself a cyberfeminist?

● yes
● no
● don't know
● other/else: ...

*""What is, in the context of contemporary cyberfeminist art,
your vision of a yet unknown cyberfeminist art?""*

What a question. What a task, to think here seriously
about what is being asked for. However, complications
occur, and this is the case not only on the level of
aesthetic reflection where you'd automatically enter
a contested zone whenever definitions of art are on
demand.
Until today, my text processor still underlines the
word "cyberfeminism" (as well as "cyberfeminist,"
"cyberfeminists," and so on) in flaming red to indicate a "wrong spelling," or an unknown phrase at
least. Why did I never 'teach' the program to use it?
Did I just forget to include it into the program's
dictionary? Was it because I still like the suggestion that I was making use of an unfamiliar, 'fresh'
vocabulary when thinking and writing about artistic
processes in the age of digital production? Which, at
least after the turn of the century, was definitely
not the case. At least when taking a look at academic
discourse, one would easily find related lectures,
roundtables and courses announced, even the first
Ph.D. projects to be devoted to "cyberfeminism."
What a recognition.

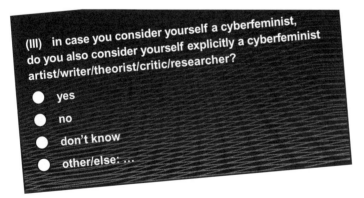

(III) in case you consider yourself a cyberfeminist,
do you also consider yourself explicitly a cyberfeminist
artist/writer/theorist/critic/researcher?

- yes
- no
- don't know
- other/else: ...

But what made me sometimes feel so uneasy when I read
articles or announcements that just indicated it?
Was this the case because, taking a closer look on
how the term "cyberfeminism" was used in the related
context, I would have to realize that others seemed
to use it in a way quite different to my own understanding of what "cyberfeminism" was (is, could be)?
Probably not, taking into account that from the
beginnings of my own encounters with cyberfeminisms,
I appreciated the idea of a multi-focal and multi-
voiced cyberfeminist pluriverse without stable definitions of what could be considered as cyberfeminist
(and not).
Did the uneasiness occur because I often discovered
the negative or at least sceptical attitudes against
"cyberfeminism" being discussed in the context of
(net.)art and (net.)culture, obviously combined with
the prejudice this would automatically exclude or at
least blur any serious political impact 'true' cyberfeminists should strive for? Or was it maybe just
because of an unspoken scepticism against the recognition itself?
But what, being an academic myself, should have nour-
ished related feelings? Was it because, while having
started myself as a theorist writing about "cyberfem-
inism(s)," in the meantime my own relationship to
cyberfeminism had developed in different directions,
including practices not easily to be subsumed under
the category of academic discourse? Or was it for reasons more closely related to my experiences with and
within the area of academic discourse itself, especially the one I am most familiar with: art history?
Hence, was it a fear against what might be called a
process of "framing cyberfeminism" within the institutions of art, and the discourses they necessarily
produce to exist?
Or was it rather because, seriously asking myself

about what would be my vision of a yet unknown cyberfeminist art, in the context of contemporary cyberfeminist art, I had to realize that before answering
this question I would have to come up with a convincing answer for another one: What is, in the context
of contemporary art, a vision of contemporary cyberfeminist art?

What is "contemporary cyberfeminist art"? Who is producing, who is processing it? Where is it to be
found? How is it to be defined? Are there even any
"contemporary cyberfeminist artists"? And if so, what
about their public recognition? Have "cyberfeminism,"
"cyberfeminist art," "cyberfeminist artists," together
with the academic discourses on cyberfeminism, proudly
entered the processes of institutionalization, and
occupied their places within contemporary art history's
Hall of Fame?

If so, what are the profits and gains of this process
on the one hand – and what are disadvantages and
losses on the other? And if not, is there anyone
demanding it?

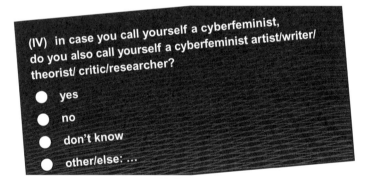

(IV) in case you call yourself a cyberfeminist,
do you also call yourself a cyberfeminist artist/writer/
theorist/ critic/researcher?

- yes
- no
- don't know
- other/else: ...

""Cyberfeminism has had an enormous impact on the visual arts today.
whereas the majority of political movements have employed art
and artists for propaganda purposes, cyberfeminism has worked to
transform art – and artists themselves.""

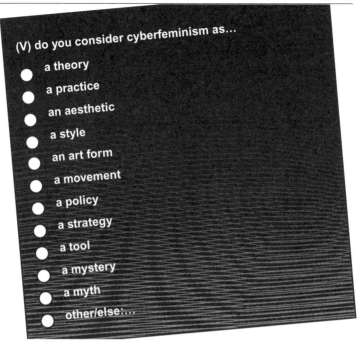

(V) do you consider cyberfeminism as...

- a theory
- a practice
- an aesthetic
- a style
- an art form
- a movement
- a policy
- a strategy
- a tool
- a mystery
- a myth
- other/else:...

""The paradox for cyberfeminism has always been that it speaks from a feminine position that it is simultaneously trying to transform.""

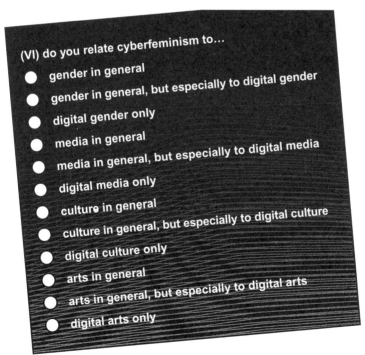

(VI) do you relate cyberfeminism to...

- gender in general
- gender in general, but especially to digital gender
- digital gender only
- media in general
- media in general, but especially to digital media
- digital media only
- culture in general
- culture in general, but especially to digital culture
- digital culture only
- arts in general
- arts in general, but especially to digital arts
- digital arts only

""The cyberfeminist challenge to accepted ideas of what constitutes great art and great artists was part of a broad attack on the art establishment.""

(VII) how would you define the
relation between art and cyberfeminism

● necessary

● superfluous

● possible

● impossible

● productive

● dangerous

● constructive

● destructive

● other/else: :...

""The cyberfeminist problematic in art history is shaped by the terrain in which we work but is ultimately defined within that collective critique of social and economic power which is the women's movement.""

(VIII) would you say art has had/has/will have
an impact on cyberfeminism?

● yes

● no

● don't know

● other/else: ...

""Cyberfeminist art, for instance, cannot be posed in terms of cultural categories, typologies or even certain insular forms of textual analysis, precisely because it entails assessment of political interventions, campaigns and commitments as well as artistic strategies.""

(IX) would you say cyberfeminism has had/has/will have an impact on art?

- ⬤ yes
- ⬤ no
- ⬤ don't know
- ⬤ other/else: ...

>""There have to date been several attempts to map out the field
>of cyberfeminist artistic practice. All disdain the idea of
>answering the question 'What is cyberfeminist art?'. There is no such
>entity; no homogenous movement defined by characteristic
>style, favored media or typical subject-matter. There are instead
>cyberfeminist artistic practices which cannot be comprehended
>by the standard procedures and protocols of modernist art history
>and criticism which depend upon isolating aesthetic
>considerations such as style or media. The somewhat clumsy phrase
>'cyberfeminist artistic practices' is employed to shift our
>attention from the conventional ways we consume works of art as
>objects and stress the conditions of production of art as a matter of
>texts, events, representations whose effects and meanings depend upon
>their conditions of reception – where, by whom, against the
>background of what inherited conventions and expectations.""*

(X) would you say it is possible/interesting/ useful/necessary to use the phrase...

- ⬤ cyberfeminist imagination
- ⬤ cyberfeminist imagery
- ⬤ cyberfeminist image
- ⬤ cyberfeminist design
- ⬤ cyberfeminist style
- ⬤ cyberfeminist aesthetic(s)
- ⬤ cyberfeminist art
- ⬤ cyberfeminist art work
- ⬤ cyberfeminist work of art
- ⬤ cyberfeminist artistic practice
- ⬤ cyberfeminist artist
- ⬤ other/else: ....

""A problematic, borrowed from the developments in Marxist philosophy, defines the underlying theoretical or ideological field which structures the forming of concepts and the making of statements. Thus, for instance, the concept 'cyberfeminist art' is the product of a bourgeois problematic in which 'art' is assumed to be a discrete and self-evident entity in which a knowing, conscious individual expresses herself in terms of an object which contains – acts as a repository for – a recognizable content called a cyberfeminist point of view or cyberfeminist ideology. M.K. uses the notion of the ideological developed in structuralist Marxism to counter this: 'the ideological is the non-unitary complex of social practices and systems of representation which have political consequences'. Thus, cyberfeminist artistic practice has initially to begin to define a problematic in relation to an understanding of the ways in which it can be effective – not by expressing some singular and personal set of ideas or experiences, but by calculated interventions (often utilizing or addressing explicitly women's experiences ignored or obliterated in our culture). Therefore, the study of cyberfeminist cultural practices leads to a series of tactical activities and strategically developed practices of representation which represent the world for a radically different order of knowledge of it. These interventions occur in the context of established institutions and accepted limits of what is ratified as art and how it should be consumed.""

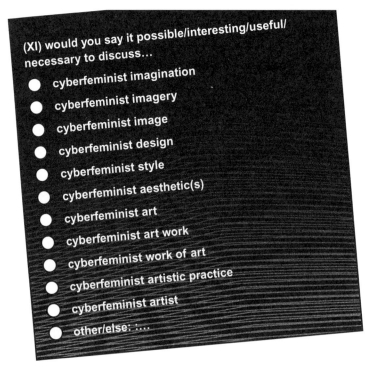

(XI) would you say it possible/interesting/useful/ necessary to discuss...

● cyberfeminist imagination
● cyberfeminist imagery
● cyberfeminist image
● cyberfeminist design
● cyberfeminist style
● cyberfeminist aesthetic(s)
● cyberfeminist art
● cyberfeminist art work
● cyberfeminist work of art
● cyberfeminist artistic practice
● cyberfeminist artist
● other/else: :...

""Cyberfeminist artistic practices cannot pretend to a greater effectivity in political change than the relative position socially designated for such activities by the society as a whole. But equally they cannot be denied a strategic necessity within a broader spectrum of contemporary political activities.""

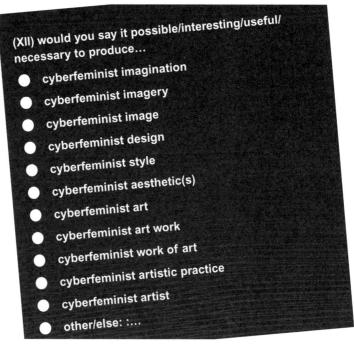

(XII) would you say it possible/interesting/useful/necessary to produce...
- cyberfeminist imagination
- cyberfeminist imagery
- cyberfeminist image
- cyberfeminist design
- cyberfeminist style
- cyberfeminist aesthetic(s)
- cyberfeminist art
- cyberfeminist art work
- cyberfeminist work of art
- cyberfeminist artistic practice
- cyberfeminist artist
- other/else: :...

""Cyberfeminist art practices do not in general subscribe to the myths of essential femininity but are consciously addressed to questions of gender and subjectivity.""

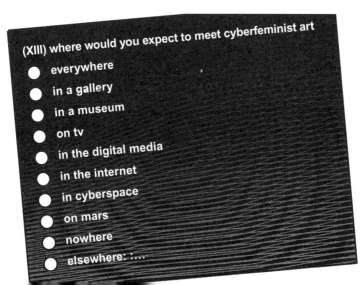

(XIII) where would you expect to meet cyberfeminist art
- everywhere
- in a gallery
- in a museum
- on tv
- in the digital media
- in the internet
- in cyberspace
- on mars
- nowhere
- elsewhere: :....

""Cyberfeminism is the conviction that gender has been, and continues to be, a fundamental category for the organization of culture. Moreover, the pattern of that organization usually favours men over women. Such a definition will not suit everyone who claims the identity 'cyberfeminist'. Nonetheless, it helps to clarify the role of the writer in shaping the interpretation of predominantly non-verbal artworks. While the very act of creating verbal categories for artwork risks deforming and consolidating the art itself, the particular risks in invoking the term 'cyberfeminist art' expose the often hidden ideologies at work in the formation of art disciplines. Although there are nascent ideological meanings in descriptive terms such as neo-realist or abstract expressionist, the effect of the term 'cyberfeminist artist' is quite different. Moreover, the appellation 'cyberfeminist' is sometimes spurned by artists whose work seems sympathetic with a cyberfeminist project.""

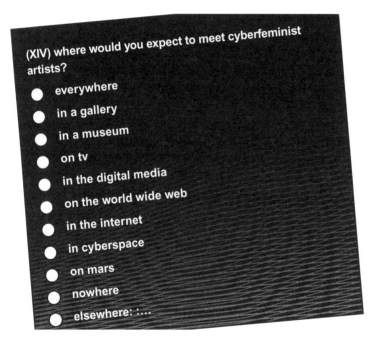

(XIV) where would you expect to meet cyberfeminist artists?
- everywhere
- in a gallery
- in a museum
- on tv
- in the digital media
- on the world wide web
- in the internet
- in cyberspace
- on mars
- nowhere
- elsewhere: :...

""Is cyberfeminism a useful descriptive term for art that employs radically different modes of address, aspiration and genre? The difficulty of answering this question helpfully reminds us of the sharp difference between the conceptual possibilities and limitations of art discourse and the often anarchic specificity of art. Or to put it slightly differently, these persistent questions remind us that rationality gives us ways to make categories while art gives us ways to resist them.""

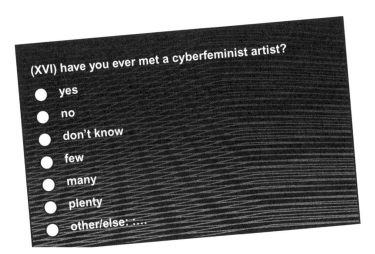

(XV) have you ever met an artist calling
herself a cyberfeminist?

- yes
- no
- don't know
- few
- many
- plenty
- other/else: :....

""Cyberfeminist art is neither a style, nor a movement, but rather a value system, a revolutionary strategy, a way of life.""

(XVI) have you ever met a cyberfeminist artist?

- yes
- no
- don't know
- few
- many
- plenty
- other/else: :....

""Cyberfeminist art is work that is rooted in the analyses and commitments of contemporary cyberfeminisms and that contributes to a critique of the political, economic and ideological power relations of contemporary society. It is not a stylistic category nor simply art produced by women.""

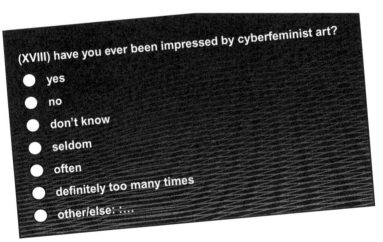

(XVII) have you ever been exposed to cyberfeminist art?

- yes
- no
- don't know
- seldom
- often
- definitely too many times
- other/else:...

*""There is no perfect marriage between cyberfeminism
(as a political ideology) and art (as a cultural activity).
Cyberfeminism promises at the same time to enrich the products
of art, to expose the pretensions and vested interests in art and
to break open the categories of art altogether.""*

(XVIII) have you ever been impressed by cyberfeminist art?

- yes
- no
- don't know
- seldom
- often
- definitely too many times
- other/else: :...

""'Cyberfeminism' is not necessarily a consciously determined ingredient
of the work, but a product of the relation between the work
and the representations of a dominant culture, a particular audience,
and the uses to which it is put. It has also been argued that there is
no cyberfeminist art but only art that can be read as cyberfeminist.""

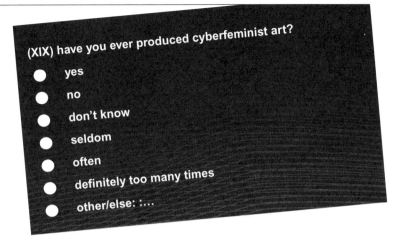

""New Media is not essential for cyberfeminist art practice, but it does offer possibilities for working directly with the artist-audience relationship, and exposing multiple, complex, overlapping meanings within the same piece – useful for cyberfeminists determined to challenge the certainties of our society.""

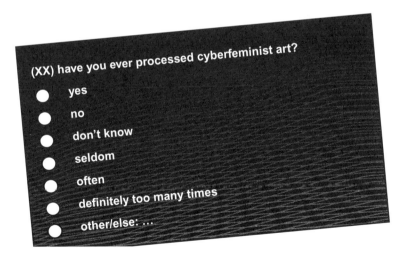

""Cyberfeminism has raised other, even more fundamental questions for art history, questions that are now affecting its function.""

The function of art history? Maybe, not only – or even: rather than "in the context of (a) contemporary cyber-feminist art," in the context of contemporary cyberfeminism, the function(s) of cyberfeminism(s) as well.

Appendix:
Thanks to Mary Kelly, Lucy Lippard, Roszika Parker, Griselda Pollock, Peggy Phelan, Lisa Tickner and many, many others, including the legendary Old Boys Network. Inspirational source texts to be found among others in: *Framing Feminism. Art and the Women's Movement 1970-85,* Roszika Parker / Griselda Pollock, Eds., London / New York 1987; *Art and Feminism,* Helena Reckitt Ed., Survey by Peggy Phelan, London, 2001.

If you do not want to read my lips, you might like to read the headlines of my texts. If you do not want to read between the lines only, you might like to read the texts as well.

Related Texts:
Kuni, Verena (1998): 'Cyberfeminismus ist kein grünes Häkeldeckchen'. Zur kritischen Netzpraxis von Künstlerinnen. In: *kritische berichte,* vol. 26, no.1, 1998, 65–72 [= Kuni 1998a]
Kuni, Verena (1998): The Future is Femail. Some Thoughts on the Aesthetics and Politics of Cyberfeminism. In: *First Cyberfeminist International Sept. 20.–28. 1997, hybrid Workspace, Kassel,* Cornelia Sollfrank / Old Boys Network, Eds., Hamburg, 13–18 [= Kuni 1998b]; slightly revised version (2001) online under: http://www.obn.org (reading room) [last access: 07/30/2002] **Kuni, Verena** (1999): Die Flaneurin im Datennetz. Wege und Fragen zum Cyberfeminismus. In: *Konfigurationen. Zwischen Kunst und Medien,* (= Papers of the Conference 'Konfigurationen…', Kassel, Juli 1997), Sigrid Schade-Tholen / Georg Christoph Tholen, Eds., Munich, 1999, 467–485 [= Kuni 1999a] **Kuni, Verena** (1999): Performing Cyberfeminism. In: *Next Cyberfeminist International, Old Boys Network, Rotterdam, March 8–11, 1999,* Cornelia Sollfrank / Old Boys Network, Eds., Hamburg, 69–72; slightly revised version (2001) online under: http://www.obn.org (reading room) [last access: 07/30/2002] [= Kuni 1999b] **Kuni, Verena** (2000): Cyberfeminism? Just Do it! Eine Einladung zur Infektion. In: *infection manifesto,* Andrea Knobloch, Ed., no. 3, Düsseldorf, 35–39 [= Kuni 2000a] **Kuni, Verena** (2000): Ganz automatisch ein Genie? Cyberfeministische Vernetzung und die schöne Kunst, Karriere zu machen. In: *Musen Mythen Markt. Jahrbuch VIII der Frauenbeauftragten der Hochschule der Künste Berlin,* Sigrid Haase, Ed., Berlin, 41–49; slightly revised version (2001) online under: http://www.obn.org (reading room) [last access: 07/30/2002] [= Kuni 2000b] **Kuni, Verena** (2001): geschlecht macht schwierigkeiten. gender troubles beim schreiben über kunst. In: *lesebuch,* Angelika Stepken, Ed., Karlsruhe, 92–101 [= Kuni 2001a] **Kuni, Verena** (2001): Der Widerspenstigen Zähmung. Webbasierte Kunst im etablierten Ausstellungsbetrieb. In: *Kunst-Bulletin, no. 11,* November 2001, 28–31 [= Kuni

2001b] **Kuni, Verena** (2002): In search of… (a short story), contribution to: *Anthology of Art*, Jochen Gerz, Ed., January 2002; see: http://www.anthology-of-art.net [last access: 01/27/2004]; pre-print version under http://www.kuni.org/v/nettext.htm [last access: 01/27/2004] [= Kuni 2002a] **Kuni, Verena** (2002): Some Thoughts On The New Economy of Networking. Cyberfeminist Perspectives on "Immaterial Labour," "Invisible Work" and other Means to Make Career… In: *Very Cyberfeminist International OBN Conference, Hamburg, December 13–16, 2001*, Helene von Oldenburg / Claudia Reiche, Hamburg, 2002, 120–127 [= Kuni 2002b] **Kuni, Verena** (2002): Die Legende vom Netzkünstler. In: *Borderline. Strategien und Taktiken für Kunst und soziale Praxis*, (= Papers of the Conference 'Borderline…', Wiesbaden, June 2001), AG Borderline-Kongress, Ed., Wiesbaden, 87–108.; English version upcoming as: 'What is a net artist?' On the uses and disadvantages of the legend of the artist in the era of its techno-logical reproducibility, In: *From Words to Work*, Doris Frohnapfel, Ed., Cologne (forthcoming). [= Kuni 2002c] **Kuni, Verena** (2002): Cherchez la Femme Fatale Digitale? Weit mehr als eine neue Masche – Cyberfeministische Netzwerkpraxis. In: *Frauen- und Genderforschung an der Universität Trier*, Helga Schnabel-Schüle / Claudia Winter / Verena Kuni, Eds., Trier (forthcoming). [= Kuni 2002d] **Kuni, Verena**: Framing Cyberfeminism(s). Cyberfeminismus und/als Kunst. In: *Kunstforum International. Kunst und Politik*, vol. 164 (forthcoming). **Kuni, Verena**: Legende von der cyberfeministischen Netzkünstlerin. Oder: 'Why Have There Been No Great Cyberfeminist Net.Artists?'. In: *(Neue) Medien. Medialität – Kultureller Transfer – Geschlecht*, (= Papers of the Conference '(Neue) Medien…', 7. Kunsthistorikerinnentagung, Berlin, September 2002), Susanne von Falkenhausen / Hildegard Frübis / Kathrin Hoffmann-Curtius et al., Eds., Marburg (forthcoming).

For further publications concerned with cyberfeminist theories and practices see: http://www.kuni.org/v/public.htm [last access: 01/27/2004]; for projects related to cyber-feminism(s) see: http://www.kuni.org/v/p-cfy.htm [last access: 01/27/2004]; http://www.kuni.org/v/obn [last access: 01/27/2004]

(XXI) which of the following formula is your favorite?

- art and cyberfeminism
- art or cyberfeminism
- art of cyberfeminism
- art off cyberfeminism
- art on cyberfeminism
- art in cyberfeminism
- art as cyberfeminism
- art against cyberfeminism
- other/else: …

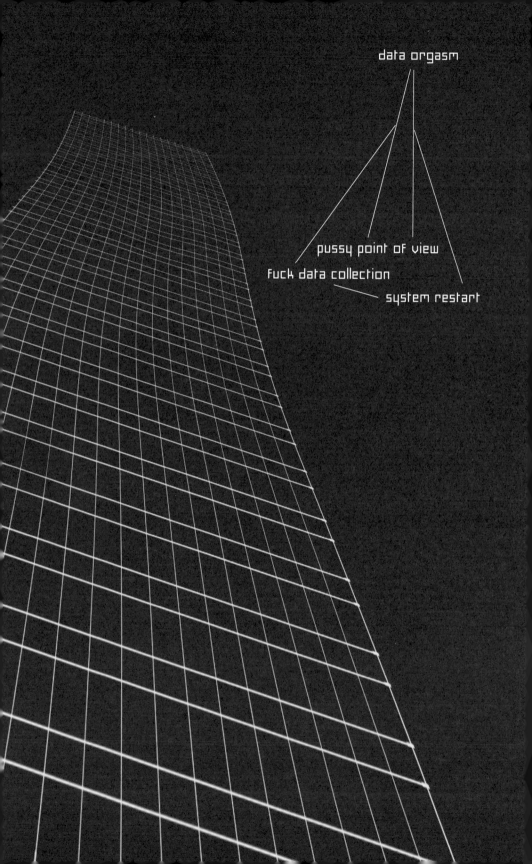

data orgasm

pussy point of view

fuck data collection

system restart

I.K.U. SEVEN PAGES

SHU LEA CHEANG

I.K.U. is a Japanese scifi porn digi movie
Produced by Uplink Co., Tokyo
Art Concept/Direction by Shu Lea Cheang
Computer graphics:
Dildo retriever by YOSIDA Amane
Data grab by Hanaoka
Chip IKU commercial by ISHIHAMA Eye

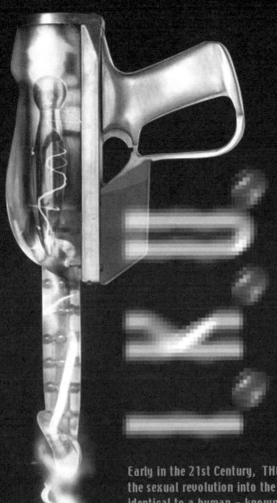

Early in the 21st Century, THE GENOM CORPORATION advanced
the sexual revolution into the GEN-XXX phase- a being virtually
identical to a human - known as an I.K.U. Coder. The GEN-XXX I.K.U.
Coders were superior in their harddrive bodies, and at least equal
in insatiability, to the programming engineers who created them.

I.K.U Coders were used in the night-world as XXX data hunters,
in the orgasmic exploration and sexualization of other couples.
After a non-stop sexing journey by a GEN-XXX I.K.U. Coder team
in the night-world, Coders were declared fulldata - ready for retrieval.

Special data collectors - I.K.U. RUNNER UNITS- had orders to fuck
to retrieve, upon detection, any fulldata I.K.U. Coders.

This was not called love.
It was called sex.

IKU is Japanese word for orgasm.

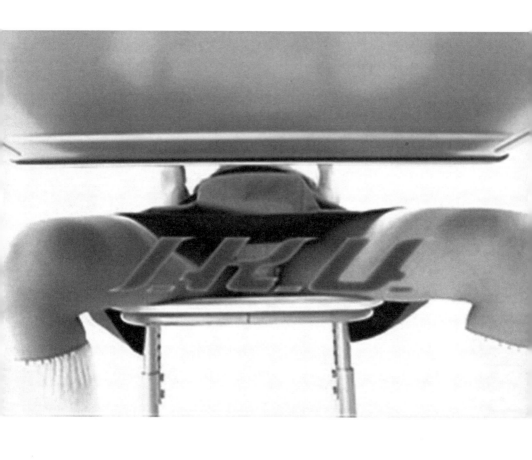

the Pussy the Matrix

LAUNCH_ME_UNPLUG_ME_HARDDRIVE_ME_RETIRE_ME

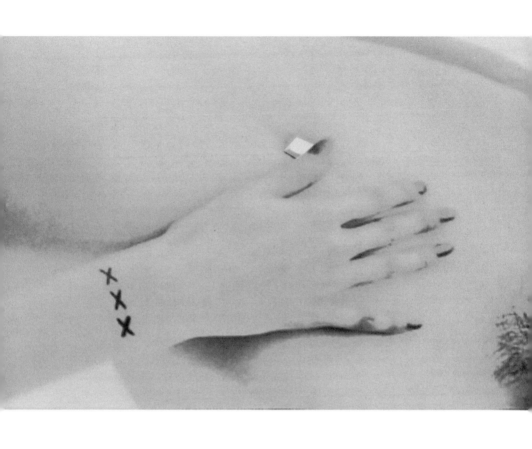

my belly button
my system restart

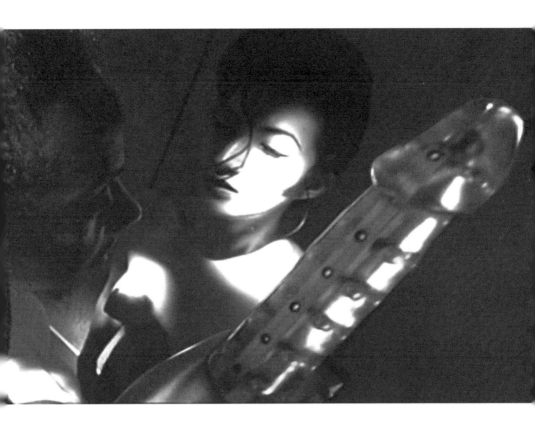

**my body
my harddrive**

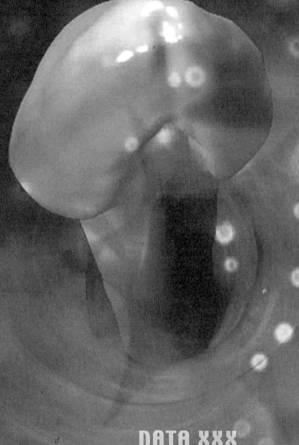

DATA XXX
Maintain: 40
Collectable: 30
R255G102B104

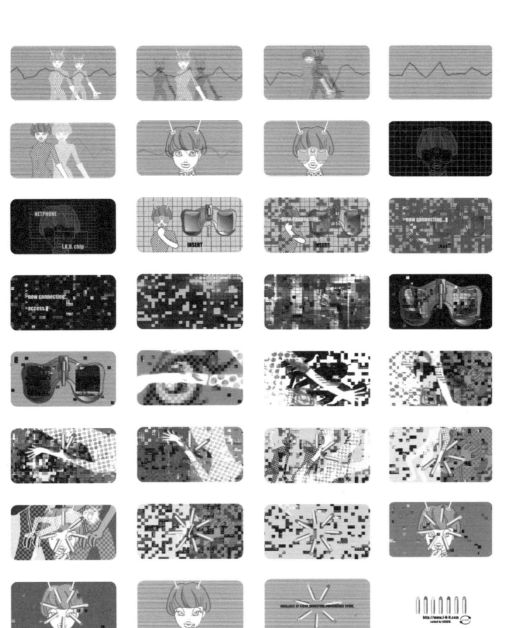

MOBILE SEX
www.I-K-U.com

obscenity of metaphysics

military medical technology

oscillation

visible human

wonders of the unseen world

ON|OFF+SCENITY MEDICAL AND EROTIC COUPLINGS IN THE CONTEXT OF THE VISIBLE HUMAN PROJECT

CLAUDIA REICHE

EPISTEMOLOGICAL FEEDBACK LOOP

> At a first glance cyberfeminist art and theory as presented in this volume, seem not to have very much in common with a major anatomical and information science's project of recording and documenting human bodies in the digital medium, as the *Visible Human Project* does. Anatomy is generally agreed to have different goals and methods from art, cultural, social, or media theory – be it (cyber)feminist or not.

It is especially the tradition of feminist theory to decipher the results of 'objective' sciences as culturally produced and producing, to analyze a so called 'nature' as a fiction that is based on cultural discourses, involving 'natural' patterns of gender. From this point of view, a scientific project in the field of anatomy could be assumed to be writing a media and gender theory implicitly, as cyberfeminist theory does explicitly.

This effort to analyze some of the discourse of the *Visible Human Project* proceeds in a cyberfeminist mode, taking into consideration that like cyberfeminism, the diverse research field of the *Visible Human Project* uses, tests and thus theorizes its object in the digital medium. This means to value most the way of presenting – data or theses – and even to claim that the way of directing representations on the different visual and verbal 'stages' designed in various interfaces is the most important result for both object of research and research itself.

OSCILLATION

Statements such as the following delivered at the renowned U.S. conference 'Medicine Meets Virtual Reality' introduce a celebratory discourse on the *Visible Human Project* in the military and scientific world:

> "The Visible Human is one of the cornerstones of a one million percent revolution in medicine. [...]If everyone develops their simulators from the Visible Human, then these things will be inter-operable. All you do is replace the Visible Human with your patient's own data. [...] It is no longer blood and guts; it is bits and bytes. It's like sending a letter or e-mail..."[1]

A 'letter' is pictured like the living human being, an 'e-mail' like the *Visible Human*. Whatever the *Visible Human* may be, its difference

---

1 **Dr. Rick Satava**, my tape-recording and transcription of his paper on 'The 5th Dimensional Human: Integrating Physical, Biochemical, and Informational Worlds' held 1998 at: *NextMed: The End of Health Care? Thought ∞ Health ∞ Immortality, A Conference on the Bio(r)evolution* ™ in San Diego, see **Reiche, Claudia** (1999): Bio(r)Evolution™, On the Contemporary Military-Medical Complex. In: *The Spectralization of Technology: From Elsewhere to Cyberfeminism and Back*, Marina Grzinic, Ed., Maribor.

2 **National Library of Medicine (US) Board of Regents** (1990): *Electronic Imaging, Report of the Board of Regents, US Department of Health and Human Sciences, Public Health Service, National Institutes of Health*, NIH Publication 90-2197, Bethesda, Maryland.

3 **Biel, Maria** (1996): Die phantastische Schöpfung des ersten (echten) digitalen Menschen. In: *P.M.*, no. 29, 90.

4 ...and can be compared to female 'cyber bodies' in realistic concretion, declared as 'cyberfeminist.'

5 **National Library of Medicine (US)**, *Visible Human Project™, Factsheet*, http://www.nlm.nih.gov/pubs/factsheets/visible_human.html, [last access: 01/27/2004].

towards a human being in this statement is regarded as negligible, as the information one gets via letter or e-mail is assumed to be identical, only that the use of the Internet for e-mailing has proven to be superior in some respects, especially in handling the fragility of the material world. The *Visible Human* thus exists in the form of globally standardized data, meant to facilitate an information "revolution" in medicine.

Dealing with the *Visible Human* seems to be risky not only in terms of the concept, but with the image-material as well that bears its name and is spread worldwide in a multitude of presentational formats. Much has been announced preliminarily: in the discourse of popular science nothing less than the presentation of images of a 'new cyber human' – as a 'cyber woman' has been in some traditions of cyberfeminism Looking at one of

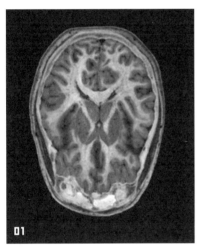

01

the first distributed images of the *Visible Human* (figure 01), you probably would not have seen such a 'new human' – without knowing about the project's claims.

In the official discourse of the project, initiated by the National Library of Medicine (US), this 'visible human being' has been summarized in a formula declaring the project to be the "first digital description of an entire human being."[2] The problem is: What will an 'entire' human being have been, that has become visible on a digital basis?

Someone who is seeing number sequences, diagrams and structures of complex networks of visual and text-based information in front of her/his inner eye after such preparation might have been 'visibly' overpowered and disappointed at the same time by the massive intrusion of old highly realistic image concretion. The meat aspects of the *Visible Human*'s imagery are reported as being associated by the general public more with a human butcher shop[3] than with a new image of the human ruled by the structure of the digital medium.[4] The National Library of Medicine's goal did not seem to offer, apart from the obvious medial transfer of data-storage, something conceptually new at first sight. Cross-sectional representations of the human anatomy as shown in the example of the head have already been documented and referenced in various anatomical publications and are common in medicine especially through the imaging technique of computer-tomography.[5] What is claimed to be done first by the National Library of Medicine with the *Visible Human Project* seems to be situated in the novelty of combining the project's image-acquisition with the digital data storage, of combining the process-ability of this data with the stimulation of visions of a future medicine (a future human condition). What can be declared effectively new about the *Visible Human Project* apparently needs to be situated within these combinations, is aneffect of operations in the technological as conceptual articulation of the 'human.' These combinations create the *Visible Human* and its context as an oscillating mode between its pretensions of literally making fantasies of invulnerable, immortal 'cyber humans,'[6] or 'cyber soldiers' and genuine achievements of new medial articulations come true. Let's have a closer look on how the *Visible Human Project* presents and changes itself from a cyberfeminist point of view, if conceptual work opens up new interpretations and visibilities between words and images.

6 **Reiche** 1999.

7 **Reiche, Claudia** (2002b): Technics of Ambivalence and Telepresence. In: *technics of cyber◇feminism <mode=message>*, Claudia Reiche, Andrea Sick, Eds., Bremen. "I find it interesting that it is possible to build every logical gate with negations only. The logical structure is stripped off the pictorial reflexes even of one's theoretical and abstract imagination. This shows the prevalence of the 'Not-operation' and gives a hint about the possibility of the machine to reach the real only through logical manipulation of the symbolic, leaving out the human including the imaginary function.", 203–204.

8 See my distinction between: 'visible,' 'not visible,' and 'invisible' in: **Reiche, Claudia** (1996): PIXEL: Experiences with the Elements. In: *Medicine Meets Virtual Reality: 4*, Suzanne J. Weghorst / Hans B. Sieburg / Karen S. Morgan, Eds., Amsterdam / Oxford / Tokyo / Washington DC, 681–689.

9 On the no longer 'living images' of cinematography in comparison to the 'living' Visible Human, see **Reiche, Claudia** (1998): "Lebende Bilder" aus dem Computer. Konstruktionen ihrer Mediengeschichte. In: *BildKörper. Verwandlungen des Menschen zwischen Medium und Medizin*, Marianne Schuller / Claudia Reiche / Gunnar Schmidt, Eds., Hamburg.

10 **Biel** 1996: 87.

NEGATIONS

In order to describe how traditions of medial representations are includ-ed and worked upon by the *Visible Human Project* it has to be defined first what the digital 'visible human' in correspondence to its massive popular scientific reception is not. In fact, recurring definitions can be detected:

• The *Visible Human* is making visible what has not been seen before.
• The *Visible Human* is no invention.
• The *Visible Human* is not mortal.

These revelations appear in different formulations in almost every report on the *Visible Human Project*. It is the oscillating figure of negation that includes various possibilities. In the ambiguous property of negation many forms (except the one that has been excluded by the negation) can appear like shadows behind a curtain or like possibilities within the arrangements of logical gates that build the Boolean algebraic operations 'and,' and 'or.'[7] 'Something that has never been seen before': something hidden that can be discovered behind a curtain on a stage or something invisible that leaves an empty stage, if the curtain is drawn – that is not for certain.[8] 'Something that has never been seen before': does that refer just to new image contents or an unknown form of representation – after the known type of images and in a different format? 'No invention' might refer to a scientifically objective representation or a 'true' image. Some-thing 'immortal' has either never lived or lives eternally.[9]

There are different variants swaying between the significances that act more or less spectacular and suggestive. The following headline referring to the *Visible Human Project* in the popular German scientific magazine *P.M.* is an example for the dissolution of oscillating negations: "The Fantastic Creation of the First (Genuine) Digital Human Being."[10]

'Fantastic' has lost here its meaning of fictitious: the creation is original, it is a living human being (who in its former existence had an identity as a male white U.S. citizen of 39 years), and it is a digital one with an immortal existence 'in the computer,' as the text furthermore explains. Categories are set into motion in the name of something scandalously new, with an euphoric and somewhat paradoxical undecidedness (if one sticks to the hitherto known reality) regarding representational states of this new 'human being': we know it is digital data, but beyond that is it a living being, an image or a concept? In the logic of the text's implicit argument the digital medium has made the differentiation between these states obsolete. Within such a fantastic medium every medial or even non-medial format, like photochemical recording, printed text or a living being is unified and – in the here-totalitarian gesture of news sensationalism – identified with one another. Is this just an extreme and insignificant example of scientific trash journalism? Contrary to that, I think that this "fantastic creation of the first (genuine) digital human being" exposes effective conceptual styles in today's sciences and representational cultures, especially to be found in theories of the posthuman, of Artificial Life as in some cyberfeminist art and theory, that continues – be it with a critical intention or not – the celebratory discourse on the digital.

IMPOSSIBLE STAGE OF A CAESURA

This specific contemporary gesture – intensified to contradictory asser-tions like the above – that presents at the same time the declaration of a cultural caesura brought about by the digital medium[11] and the positive, hence paradoxical, description of its effects has to be located. I suggest the term 'obscene' in the truest sense of the word 'ob-scene': 'before,' 'in front of,' 'out of,' thus 'off scene' (in the sense of *scaena*, Latin for stage) in order to name the space opened up by this gesture. What is not on stage, but will have shifted the focus of attention as if it was, is off scene – thus provoking oscillating figures of negation and affirmation of its point of reference. And the *Visible Human Project* can be thought of as such – 'ob scaena' – .

Off scene of the hitherto possible negation locates its object by claim-ing that the *Visible Human* opens up a visibility not seen before. The pos-itive descriptions of what is 'visibly' new about it – with the notions of an original creation, an unprecedented true document and an immortal, 'liv-ing' data-image – though neither leave nor claim its point of reference, the stage of the visual, with the most rude and dirty effects on organized thinking. As exciting and productive as this may be, I propose to explore

---

11 On the problematic belief and location of the 'digital caesura,' which rarely
   is reflected as such, see **Tholen, Georg, Christoph** (1997): Digitale Differenz, Zur Phantasmatik und Topik des Medialen. In: *Hyperkult. Geschichte,
   Theorie und Kontext digitaler Medien*, Martin Warnke / Wolfgang Coy /
   Georg Christoph Tholen, Eds., Basel / Frankfurt am Main.

12 The following six subtitles are transcripts from the German dubbed version
   of *Tron*.

13 Media Festival Osnabrueck 2000, mix by the group 'Nog Harder', *N3 Vee Jay
   Night*, N3 (German TV station), 03/03/2001.

a possible ob-scenity of the *Visible Human* in a different way, following the effects of this oscillation, shifting the point of reference as the scene.

This first requires the building of a new, more adapted scene, thus achieving a possible representation. A possible visual prequel of the *Visible Human* is to be constructed in the following by means of a number of fragments from Hollywood films, video art and the culture of computer medical visualization.

DISPLAYS

In *Tron* (U.S. 1982, director Steven Lisberger) future scientists are able to digitize objects in a way making them disappear from the material world, thus allowing them to exist as pure data. A return to material form can be accomplished as well. Such "Matter Transform Sequences" are carried out with the molecular structure of living human beings, the adventures of whom as 'transformed matter' deliver the film's screenplay. The character continues to exist as an information pattern in human form – like a figure in a computer game. (figure 02–05)

02 "Asking admission to code group 6" "You know I can't allow that"[12]

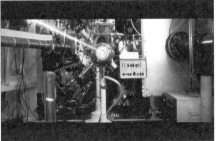

03 "Hey, hey, the almighty Master Control Program [...] come on, show what you can do, you show-off"

04 "I am warning you [...] I will get you on the game frame."

05 "You want to play around with me [...] you can get that..."

A current design of continuous fast motion in a central perspective into the image should be compared to a still from a computer-animated music video.[13] The tunnel journeys into artificial worlds whose smooth round walls are covered with numbers are being mixed with images from the 1970s of a dancing disco girl, respectively close-ups of her lower abdomen directly above the camera. (figure 06–07)

06 "We don't want to shock people..."[14]   07 "...we don't show extreme porn."

The following images come from the movie-trailer for *Fantastic Voyage* (U.S. 1966, director Richard Fleischer). It is about intruding into a human body and surviving it. Scientists in a submarine have been miniaturized with the help of a computer and are injected into the blood circuit of a patient to treat a blood clot in his brain. The computing center of this operation corresponds to the one of a rocket launch into outer space. According to the logic of the film, both spaces are regarded as unrevealed reservoirs of visibilities that can be explored by computer technology. The penetration of this outer/inner space by traveling across the body is accomplished as follows: the natural human measure appears as a giant cave-like landscape that is explored with new possibilities and risks by the miniaturized scientists and the camera. Therefore, the dynamic voice in the movie-trailer hardly promises too much: "You are going where no

---

14 This and the following subtitle come from an interview with 'Nog Harder', *N3 Vee Jay Night*.

15 Fox Video with 'Original Theatrical Trailer', *Fantastic Voyage*.

16 The following legends are transcripts from the trailer to *Fantastic Voyage* ibid.

17 The views displayed in the video are based on the program VOXEL-MAN, http://www.uke.uni-hamburg.de/institute/ imdm/idv/ [last access: 01/28/2004].

man or camera has ventured before."[15] However, the significance of "you" turns into a question: "And when you come out you may never look at yourself in the same way again."[16] (figure 08–09)

08 "A startling new kind of excitement plunges you in the most incredible adventure that men would ever achieve."

09 "Four men and a beautiful girl actually entering the human body [...] exploring an unknown universe, unknown dangers."

The following series of images comes from the video *Professor Roentgen meets the virtual body*, produced by the Institute for Mathematics and Computer Science in Medicine at the University of Hamburg in 1994. The sequence is called "Journey Through Cerebral Vessels." On this scientific journey through cerebral vessels, computed images are introduced like the ones being generated as three-dimensional representations derived from cross-sectional images of the human body, for example those in computer tomographies.[17] The camera's journey through a cerebral artery corresponds to the staging of the inner body in Hollywood's *Fantastic Voyage*. A fictional viewer's perspective formulates the commentary to these images: "But we can also put ourselves onto the tip of a catheter and view the vessel from inside." (figure 10–11)

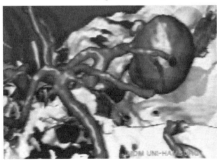 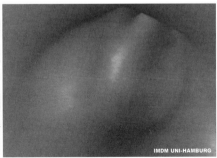

10 "The virtual body offers novel possibilities of vesicular imaging as shown with this aneurysm [...] acquired with CT and angiography."[18]

11 "We enter the anterior cerebral artery, proceed into the middle cerebral artery, follow the path to the aneurysm and look back [...]"

For the time being, it can be asserted as subject of representation in the mentioned film and video examples that a borderline is being staged visually: the borderline of the visible that is intended to be crossed.

The persistence of a similar motive in combination with a typical motion points to the crossing of a borderline that does not only prolong the section of the visible but also intends to visually construct something invisible. In each case, it refers to a central motion of the camera point into the depth of the image, as if driving into a tunnel. It appears as if the spectator has the position of a 'flying object' moving into the depth of the opened image. Computer calculations are the basis for each motion into the many visual tunnels, be it on the level of film narration or as media-technological basis of image creation itself.

On a more speculative level of comparison, another common characteristic may be the statement that each example is a matter of life and death, or rather the borderline between them. *Tron* dealt with survival in an impossible world 'in a computer.' The cross-fading of computer-generated tunnels with the dancing girl are a component of a visual and acoustic technology of ecstasy, possibly producing fainting fits. *Fantastic Voyage* staged the survival with an almost disappeared body. The current scientific side of the persisting tunnel motif manifests itself in *Professor*

18 All legends are transcripts from the video *Professor Roentgen Meets the Virtual Body*.

19 Compare **Elisabeth Strowick**'s contribution in this volume, on the question of arriving at a similar moment of paralysis and disappearing (flickering) visibility, that represents its own technical condition as the marker of the digital: "The performative surface structure of the interfaced body cannot be reduced to a logic-of-presence concept of visibility, but persists as a flickering/paradoxical imagery that, by performatively paralyzing the visibility paradigm, refers images to their media-constituent conditions."

20 See on the Ego as mobile point with no extension in information space: **Reiche, Claudia** (2001): Die avatarische Hand. In: *Hand. Medium¬Körper¬ Technik*, Ulrike Bergermann / Andrea Sick / Andrea Klier, Eds., Bremen.

21 ...since Renaissance at the latest, it is a continuous, homogeneous, three-dimensional void. See **Reiche** 2002a: 200.

22 Cf. **Reiche, Claudia** (2002c): Vom Ursprung des Lebens im Bild – Der weibliche Orgasmus, das Visible Human Project und die Versprechungen der Genomtechnik. In: *Techniken der Reproduktion. Medien, Leben, Diskurse*, Ulrike Bergermann / Claudia Breger / Tanja Nusser, Eds., Königstein, 17–34.

Roentgen Meets the Virtual Body by visualizing organs of a living body, with remarkable similarities to computer-generated music videos. From a potentially all-seeing perspective, the visual intrusion into a computed virtual body allows impossible access into an inner body that would not be possible with a living person on an operating table, even by inserting endoscopic cameras.

It is my opinion that each image deals with a new scene as with a transformation of the scene itself, intended to be signified in the hypnotizing wake of the visual tunnel journeys or flights: entering and leaving stage like entering or leaving life? Their most intimate visibilities in the sense of the representation of crossing or transition into the 'other' are connected to the imagined tunnel: someone who imagines to have seen the light of day through a birth channel might also imagine the experience of approaching death as seeing a faraway yet approaching light – the imagined tunnel. Consequently let me claim that the four selected visual examples always deal with one topic – ob-scenities, crossing and transforming scenes (in)to 'other' scenes, images on the borderline of the visible.

An oscillation of being 'on scene' and 'off scene' – 'on/off-scenity' – best describes this ob-scene mode set on the borderline of an almost disappearing tunnel-vision that gives way to conceptual patterns and pictorial reflexes.[19] The recurring image of moving forward in a tunnel, intimately linked with the empty, but metaphysically heavily loaded space 'in the computer,' as illustrated in *Tron*, signifies fast motion with minimal change in the center of the field of vision, and thus combines immobility with the notion of transgression. The futile chase of the vanishing point in the perspective's representation – which could give a rational description of a straight tunnel-movement in the logic of pictorial construction – is nevertheless linked with the fantasy to reach beyond the scene, as if one could touch the represented objects as real ones, transgressing through the imaginary to the image itself. It is the phantasm of entering (and thus annihilating) the image, bound since the Renaissance and in the optical-mechanical construction of every film camera to the laws of central perspective. But even fantasizing about reaching and surpassing the vanishing point in an impossibly fast tunnel-motion – where would the spectator end? A point has no extension[20] and space is empty by definition.[21] Even by slitting the screen in the cinema or shooting the TV-display one will end up and arrive at the material base of the imaginary projection: the medium's concretion. In contrast the ob-scene fantasy of the tunnel reaches through the visible into the next world,[22] confounding the border of the imaginary and the symbolic in the Lacanian sense with the limits of the Ego.

The scene and visual prequel of the *Visible Human* as constructed by the four examples of movements into visual tunnels has in such a way built the ob-scene: as on/off-scenity of difference.[23] This is meant to reveal a new (in)sight on the ambivalent notion of depth, aimed at through the symptomatically recurring penetrations of the two-dimensional image (from film to computer-animation). Examples used for data processing of the *Visible Human Project* allow to draw a connection between the already activated elements of image and imagination. These elements include insecurities, fascinations and confusions that are activated with the (un)representable process of medial transformation of and by the digital.

A DIGITAL IMAGE LIBRARY

The National Library of Medicine's plan to have launched the development of a database with the purpose of collecting and generating a new type of digital images serving the medical description of human beings as early as the middle of the 1980s has to be regarded as technologically advanced:

> "NLM should undertake a first project building a digital image library of volumetric data representing a complete, normal adult male and female. This *Visible Human Project* will include digitized photographic images from cryosectioning, digital images derived from computerized tomography and digital magnetic resonance images of cadavers."[24]

Though the 'Image Library's' goal to present a universal and standardized new visual *knowledge* about 'the human being' in the bio-medical field

---

23 The concept of the 'flickering signifier' developed by N. Katherine Hayles draws a similar figure, concerning a sort of 'instability' of signifying in the digital, involving the different levels of signification in a program's functions. I would agree with: "[...] information technologies create, what I will call *flickering signifier*, characterized by their tendency toward unexpected metamorphoses, attenuations, and dispersions. Flickering signifiers signal an important shift in the plate tectonics of language." **Hayles, N. Katherine** (1999): *How We Became Posthuman, Virtual Bodies in Cybernetics, Literature, and Informatics*, Chicago / London, 30. But I would not describe this "important shift" as Katherine Hayles does, by shaping the 'flickering' in contrast to Lacan's 'floating signifier.' The new dialectic of pattern and randomness, that discriminates for Hayles the digital from the old dialectics of

has been called for since Renaissance times, it is, however, a new one. And it remains a new goal as long as this knowledge is going to be organized in a new media format.

> "The Visible Human Project data sets are designed to serve as a common reference point for the study of human anatomy [...] This is the larger, long-term goal of the Visible Human Project: to transparently link the print library of functional-physiological knowledge with the image library of structural-anatomical knowledge into one unified resource of health information."[25]

The new digital image is no longer only image but credited with the potential of new knowledge representation, articulated as linking between physiological and anatomical nomenclature and dynamic organization of the thus-labeled objects. The medial-material unification of images and texts by the computer is followed by the re-formulation of the form of knowledge under such conditions, leading to the verbal replacement of the different knowledges with the unifying term "health information." As 'information', the methodologically and medially transformed image is even in this short factsheet of the "first digital description of an entire human being" and representation of a "complete, normal adult, male and female" credited with more completeness, closeness or even identity to the pictured 'original.' The seemingly modestly formulated project of the National Library of Medicine thus indicates a lingual and media-technological transformation of utmost extent: transformation of 'knowledge,' 'words,' 'images,' and the 'human being' itself.

The use of cadavers and photography to enter into the digital era of image is spectacular and obviously contradictory. That's new. To be

---

absence and presence, stages the main characteristics of signifiers, their arbitrariness, as perceptible in the effects of the digital medium and identifies signifiers with their matter, be it marks on paper or patterns of absence/presence commands (electrical current or not). Hence the topical analogy she posits between 'castration' (Lacan) and the shift to the new 'mutation' in the flickering signifier's realm, is based on the false assumption that such castration is conceived as literally taking place. Cf. ibid. 33. Instead I propose to read castration as a paradoxical staging of difference and as 'flickering.'

24 **National Library of Medicine (US)**, *Visible Human Project*™, *Factsheet*. http://www.nlm.nih.gov/pubs/factsheets/visible_human.html, [last access: 01/28/2004].

25 Ibid.

concrete: to be photographed, the inner body has to be opened by knives and has to be planed off layer by layer from head to toe into one cross-section after the next, until thawed cuttings in the submillimeter range are all that is left from the human body – after the image series has been completed.

This procedure has already been conducted on "a complete, normal adult, male and female." As early as 1995, television and print media celebrated 'digital Adam' and 'digital Eve'[26] as new human beings and declared the plain computer-stored digitized photographs to represent the beginning of the new digital era of the human being. The alleged total identity, the idea of availability and changeability of data material are regarded as guaranteed for future medical use. The processed cadavers are regarded as paradoxical 'images' – too complete to be treated as conventional images any longer.

To be objective: color and detail are the sole advantage of the acquired photographic data in contrast to the usual virtual cross-sections by computer-tomographic and magnetic resonance images.[27] While data are being further processed in many projects working with the *Visible Human* data set[28] the following is achieved: the volumetric reconstruction of the cross-sectional two-dimensional images into a virtual body in three-dimensional presentation mode of the computer. This means that the fixed images are calculated into to a three-dimensional image-object of Virtual Reality. This can be realized with more or less degrees of immersion, ranging from mouse-controlled navigation through a three-

---

26 On the specific differences between the reception of the male and the female Visible Human dataset see **Cartwright, Lisa** (1998): A Cultural Anatomy of the Visible Human Project. In: *The Visible Woman, Imaging, Technologies, Gender, and Science*, Paula Treichler / Lisa Cartwright / Constance Penley, Eds., New York / London.

27 On the long history of animating serial cross-sectional anatomical samples: **Reiche, Claudia** (2002a): "Lebende" Anatomien 1900/2000: Kinematographische Serienschnittanimationen und voxelbasierte Volumen Visualisierung. In: *Filozofski vestnik, The Body / Le corps / Der Körper / Telo*, vol. 23, no. 2, Ljubljana, 287–312.

28 See especially the **Institute of Mathematics and Computer Science in Medicine**, University Hospital Hamburg-Eppendorf, *Work with the Visible Human Data Set using the VOXEL-MAN program*, http://www.uke.uni-hamburg.de/institute/imdm/idv/forschung/vhp/index.en.html [last access 07/08/2002].

dimensional environment on a graphics monitor, where one can visually access the virtual human body from arbitrarily chosen points of view, to more 'realistic' interactions in surgery simulations with stereotactic view. The objects, here a human body, can thus be virtually explored by an individually calculated turn of the imaginary camera-view from any angle or axis. And more: sections or penetrations along anatomic tunnel-structures like blood vessels are possible, thus the user is able to get 'unlimited' access to the object. With this mode of 'fly through' the inner walls and cavities become visually accessible, too. The spectator is no longer in the situation of wish-fulfilling imagination in front of a pictorial presentation but set as her/his point of view into visible motion to access the cavities and tunnels of the enlarged inner body thus taking the form of an extent-less, yet 'seeing' point – or a minute submarine. For such an exploring look the virtual body is frankly turned inside out. The user is invited to take part in an imaginary de-materialization to understand 'her/himself' as an element of the virtual image space – just like a *Visible Human* that explores its interior, flying through the data landscape. A borderline is crossed in a new way – the one between image and spectator, and a differentiation between dead and alive has again been set into motion. Here, the virulent fantasies about 'living' images cover all other forms of reaction.

In this way, something is being visualized that cannot be directly illustrated. The factualness of newly computer-generated images does after all transgress existing taboos of scientific rationality, the traceless manipulability transgresses the certain differentiation between reality, document and fiction. The virtual human being is consequently fantasized as 'real' in this motion of transgression. Or could direct access to the reference object of the image be possible by manipulating digital images: a living body?

In the field of telepresentic surgery, surgical environments in the modus of Virtual Reality are being created with the computer that can simulate surgery with tactile output and input devices. Surgeons can rehearse complicated operations, e.g. in neurological surgery, with the patient's individual data material, or perform real surgery on the patient without having to use the devices differently in relation to these methods. The difference is that a robot may or may not carry out the commands given in the Virtual Reality mode. Thus surgery is performed on the 'image' with life-deciding consequences for those being pictured in it.

An incision into a novel 'image body' can act as calculation and incision into a living body at the same time. Transmitting a spatial motion sequence like using a virtual scalpel results in a three-dimensional spatial curve that is followed along by the robot-guided real scalpel. This transmission has decisive practical, surgical advantages: a proportional miniaturization of the robot-guided gesture makes it possible to perform micro-surgical operations on enlarged visual and tactile organic phantoms with greater dexterity and precision. or the hand's tremor in case of weariness can be filtered with algorithms of stabilization[29]. Journalistic and medical jargon calls it:

JOYSTICK SURGERY

The example of *OP 2050* can illustrate how the category of the ob-scene is pushed forward in relations between patients' and surgeons' bodies. It is about a project transferring the miniaturized surgeon into the patient's body while using the virtual representation, thus positioning her/his visual focus at the tip of the endoscopic instrument. Following the known example that means programmatically: "The goal is to give the surgeon the illusion of being located on the tip of the endoscope and that he is working within a greatly enlarged anatomy."[30] Here, the surgeon is very obviously attributed as male.

> "In the operating room of the future [...] the doctor is supposed [...] to sit comfortably in the operation cockpit. He operates the robot from a distance with a joystick. [...] During surgery every motion of the instrument is being transferred to the chair: when the endoscope glides along the nerve tracts the cockpit tilts forward in the same angle – if the endoscope moves to the right the doctor's chair tilts to the right at the same time. The surgeon is under the impression he is riding through the patient's body on

29 Volz, Tanja (1998): Ausgezittert. In: *bild der wissenschaft*, no. 7, 33.
30 Wapler, Matthias / Urban, Volker et al. (1998): Motion Feedback as a Navigation Aid in Robot Assisted Neurosurgery. In: *Medicine Meets Virtual Reality, Art, Science, Technology: Healthcare (R)evolution™*, James D. Westwood / Helene M. Hoffman / Don Stredney / Suzanne J. Weghorst, Eds., Amsterdam / Berlin / Oxford / Tokyo / Washington DC, 218.
31 Volz 1998: 34–35.
32 Cf. Reiche, Claudia (1998): Feminism is digital. In: *First Cyberfeminist International, Sept. 20.-28. 1997, Hybrid Workspace*, Kassel, Cornelia Sollfrank / Old Boys Network, Eds., Hamburg, 24–32.

the back of the endoscope. [...] If, for example, the endoscope meets tissue, a blood vessel or vagabond cell clots in the human body, the surgeon
will feel it by receiving a heavy blow to his cockpit."[31]

In such telepresentic surgery, points in the virtual and the so-called real
world are confused (and do not become identical) thus directing the
looking angle at the same time 'into' the simulation as well as 'to the outside' into the operational field. The spaces of virtual presentation and the
involved bodies are projected onto each other. The illusion is oscillating
between imaginary projection and symbolic dislocation, introducing a
new location for the subject: an ob-scene one in a formal sense. This
would enable a surgeon to walk 'in her/himself', even operate 'her/him-
self' until physical limits have been reached. A representation can only
be uncertainly distinguished from its represented, a stage, a scene can
hardly be distinguished from its beyond anymore.

To give imagination to it, to drive the ob-scene in a paradox formulation even further towards the limits of the imaginary, one could now
conclude that a new tunnel between what words and images will formerly
have been, has come into existence. And this in the sense that something
invisible and unspeakable is imaging, for example, as a tunnel. Words
and images would transform into a new projection now to be called
'body.' Such a strange body maybe would in the future connect every
look into a display with the expectation that this might be an image eligi-
ble from any number of perspectives, animations and simulation of operations with the image or with its reference, as well as one of many sur-
faces, topical intersections and labyrinthine choices. Who would know if
an intrusion into the computer image might still have effects in reality?
The distinction between an inner and an outside world as fixed realities
would then become senseless, just like the over-determined image perception of a tunnel as breakthrough 'behind' the veil of the image surface.

Media-change, as well as technical realization of new digital imaging
parameters, tends towards ob-scene characteristics, triggering the oscillation between transgressive fantasies (as omnipotence hallucinations) and
basic research at the new technical border of image-generation and perception. What may be called 'on/off-scenity' in this respect is a marker
for the old trap of a mistaken identification of the visible with presence[32],
which is pushed to the paradoxical limit and revealed as phallogocentric
speculation of 'mind over matter' in the image of the tunnel flights. The
term is in a way ob-scene as associated with metaphysical implications.
At the same time, 'on/off-scenity' is meant to remind of the difference

between signifiers as the basis of articulation itself. "[The signifiers'] most precise characteristic lies therein to be something what the others are not."[33] What switches ambivalently 'on' and 'off' the scene, is the difference between the elements, hidden and presented at once within their individual characteristics. Ob-scene in this respect would be a notion of difference itself, based on the figure of negation, effect of a structural exclusion, and thus beyond the presentic logic of the visible.[34]

UNCANNY SCENE

But can formal ob-scenity become completely freed from obscenity in the simple word sense?[35] This would probably happen at the cost of rendering the sensational caused by the digital image world of the *Visible Human* banal, making the same mistake as the official presentation of the project did before. The multitudinous wanderings of images in different contexts as analyzed in historical cultural research apply as well to the erotic and the scientific that can be close to each other in a visibility.[36] Early pornographic films that once were exclusively available for a male audience can be of special interest here. A title from 1927, *Wonders of the Unseen World*, illustrates this.[37] Anatomic science and sexual voyeurism may have met here in so far as female genitals represented the wonders of 'things never seen before.' Could this give the gender-polarized perspective

---

33 **Reiche** 1998, quoting Ferdinand de Saussure's *Cours de linguistique génerale*.

34 The technical oscillation of the cathode ray tubes of the computer displays may often be regarded as subliminally visible expression of a sort of 'on/off-scenity' but are not to be paralleled to the logical 'on's' and 'off's', current or no current – written as zeros and ones – in a computer's logical gates. Technically, this oscillation just rebuilds the cinematographic, flickering hallucination of the moving image and simplifies, if installed theoretically as 'visible difference', the paradoxical structure of difference as ob-scene and in itself transferred.

35 A similar, but slightly different gesture of confronting formal ob-scenity of new visual media of the 19th century (like stereoscopic photography) with pornographic obscenity is presented by **Williams, Linda** (1997): Pornographische Bilder und die "Körperliche Dichte des Sehens". In: *Privileg Blick, Kritik der visuellen Kultur*, **Christian Kravagna**, Ed., Berlin, 65–97. Williams defends a point of view, which does not 'disembody' sexual pleasures caused by the act of viewing erotic subjets in favor of an repressing intellectual abstraction, like the feminists' critique of a 'phallic gaze' or like a

on the present flood of 'fantastic (computer-calculated) journeys' into the inner body?

I would agree with this, but only with such transmitted manner where technical media is linked to femininity. This very early pornographic film illustrates how to solve the question of the relation of femininity with mediality which I am intending to suggest here.

Like in an educational film, this film shows different heterosexual practices to the male viewer that have all been filmed with the visual focus on the female genitals. As far as anatomical and physiological knowledge are concerned, it is thus attempted to fulfill the title's promise to show the wonders of the unseen world. I would like to explore the promised wonders in a different manner by giving the introductory sequences a closer look .

We see the male protagonist from behind – a close-up shows him opening a photo magazine – and our look is plainly identified as that of the man. The subtitle: "This is the way Mr. Evil Minded saw the photographs" comments on the transformation of a photo arranged like a pompous *tableau vivant* with a reclining

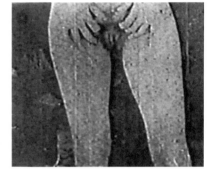

12 "This is the way Mr. Evil Minded saw the photographs."

theoretic 'sexualization' of the cinematographic apparatus. I can't agree with the underlying opposition of bodily sensations as original and language/theory as secondary, but with her demand for an intense research on pornographic traditions in relation to other cultural discourses.

36 "[…] the VHP as a kind of fantasy object for medicine, a form of pornography which plays out medicine's imaginary anatomies in unprecedented ways. Pornographic and medical genres frequently converge around the quest for a maximized bodily visibility […]." Catherine Waldby analyzes in her extended and brilliant discussion of the Visible Human Project the uncanny openness of the category 'human' to technical production and reproduction, relating to its pornographic aspects in various ways. **Waldby, Catherine** (2000): *The Visible Human Project, Informatic Bodies and Posthuman Medicine*, London / New York, 8, 114–115.

37 **Williams, Linda** (1989): *Hard Core, Power, Pleasure and the 'Frenzy of the Visible'*, Los Angeles, Williams emphasizes the artless image practice of genital action reminding of medical, anatomic displays and pursuing the main goal to explain about the hidden female sexual function, 58–92.

naked woman, which is being replaced by a 'living' woman standing naked in front of a black background. The following subtitle: "His eyes were on the photos but not on the faces" choses an interesting paraphrase for the female sex characteristics: "photos." An interlock has been linguistically accomplished that links the erotic attraction to the technical medium as the medium for desire while being transferred from photography to film. A self-referentiality of the film is installed here as the erotic attraction par excellence in the viewing situation. Medium and female are arranged to become undistinguishable. (figure 12) So the allegedly direct gesture where the woman spreads her labia with her fingers and shows her clitoris is much more than just unpretentious. It is of obscene beauty, staging something that will have been before, in front of and out of the scene, and at this point the wonders of the 'unseen' world intensify to an ob-scene oscillation between the visible, the not visible and the invisible. In this case, 'medium' refers to the photo-chemical recording and motion deception in film that in the early era of the medium was regarded as 'living photography.' Following this introduction to the obscene, epistemologically oscillating female body the film's protagonist consequently proceeds from the exploration of photography to the exploration of the female protagonist and the so-called story, the fiction of the film, begins.

The 'journeys into the inner body' that in this case are erotically charged with forbidden looks thus represent a gender-specific key to present image worlds of the *Visible Human Project* and its robot-based transmissions to present patients' bodies. In a broader sense, this interpretation is also supported by many factors, if a relation to the problem of representation and interpretation of the media-technical new image is constructed following the recognition of the 'female' as a problematic structure of representation. But this also means that the rash assumption of regarding the many tunnel flights as images of plain male fantasies about penetration should not necessarily mark the end of discourse. The tunnel flight could rather be read as journeys into the own stage-like produced head, into the imaginary Ego of the spectator, where this Ego can

---

38 Translation Sabine Melchert, compare **Freud, Sigmund** (2000[1919]): Das Unheimliche. In: *Studienausgabe, Band IV, Psychologische Schriften*, Alexander Mitscherlich / Angela Richards / James Strachey, Eds., Frankfurt am Main, 266–267.

be seen in the guise of a thought figure of a little man inside a little man inside a little man in endless narcissistic and idealistic misappreciation.

The tunnel images into the alleged depth of two-dimensional images, into the 'unseen', is directed towards the borderline between the symbolic and the imaginary. The gesture to get behind the surface of each image but still to be linked to the spatial geometry of the mirror – the imaginary – is however futile and in the virtual three-dimensional worlds of interactive computer imagery only raised to a higher power. This also allows interpretation as ob-scene in another way, as the pornographic genre seems to offer only too readily.

It appears to me that the *Visible Human Project* is being driven as well as haunted by the history of its creation, the obscenity of death. Facing the colorful 're-animated' image of digital body reconstruction the images of the dissection of a cadaver become obscured into a vibrating background. A swaying scene has been staged here that has to hold distance to the deadly origin, that is so far away but yet so close.

If one follows Sigmund Freud's statements in his essay on the 'uncanny', one can conclude a bond to familiar imaginary worlds, if an uncanny feeling occurs – like the amputation of limbs, disappearance into a monstrous abyss, or even the fear of being buried alive – and at the same time interpret an attempt to overcome the uncanny feeling. The castration complex and the uncanny of the female genitals perspectively figures as vanishing point.

> "For the uncanny is nothing really new or strange, but something long-time familiar to the soul that has been alienated by the process of repression. [...] Severed limbs, a chopped off head, a hand severed from an arm [...], feet dancing on their own [...] have something really uncanny about them, especially if [...] an independent activity is conceded to them.[...] Neurotic men often declare that female genitals are uncanny for them."[38]

But what would happen if the process of assimilating a new technology was structured according to the assimilation of male gender identity? Will the procedures of computer-generated images with the transgressions of previous image possibilities change something? And what could come into existence? Something ob-scene? In the best sense, of course. Because, if we are dealing with something 'never seen before,' we have hope that something is being articulated that is going to change the imagination of a scene itself, as if a paradox tunnel between words and images would open new possibilities of female representation. And it would finally include the invisibility of phallus and castration as a secured component into the scientific as well as the popular epistemological assumptions, thus transgressing the traditional claim of 'living' media artifacts, in film or in the case of the computer-animated *Visible Human*.

With the term of on/off-scenity, this constitutive invisibility that opens the visible is marked as a specific ob-scene location in media-theory: not 'in the computer,' but at the slash, at the graphical marker of a paradoxical border between 'on' and 'off', that is no border and no location at all.

This would mean to intervene into the uncertain relations between medial and bodily traces and to play them off as an ob-scene possibility of ambiguous negation and shift in a digital matrix: cyberfeminist uses of on/off-scenity, which reflect and subvert the metaphysical and gender stereotypes in cyberfeminism as in global military and technological plans for 'our' future.   <

TRANSLATION: **Sabine Melchert**

BIBLIOGRAPHY
Print

Biel, Maria (1996): Die phantastische Schöpfung des ersten (echten) digitalen Menschens. In: *P.M. – Peter Moosleitners interessantes Magazin*, no. 2, Munich, 86–91 **Cartwright, Lisa** (1998): A Cultural Anatomy of the Visible Human Project. In: *The Visible Woman, Imaging, Technologies, Gender, and Science*, Paula Treichler / Lisa Cartwright / Constance Penley, Eds., New York / London, 21–43 **Freud, Sigmund** (2000[1919]): Das Unheimliche. In: *Studienausgabe, Band IV, Psychologische Schriften*, Alexander Mitscherlich / Angela Richards / James Strachey, Eds., Frankfurt am Main, 241– 274 **Hayles, N. Katherine** (1999): *How We Became Posthuman, Virtual Bodies in Cybernetics, Literature, and Informatics*, Chicago / London **National Library of Medicine [US] Board of Regents** (1990): *Electronic Imaging, Report of the Board of Regents, US Department of Health and Human Sciences, Public Health Service,*

National Institutes of Health, (NIH Publication 90-2197), Bethesda, Maryland **Reiche, Claudia** (1996): PIXEL: Experiences with the Elements. In: *Medicine Meets Virtual Reality: 4*, Suzanne J. Weghorst / Hans B. Sieburg / Karen S. Morgan, Eds., Amsterdam / Oxford / Tokyo / Washington DC, 681–689 **Reiche, Claudia** (1998): Feminism is digital. In: *First Cyberfeminist International, Sept. 20.-28. 1997, Hybrid Workspace, Kassel*, Cornelia Sollfrank / Old Boys Network, Eds., Hamburg, 24–32 **Reiche, Claudia** (1999): Bio(r)Evolution™, On the Contemporary Military-Medical Complex. In: *The Spectralization of Technology: From Elsewhere to Cyberfeminism and Back*, Marina Grzinic, Ed., Maribor, 33–54 **Reiche, Claudia** (2001): Die avatarische Hand. In: *Hand. Medium¬Körper¬Technik*, Ulrike Bergermann / Andrea Sick / Andrea Klier, Eds., Bremen, 120–134 **Reiche, Claudia** (2002): "Lebende" Anatomien 1900/2000: Kinematographische Serienschnittanimationen und voxelbasierte Volumen Visualisierung. In: *Filozofski vestnik, The Body / Le corps / Der Körper / Telo*, vol. 23, no. 2, Ljubljana, 287–312 [=Reiche 2002a] **Reiche, Claudia** (2002): Technics of Ambivalence and Telepresence. In: *technics of cyber<>feminism <mode=message>*, Claudia Reiche, Andrea Sick, Eds., Bremen, 197–208 [=Reiche 2002b] **Reiche, Claudia** (2002): Vom Ursprung des Lebens im Bild – Der weibliche Orgasmus, das Visible Human Project und die Versprechungen der Genomtechnik. In: *Techniken der Reproduktion. Medien, Leben, Diskurse*, Ulrike Bergermann / Claudia Breger / Tanja Nusser, Eds., Königstein, 17–34 [=Reiche 2002c] **Tholen, Georg, Christoph** (1997): Digitale Differenz, Zur Phantasmatik und Topik des Medialen. In: *Hyperkult. Geschichte, Theorie und Kontext digitaler Medien*, Martin Warnke / Wolfgang Coy / Georg Christoph Tholen, Eds., Basel / Frankfurt am Main, 99–116 **Volz, Tanja** (1998): Ausgezittert. In: *Bild der Wissenschaft*, no. 7, Stuttgart, 32–36 **Waldby, Catherine** (2000): *The Visible Human Project, Informatic Bodies and Posthuman Medicine*, London / New York **Wapler, Matthias / Urban, Volker** et al. (1998): Motion Feedback as a Navigation Aid in Robot Assisted Neurosurgery. In: Westwood, James D. / Helene M. Hoffman / Don Stredney / Suzanne J. Weghorst, Eds. (1998): *Medicine Meets Virtual Reality, Art, Science, Technology: Healthcare (R)evolution™*, Amsterdam / Berlin / Oxford / Tokyo / Washington DC , 215–219 **Williams, Linda** (1989): *Hard Core, Power, Pleasure and the 'Frenzy of the Visible'*, Los Angeles **Williams, Linda** (1997): Pornographische Bilder und die "Körperliche Dichte des Sehens". In: *Privileg Blick, Kritik der visuellen Kultur*, Christian Kravagna, Ed., Berlin, 65–97

Web | **Institute for Mathematics and Computer Science in Medicine**, University of Hamburg, for the program VOXEL-MAN, http://www.uke.uni-hamburg.de/institute/imdm/idv/ [last access 01/28/2004] **National Library of Medicine** (US), Visible Human Factsheet, http://www.nlm.nih. gov/pubs/factssheets/visible_human.html [last access 01/28/2004] **University of Colorado**, Center for Human Simulation, Visible Human Head, http://www.uchsc.edu/sm/chs/gallery/images/headcrosssections. html [last access: 04/20/2004].

Film, TV

Fantastic Voyage (US 1966), 1'41'', Production: Twentieth Century Fox / Saul David, Director: Richard Fleischer, Screenwriter: Jerome Bixby, David Duncan, Harry Kleiner, Otto Klement, Performers: Stephen Boyd, Raquel Welch, Edmond O'Brien, Donald Pleasence, Arthur O'Connell et al., Cinematography: Ernest Laszlo, Editor: William B. Murphy, Music: Leonard Rosenman. Accessible at: Fox Video with 'Original Theatrical Trailer', Fantastic Voyage W/S, FOX 201249

Professor Roentgen Meets the Virtual Body (GER 1994), 10'', involved Scientists: Computer Science: M. Bomans, Th. Dahlmanns, N. Hausig, K. H. Höhne, B. Pflesser, A. Pommert, K. Priesmeyer, M. Riemer, Th. Schiemann, R. Schubert, U. Tiede / Medicine: Z. Halata, W.-J. Höltje, C. Koch, H. Kraemer, W. Lierse, R. Maas, J. Nuthmann, U. Rehder, Chr. Seebode, V. Wening, Video VHS, generated with the VOXEL-MAN volume visualization software, Institute for Mathematics and Computer Science in Medicine, University of Hamburg

Tron (US 1982) 1'36'', Production: Walt Disney Productions / Donald Kushner et al., Director: Steven Lisberger, Screenwriter: Steven Lisberger, Bonnie Macbird, Performers: Jeff Bridges, Bruce Boxleitner, David Warner, Cindy Morgan, Barnard Hughes et al., Cinematography: Bruce Logan, Editor: Jeff Gourson, Music: Wendy Carlos

N3 Vee Jay-Night – Media Festival Osnabrueck 2000, Rave Night, (GER 2000), 2', Production: Experimentalfilm Workshop e.V. European Media Art Festival / Kunsthochschule für Medien Köln, Director: Egon Blume, Screenwriter: Oliver Held, Cinematography: Oliver Schwabe, Richard Bade, Daniel Gräbner, Thorsten Pengel, Daniel Müller, Christoph Döring, Editor: Tobias Aman, Oliver Held, Egon Blume / Matthias Neuenhofer, David Larcher. German Television Station: N3, 03/03/2001

Wonders of the Unseen World (US 1927), 11'', "Allcock Production Inc. presents Wonders of the Unseen World, Copyright 1927, Seduced by A. Prick, Directed by Ima Cunt, Photographed by R.U. Hard" as credited in the film. Accessible at: Filmfare Video Labs. Inc., Classic Stags – 1914 to 1940s, Tape 139

Illustration | **01** Cross-section through the Visible Human head, University of Colorado, Center for Human Simulation, **http://www.uchsc.edu/sm/chs/gallery/ images/headcrosssections.html** [last access: 07/07/2002]
02–05 *Tron*
06–07 *N3 Vee Jay-Night* – Media Festival Osnabrueck 2000, Rave Night,
08–09 *Fantastic Voyage*
10–11 *Professor Roentgen Meets the Virtual Body*
12 *Wonders of the Unseen World*

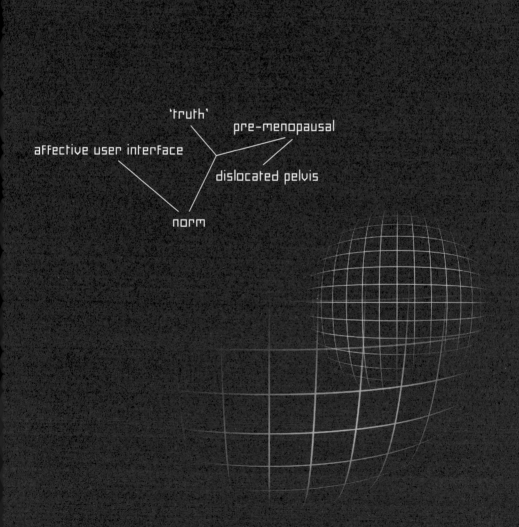

affective user interface

'truth'

pre-menopausal

dislocated pelvis

norm

Virtual Ideals: Art, Science and Gendered Cyberbodies

JULIE DOYLE | KATE O'RIORDAN

> Historically reliant upon technologies of imaging for the promotion of its practices, science inscribes the body through a specular logic, delineating the anatomical structures as a compendium of visible knowledge. Illustrative of this logic is the figuration of gender norms as conditions of the body, where anatomy is privileged as the authoritative marker of difference. Yet, while scientific discourse operates through a naturalization of the normative ideals of identity, an acknowledgement of the socio-historical intersections between the discourses of art and science problematizes scientific authority over gendered bodily matters. This chapter will thus consider the trajectories of medical and artistic imaging processes in the representation of the female

body. These will be discussed through an analysis of the *Visible Female* website hosted by Stanford University and the *Brandon Teena Site* hosted by the Guggenheim Museum. These installations are understood here as instances of intersecting representations of art and science in cyberspace. The *Stanford Visible Female* (*SVF*) site is an example of digitized anatomical images available on the Web. It is deployed here as a representation of contemporary medical imaging processes dealing with the gendered body as an anatomically definable form. The *Brandon* site is a virtual art installation and represents an example of contemporary artistic practice which critically engages with the gendered inscription of the body as an effect of medical discourse. We have selected these sites to discuss the (inter)relation between the discourses of art and science in order to problematize scientific assumptions concerning the representation of the body as a normatively gendered form. The *Brandon* site visually engages with these relations by disrupting the specular logic of the scientific body, calling attention to the psychical investments in embodiment through its deployment of an affective user interface. The Stanford site reinstates normative notions of gendered embodiment through its adherence to representational user interaction which fails to disrupt the scientific correlation of specularity with notions of 'truth'. What we hope to offer here is a consideration of how the processes of artistic and medical imaging intersect in digital presentations of the body. A resituation of the discourses of art and science as interrelated provides a contextualization lacking in both medical figurations of the body and conceptualizations of cyberspace.

The publication of Vesalius', *De Humani Corporis Fabrica*, in 1543 marked the beginnings of the proliferation of illustrated anatomical texts, representative of a developing discourse of scientific and medical knowledge. The constitution and dissemination of scientific knowledge has thus been historically contingent upon such images and the artistic conventions of display within which they emerge. Such conventions include the perspectives of classical realism in the content of the images, marked especially in the pose and features of the female figure in D'Agoty's 1773 text, for example (Figure 01), and techniques such as engraving and mezzotint in the form. The trajectory of the visual culture of medical imaging thus arises from the conventions of the artistic. The historical interstices of art and science in the constitution of gendered knowledge is represented more explicitly by the eighteenth century medical preoccupation with anatomical images of the pregnant female body. Presented as exemplary

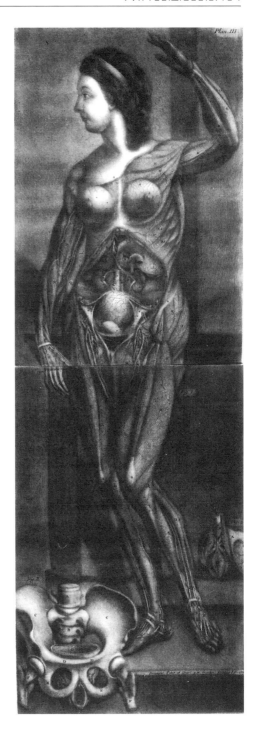

Figure 01
D'Agoty (1773)

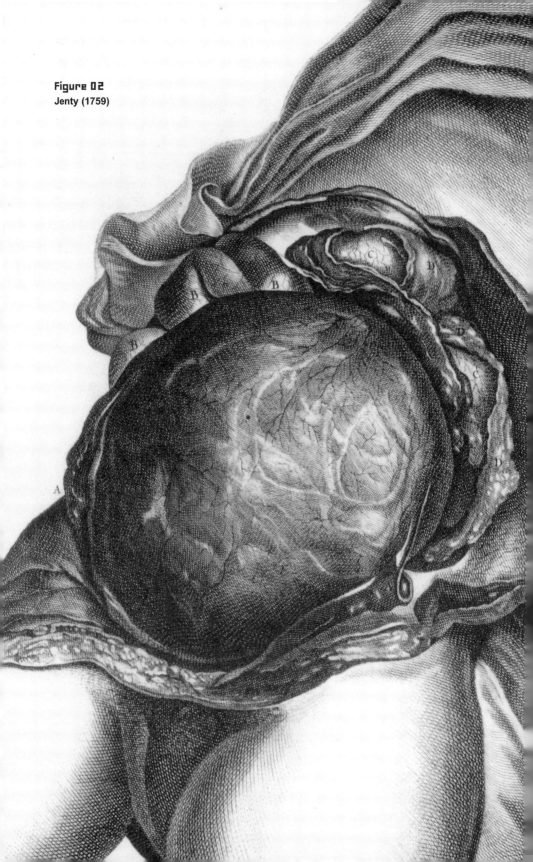

Figure 02
Jenty (1759)

in an emergent discourse of scientific objectivity, these illustrations clearly deployed the aesthetic conventions of display (Figure 02), while inscribing the female body through the ideological remit of heteronormative reproduction. A resituation of the discourses of medicine and science as conceptually contingent upon artistic processes of representation, therefore disinvests the body as the presumed site of 'objective' knowledge, calling into question the normalizing conceptualizations of gender identity, and relocating these as the interarticulated effects of the discourses of art and science.

This paper discusses the divergences between the discourses of so-called objective and empirical medicine on the one hand, and the subjective, exploratory and expressive discourse of art, on the other. A theoretical underpinning to this is the model of abjection and othering central to psychoanalytic theory (through both Freud and Lacan) and rearticulated in the more recent work of Judith Butler. Of the formation of subjectivity Butler writes:

> "the subject is constituted through the force of exclusion and abjection, one which produces a constitutive outside to the subject, an abjected outside, which is, after all, 'inside' the subject as its own founding repudiation."[1]

This model of subject formation relates to the discursive mobilization of art and medicine in the following way. Medical discourse legitimates itself as empirical and objective through the abjection of the subjective and expressive. The positive and inductive logics of science are polarized against the subjective and emergent discourse of art. In this way, medicine seeks to abject its cultural context and evict itself from all social conditions in order to obtain a universal position. Yet as a discourse involved in the historical formation of notions of identity – through the promotion of anatomy as representative of scientific knowledge – medicine as a model of subjectivity is already destabilized by its emergence from the conventions of art, which constitute its abjected other. A recontextualization of the discourse of science in its cultural specificity is, we suggest, a more productive mode of viewing.

Articulating the discursive interrelations between art and science as representative of the tensions constitutive of subjectivity, this paper acknowledges the return of the 'repudiated' which is occurring in contemporary art. Contemporary artistic practice, in a return to the body,

1 **Butler, Judith** (1993): *Bodies that Matter: On the Discursive Limits of Sex*, London / New York, 3.

now draws on, critiques and deploys both the conventions and content of anatomical imaging. Artists such as Helen Chadwick, Critical Art Ensemble, Damien Hirst, Tiffany Holmes, VNS Matrix, Orlan, Friederike Paetzold and Eugene Thacker draw material directly from anatomical models such as the *Visible Human Project* and other diagnostic and teaching materials which represent the body, often to overtly critique normative anatomical and biomedical discourse. We suggest that the visual culture of science needs to engage with such a return.

The Stanford Visible Female (SVF)

While the processes of engraving and mezzotint were relied upon in the promotion of anatomical knowledge during the late eighteenth and early nineteenth centuries, these have now been taken over by advanced imaging technologies such as computer tomography (CT) and magnetic resonance imaging (MRI) which, along with graphic design software, are utilized to present anatomical images through the virtual medium of cyberspace. The *Stanford Visible Female* project, hosted by Stanford University, is part of a widening collection of these medical images which can be accessed through the World Wide Web. The *SVF* is "a collection of digitized serial photographs of a cryosectioned 32-year old cadaveric female pelvis"[2] (Figure 03). The 32-year old woman whose body provided the raw material for the *Stanford Visible Female* – a project which translates the flesh of the body into digital imagery – is signified within the project as a dislocated pelvis. It is the reproductive potential represented by this female body that provides the particular reasoning behind this project – a fact which

2   *Stanford Visible Female* http://summit.stanford.edu/RESEARCH/Stanford-VisibleFemale [last access: 10/11/1999].

3   *Stanford Visible Female* (*SVF*) hosted by Stanford University (1997): http://summit.Stanford.EDU/RESEARCH/StanfordVisibleFemale [last access: 10/11/1999].

4   See **Waldby, Catherine** (2000): *The Visible Human Project: Information Bodies and Postman Medicine*, London / New York for a full exposition of this project and the project's website: *Visible Human Project* (*VHP*) hosted by the NLM – National Library of Medicine, http://www.nlm.nih.gov/research/visible/ [last access: 01/28/2004] for the primary material.

5   *Visible Human Project* (*VHP*) hosted by the NLM – National Library of Medicine (1999): http://www.nlm.nih.gov/research/visible/ [last access: 01/11/1999].

6   *Stanford Visible Female* website.

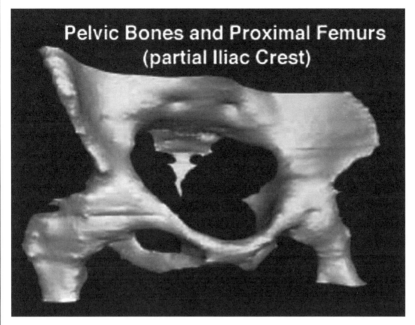

Figure 03
Image of the pelvis from the data sets of the Stanford Visible Female Project

renders it "unique in a very important way" by virtue of its difference from "the 59-year old post-menopausal Visible Human Female"[3] used in the National Library of Medicine's *Visible Human Project*™[4]. Where the *Visible Human Project* (*VHP*) presents "complete, anatomically detailed, three-dimensional representations of the normal male and female human bodies,"[5] the representation of the female body within the *SVF* is focused upon the pelvic region alone.

The declared goal of both projects is to create anatomical images for use in medicine, surgery and biomedical research, with the specific aim of the *SVF* being the development of "accurate 3-D models of female pelvic anatomy for use in surgical simulation." However, the medical focus upon the generative parts and organs of the female body, as presented in the *SVF*, represents an ideologically specific figuration of the female body. It is not the female subject who is described in terms of age here, rather it is the "reproductive-age cadaveric pelvis"[6] which synecdochelly represents this 32-year old female. This particular figuration of the body involves a rearticulation of conventional notions of gendered embodiment within cyberspace, where anatomical knowledge of the female is reduced to, and signified by, her reproductive parts.

While the associated *VHP* has attracted much critical attention and is discussed both through the medical discourse from which it emerged and also as a free-standing cultural artefact, the *SVF* has not received the same attention. The representation of the female body in the *SVF* is intended to be that of the 'normal' female human body. The images in the *SVF* are created from the corpse of a female body and supply a representation of the pelvic region of a pre-menopausal female using cryosectioning, MRI and CT techniques. The images are placed into a sequence that performs a reconstituted body – creating the illusion that these technologies of imaging allow the medical vision to actually penetrate the body. Some techniques do perform an x-ray model of imaging such as MRI. However, the process of cryosectioning which underpins the *SVF* is a process whereby the corpse is filled with fluid, frozen and then sliced thinly, with an image taken of each slide. (Figure 04)

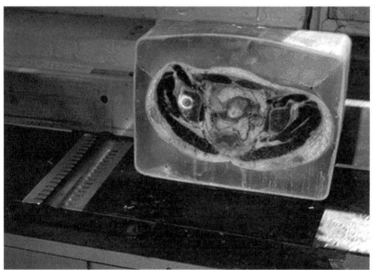

Figure 04
Cryosection from the Project Overview of the Stanford Visible Female

7   Debord, Guy (1983): *Society of the Spectacle*, Detroit.
8   Kember, Sarah (1999): NITS and NRTS: Medical Science and the Frankenstein Factor. In: *Desire By Design: Body, Territories and New Technologie*, Cutting Edge: The Women's Research Group, Eds., London.
9   Jordanova, Ludmilla (1989): *Sexual Visions: Images of Gender in Science and Medicine Between the Eighteenth and Twentieth Centuries*, Madison.
10 Cartwright, Lisa (1995): *Screening the Body: Tracing Medicine's Visual Culture*, Minneapolis.

The processes of freezing, slicing and photographing are followed by design processes which are then assembled into a filmic presentation. A variety of techniques and packages are used, such as Adobe Photoshop, before the images are presented on the Web and CD-ROM; techniques identical to those used in the production of digital art. The process before the material is marked up into web pages and data sets involves different stages of dissection, imaging, storage, reassembly, design and editing. The data sets are produced in the same way that any mediated information is assembled. Elements are selected according to various filters and presented in a particular way. Yet the rhetoric of the project refers to the 'normal' as though this were naturally occurring data which has been found and neutrally collected rather than constructed. These two factors, the obscuring of the means of production of the representation, and the modelling of the 'normal' living body on a single, processed corpse, serves to separate the representation from the body that it is taken from and to free it as a simulation without referent other than itself.[7] This simulation is then affixed to the ideology of the natural body as though this existed other than in the realm of representation.

The pelvis can be viewed in a variety of ways, from individual files of the cryosections to fully animated tours through the reconstituted pelvic area. The individual images can be viewed separately or strung back together in an animation which allows the viewer's point of view to survey the body. This perspective, where the point of view moves through the body, has been simulated before, and endoscopy has been deployed in many forms of visual communication from surgery to popular film but here it is innovative on two counts. Firstly because it is a representation constructed from images of an actual corpse rather than a simulation; and secondly because it allows a cross-body vision of everything enveloped by the outer skin as opposed to that enveloped by a single passage or membrane, as with endoscopy. Yet the radical technologies of imaging and animation employed by the *SVF* represent a limited psychical interaction between participant and cyber body which redeploys conventional notions of gender through anatomy. Navigation of the reconstituted pelvic region – from the individual files which present textual and diagrammatic information on the pelvic organs to the rotating pelvic structures – maintains a normative female body as its referent. Interaction is negotiated through the heteronormative conceptualization of female anatomy as signified by the reproductive organs, where the referent in the *SVF* remains the 32-year old pre-menopausal female, signified by the pelvic parts.

The *SVF* deploys advanced imaging techniques and technologies which have been described in terms of their "Frankenstein factor", by Sarah Kember[8], Ludmilla Jordanova[9], Lisa Cartwright[10] and Karen Newman[11] have all discussed the specular construction of normative bodies through scientific discourse. Catherine Waldby[12] further discusses the images produced through the visual culture of science in her study of the *VHP* which is also associated with the *SVF*. Contemporary artistic interest in biotechnologies as art media also reflects current widening cultural concerns with constructions of the body and narratives of science. An example of such interest is the work of the Critical Art Ensemble and Friederike Paetzold which contests the imaging techniques of anatomy while deploying their form. The work of Eugene Thacker also reflects this interest in his appropriation of the data sets of the *VHP* for his piece *FTP_formless_anatomy*.

The logic underpinning the figuration of the female by virtue of the pelvic region can be read as emblematic of scientific induction. However the images of pelvic anatomy available on the *SVF* website can also be understood as artistic representations, where the brightly colored computer animations of the pelvic structures function as aesthetically mediated representations of the female form. Thus, while The *SVF* represents a contemporary example of how radical imaging technologies are being utilized to reinforce existing orthodoxies of gender identity, at the same time, the *SVF* project foregrounds how the specular logic of scientific discourse is dependent upon artistic conventions of representation. Here the body is revealed as a technologically manipulated form, thereby calling into question the normalizing representation of gender as a natural condition of the body.

Drawing an analogy between representations of the female body within a discourse of art and that of science emphasises the instabilities of the visual culture of medical imaging. The conventions of art which have always been present but elided in medical discourse are brought to the fore. Thus, moving on from an analysis of the *SVF*, we will examine the *Brandon* website as an example of how contemporary collaborations

---

11 **Newman, Karen** (1996): *Fetal Positions: Individualism, Science, Visuality*, Stanford.

12 **Waldby, Catherine** (2000): *The Visible Human Project: Information Bodies and Posthuman Medicine*, London / New York.

13 *Brandon* site, http://brandon.guggenheim.org [last access: 10/11/1999].

Figure 05
'Bigdoll Interface' – part of the *Brandon* site

between art, science and technologies of imaging are being used to question the normative prescriptions of bodily identity within cyberspace.
Disinvesting the body as the imagined site of gender identity involves a
foregrounding of the psychical and institutional construction of gender
norms, as presented by the *Brandon* website; a move which calls into
question the assumed determinacy of the specular logic of science in the
production and maintenance of normative notions of bodily identity.

The Brandon site

While medical discourse fantasizes about a body fixed by the dominant
sex/gender ideology, other sites represent bodies resistant to the prescriptions of this imaginary. The *Brandon* site (Figure 05) hosted by the
Guggenheim Museum[13] is concerned with representing both emergent
bodies and relations between bodies. The site deals with themes such as

boundaries and borders between actual/virtual and male/female and also questions hegemonic and institutional bias towards the clearly defined and conformist body. Deploying the metaphor of the panopticon, the road trip and the court room, this site re-stages court sessions on the Brandon case. This case was concerned with the 1993 rape and murder, in Nebraska, of Brandon Teena who was a pre-operative transsexual. Two films, *The Brandon Teena Story* (1998) and *Boys Don't Cry* (1999) have been made about the story. The *Brandon* site is organized by the artist Shu Lea Cheang and represents a commentary on the interactions of law, sexuality, and identity. Both Allucquère Stone and Del LaGrace Volcano who have also been involved with the site, make a direct connection between the boundaries of actual and virtual and those of gender. Stone's theoretical work on actual/virtual/multiple identity[14] is correlated to Brandon's bodily performance and to the representation of different identities in a single body, through this site. Lisa Cartwright, a critic of medicine's visual culture is also involved in the project.

The *Brandon* site was an interactive, multi-user forum for the first year that it opened. It can be discussed as a virtual exploration of performativity of the body on many levels. The site incorporates historical references such as Herculine Barbin[15] and contemporary figures such as Venus Extravaganza.[16] It is an attempt to engage with the boundary tensions between virtual and actual bodies, the body as performance, medical intervention and the experience of 'living in the skin.' The *Brandon* site deploys anatomical line drawings in the interface along with photographs of both flesh and of prosthetic body parts (Figure 05). Other parts of the site depict surgery itself through representations of operations in action. In the Panopticon Interface gloved surgeon's hands are imaged making incisions into the flesh of the body which is draped with fabric like Jenty's image of 1759. The convention of draping or shrouding the nude body is played across art and imaging to surgery and burial, from live bodies to dead ones. Its exploration of the body meshes with contemporary concerns about heteronormativity, bodily ownership and design in the context of a society which incorporates both augmented and margin-

14 Stone, Alluquère Rosanne (1995): *The War of Desire and Technology at the Close of the Mechanical Age*, Cambridge Mass.; Benedikt, Michael, Ed. (1993): *Cyberspace: First Steps*, London / Cambridge.

15 See Foucault, Michel (1978): *Herculine Barbin, dite Alexina B.*, Paris.

16 *Paris is Burning* (US 1990) Director: Jennie Livingston.

alized bodies, regulated by corporate law. These sites form part of a wider discourse which articulates the decentralization of the objective body and an exploration of emergent bodies through artistic and critical activity.

The theme of identity as performed and how it relates to identity as embedded in the material substance of the body, is represented in the *Brandon* site. This representation occurs through the depiction of Brandon Teena and the inclusion of other material relating to multiple or transitional identities. The theme of performativity emerges on two levels: the first is in the form of the site, a virtual art installation based on a juxtaposed, actual event, where the site designers deploy the disembodied realm of cyberspace to represent events and issues centred in embodiment. Secondly, the site thematically explores performance as lived experience, engaging with Brandon who signified her/his masculinity in defiance of the sex/gender binary. Explorations, which engage with work on identity politics more generally. The tensions between essential and performed identities in this field, are visible here. The performance of identity through representation on this site can be seen as a virtual embodiment of this theoretical area where the site holds in tension the poles of virtual and performed against those of essential and material. It can also be seen as an example of the merging of form and content in virtual representation, and of the difficulty in distinguishing between agent and text. The interactive elements of the *Brandon* site incorporate observations and commentary from participants, and combine them with the predesigned 'text' of the site. The *Brandon* site is an interactive forum combining display with interjection which reflects back out of virtual communication to problematize the performance of off-line identity.

The *Brandon* site is interactive, and the prior text of the site is merged with the contributions of participants in the virtual courts. That the site involves participation reinforces its contribution towards embodying the notion of representation as action. The bodies emergent in the text of the *Brandon* project challenge the inscriptions of the gender division. While the construction of gender is made evident through its transsexual narrative, the constitution of normative gender through legislation, bureaucracy and consensus is particularly evident in this project and conformity to this model of the body is questioned. The connection that one informant, involved with the site, made between the virtual/actual tension and gender disphoria was that virtuality enabled the exploration of different gender identities. The *Brandon* site interrogates the normalizing representations of the gendered body by seeking to re-embody cyberspace with participation and interaction. It also recontextualizes the body as something in relation to and emergent through psychic, cultural, and social factors, as opposed to a body discovered in objective isolation which is the implication of both the *VHP* and *SVF* projects.

Conclusion

The objective isolation of the *SVF* can be undercut by comparing the images collated in this article. The pelvis in D'Agoty's text (Figure 01) which still retains a strongly marked relation to classical realism in both the pose of the female and retention of her features, precedes the disembodied pelvis of the *SVF* (Figure 03). In the latter figure the context of both the body and of the conventions of art have been evicted from the frame but they still inform it. The *Brandon* site references anatomical images, seen here as the colored line drawings of genitalia in the 'Bigdoll Interface' (Figure 05), in order to recontextualise the body parts photographed, as informed by medical narratives. The eviction of context from medical representations is thus challenged by the contemporary resituation of the visual culture of medicine within the practice of art.

Although the techniques, tools and context of these two sites are similar, the meanings produced have very different implications. The engagement required differs significantly; where the *SVF* names, defines and directs interpretation, the *Brandon* site positions the user as the interpreter of the images. The *Brandon* site juxtaposes medical images with photographs of parts of the body, overtly encouraging an interpretation of their relation. The *SVF* uses the body as proof of the 'truth' of the medical images produced through it, foreclosing meaning and eliding the work of the production of these images.

The engagement, especially in terms of the level of interaction, also differs significantly. The prescriptive definitions and labels accompanying the *SVF* constitute a representational paradigm – the referent of this female body is the focal signifier of meaning. The *Brandon* site, which changes as you view it and which avoids the informational format of the *SVF*, constitutes an affective paradigm. That is to say that the interaction is not fixed to a single referent but the viewer is called as the referent, signified by the text. The location of the viewer within the process of interpretation repositions the user as sharing the constitution of bodily knowledge. The *SVF*'s premature eviction of the user in the process of understanding the body produces a closed text which can only offer a monolithic version of bodily knowledge which will always be troubled by the paradigm's abjection of the multiplicity of subjectivity.

The *Brandon* site thus engages directly with the inherent anxieties expressed in the *SVF*. Anxieties which can be read through the desire to fix meaning – through the informational frames for example, and through the gaps in that knowledge. Those 'parts' of the body which are not named in the *SVF* can be read as the excess which cannot be apprehended by a subject which 'repudiates' its own founding constituents. The subjective cultural context of the *SVF* is that which is evicted from the project by the foreclosure involved in adherence to the representational paradigm. It is this context which is reinstated by the acknowledgement of the originating influences of an artistic and affective paradigm.

Both the *Stanford Visible Female* and *Brandon* websites utilize advanced imaging technologies to present a version of the reconstituted body within the cyber domain. Yet where the *SVF* project is predicated upon, and rearticulates, a representational referent of normative female anatomy, the Brandon website offers an affective interaction which undermines the normalizing notions of gender and their prescription as anatomically definable instances of the body. Affective rather than representational user interaction within cyberspace here involves a psychical and visual disruption of the normative referent of gendered anatomy. The historical intersections between art and science in the conceptualization of the body are manifest in both projects. The tensions between scientific objectivity and the exploratory discourses of art which underpin the *SVF* project are thus brought to the fore in the *Brandon* website. These tensions are constitutive of the anxieties involved in the formation and regulation of gendered subjectivity, as read through the institutional authorities of medicine and law. An acknowledgement of the tensions endemic to the psychical and cultural processes involved in subject formation, and those represented by the intersections between science and art, must therefore be foregrounded as the conceptual premise from which notions of gendered identity should be examined and explored. <

BIBLIOGRAPHY

Print

Benedikt, Michael, Ed. (1993): *Cyberspace: First Steps*, London / Cambridge **Butler, Judith** (1993): *Bodies that Matter: On the Discursive Limits of Sex*, London / New York **Cartwright, Lisa** (1995): *Screening the Body: Tracing Medicine's Visual Culture*, Minneapolis **D'Agoty, Johannes Fabien Gautier** (1773): *Anatomie des parties de la generation de l'homme et de la femme*, Paris **Debord, Guy** (1983): *Society of the Spectacle*, Detroit **Foucault, Michel** (1978): *Herculine Barbin, dite Alexina B.*, Paris **Haraway, Donna** (1991): *Simians, Cyborgs and Women: The Reinvention of Nature*, London **Jenty, Charles Nicholas** (1759): *The demonstrations of a pregnant uterus of a woman at her fulltime in six tables, as large as nature, done form the pictures painted after dissections by Mr. Van Riemsdyk and disposed in such a manner as to represent, completely, this state of pregnancy, by Charles Nicholas Jenty, AM, Professor of Anatomy and Surgery*, London. **Jordanova, Ludmilla** (1989): *Sexual Visions: Images of Gender in Science and Medicine Between the Eighteenth and Twentieth Centuries*, Madison **Kember, Sarah** (1999): NITS and NRTS: Medical Science and the Frankenstein Factor. In: *Desire By Design: Body, Territories and New Technologie*, Cutting Edge: The Women's Research Group, Eds., London **Kirkup, G. James / L. Woodward, K. / Hovenden, F.**, Eds. (2000): *The Gendered Cyborg: A Reader*, London / New York **Newman, Karen** (1996): *Fetal Positions: Individualism, Science, Visuality*, Stanford **Reiche, Claudia** (1999): Bio(r)Evolution ™: On the Contemporary Military-Medical Complex. In: *Next Cyberfeminist International, Old Boys Network, Rotterdam, March 8–11, 1999*, Cornelia Sollfrank / Old Boys Network, Eds., Hamburg, 25–31 **Stone, Alluquère Rosanne** (1995): *The War of Desire and Technology at the Close of the Mechanical Age*, Cambridge Mass. **Treichler, P. A. / Cartwright, L. / Penley, C.**, Eds. (1998): *The Visible Woman: Imaging Technologies, Gender and Science*, New York / London **Vesalius, Andreas** (1543): *De Humani Corporis Fabrica*, Basel **Waldby, Catherine** (2000): *The Visible Human Project: Information Bodies and Posthuman Medicine*, London / New York

Web

Brandon site, organized by Shu Lea Cheang, http://brandon.guggenheim.org/ [last access: 10/11/1999] **Stanford Visible Female** (SVF) hosted by Stanford University (1997): http://summit.Stanford.EDU/RESEARCH/StanfordVisibleFemale [last access: 10/11/1999] **Thacker, Eugene** (1999): *Ftp_formless_anatomy*, construction of a counter-anatomical database using material from the Visible Human Project, http://rhizome.org/art

base/1699/index/splash_image.html [last access: 01/28/2004] **Thacker, Eugene** (2000): .../visible_human.html/digital anatomy and the hyper-texted body, http://www.ctheory.com/a60.html [last access: 04/02/2000] **Visible Human Project** (VHP) hosted by the NLM – National Library of Medicine (1999): http://www.nlm.nih.gov/research/visible/ [last access: 01/28/2004]

Film **Boys Don't Cry** (US 1999) 1'54'', Production: Hart-Sharp Entertainment, Independent Film Channel, Killer Films / John Hart, Caroline Kaplan, Pamela Koffler et al., Director: Kimberly Peirce, Screenwriter: Kimberly Peirce, Andy Bienen, Performers: Hilary Swank, Chloë Sevigny, Peter Sarsgaard, Brendan Sexton, Alicia Goranson, Alison Folland et al., Cinematography: Jim Denault, Editor: Tracy Granger, Lee Percy, Music: Nathan Larson
The Brandon Teena Story (US 1998) 1'30'', Production: Bless Bless Productions / Jane Dekrone, Susan Muska, Director: Susan Muska, Gréta Olafsdóttir, Screenwriter: Susan Muska, Gréta Olafsdóttir, Performers: Kate Bornstein, JoAnne Brandon, John Lotter, Tom Nissen et al., Cinematography: Susan Muska, Editor: Susan Muska, Gréta Olafsdóttir
Paris is Burning (US 1990) 1'18', Production: Jennie Livingston, Claire Goodman et al., Director: Jennie Livingston, Performers: André Christian, Dorian Corey, Paris Duprée, Shari Headley, Junior Labeija, Pepper Lebeija, Willi Ninja, Venus Xtravaganza et al., Cinematography: Paul Gibson, Editor: Jonathan Oppenheim

Illustration **01 D'Agoty, Johannes Fabien Gautier** (1773): Anatomie des parties de la génération de l'homme et de la femme, Paris
02 Jenty, Charles Nicholas (1759): The demonstrations of a pregnant uterus of a woman at her fulltime in six tables, as large as nature, done from the pictures painted after dissections by Mr. Van Riemsdyk and disposed in such a manner as to represent, completely, this state of pregnancy, by Charles Nicholas Jenty, AM, Professor of Anatomy and Surgery, London
03, 04 Stanford Visible Female (SVF) hosted by Stanford University (1997): http://summit.Stanford.EDU/RESEARCH/StanfordVisible Female [last access: 10/11/1999]
05 Brandon site, organised by Shu Lea Cheang, http://brandon.guggen heim.org/ [last access: 10/11/1999]

Acknowledgement Parts of this paper are also published in: **Booth, R. / Flanagan, M.**, Eds., (2001): *Reload: Redefining Women and Cyberculture*. Cambridge Mass.

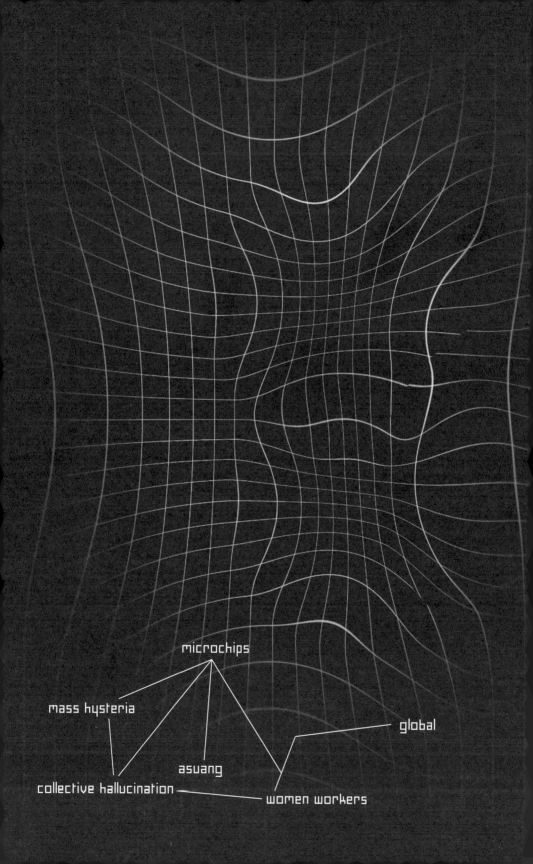

microchips

mass hysteria

global

collective hallucination

asuang

women workers

ito ay panaginip sa ibang pangungusap [1]

"This is a dream not of a common language. It is of a feminist speaking in tongues to strike fear in the circuits of the supersavers of the right."

A Cyborg Manifesto, Donna Haraway

"I feel as if I am seen as a machine for producing, and if the machine stops, management thinks we are rebels."

Mirim, a factory worker in Jakarta[2]

PREMA MURTHY

>   It has been reported that women working in the microchip factories of South Asia have experienced mass hysteria and collective hallucinations while on the job. Many have chosen to report on this 'mysterious' occurrence but few have delved into the causes or implications of this phenomenon. The complexity of these women's lives made up of an overlapping of their external (social) and internal (physical/mental) spaces may make it difficult to diagnose these women. But upon further examination, one might discover that the 'madness' located in the minds of these women is actually located beyond their borders and into their socio-political and economic environment.

site as the city

jakarta, indonesia

"At Duta Busana, a factory in Jakarta, work shifts often stretch to 14 hours a day and those who refuse overtime are simply fired. This city has at least 800,000 people who have no work or income of any kind – and 2 million people who earn less than they need to live. In these desperate conditions, it is easy to find new workers. People even pay bribes for jobs."[3]

"Hira, a young woman working at the Duta Busana factory describes the plant conditions: 'Inside it is very hot. The building has a metal roof and there is not much space for all the workers. There are over 200 people working there, mostly women, but there is only one toilet for the whole factory.'"[4]

"Hira says: 'The truth is that when we come home from work, we don't have enough energy left to do anything but eat and sleep.' Home is the upper floor of a shack that has been divided into eight rooms – each about six feet by nine feet. The small cell costs almost a week's pay every month. The house has no plumbing, so the women have to haul water they need for bathing and drinking."[5]

bangkok, thailand

Sanyan, a young Thai woman says:

"'The women in her factory work from 7a.m. to midnight. In Huay Khwang, Bangkok's crowded factory district, the workplaces are the bottom floor of three-story row houses. The second floor is apartments for the owner's family and the top floors are dormitories for young women workers. There are 5,000 to 10,000 of these factories run as family affairs – the owners often recruit girls from their home villages and barely make

1   translated: (tagalog) "This is a dream not of a common language...". See **Haraway, Donna** (1991): A Cyborg Manifesto: Science, Technology, and Socialist-Feminism in the Late Twentieth Century. In: *Simians, Cyborgs, and Women: The Reinvention of Nature*, London.

2   **Seabrook, Jeremy / Figueroa, Hector / Luciente / Avakian, Bob** (1999): Women in the Factories of the World. In: *The Revolutionary Worker Online*, no. 997, 03/07/1999, http://www.rwor.org/a/v20/990-99/997/workfem.htm [last access: 01/28/2004].

3–8 **Seabrook/Figueroa/Luciente/Avakian** 1999.

9   **Anonym**. (1998): Winged Humanoid Creature Terrorizes Village. In: *Weekly World News*, 03/10/1998.

a living themselves. The women workers live together and eat together – when they have children they keep them here for the first two or three months and then send them back to the villages to be raised.'"[6]

dhaka, bangladesh

"Twenty years ago, there was almost no factory work in Bangladesh – young girls could only find work as servants. But Bangladesh attracted capital because the price of human labor there is the lowest in the world. Now there are 1.2 million young people working in the factories in Bangladesh, 80 percent of which are young women. Their labor produces over 50 percent of the foreign exchange of the country.[7]

Many [of the women] marry [...] rickshaw drivers. Their husbands are happy for them to continue working after marriage – so long as they also do the domestic work as well: cooking, cleaning, looking after the children, fetching water and fuel."[8]

site b: the village

Talking with my Filipino grandmother and her elderly friends, I am told stories of supernatural occurrences unique to specific regions in the Philippines. The truth of these stories is not really questioned and usually confirmed by medical 'experts' in the region and in the newspapers. Liver organs and pregnant women's babies, I'm told, are commonly stolen by the *asuang* (half-demon, half-human vampires) at night. Open windows are lined with crushed garlic and salt to ward them off. It is not safe to leave the home at night especially if you have children for fear of demons or spirits coming in the house at night to steal or harm the children. One woman spoke of a mysterious fire that would appear at night and lead people away from their village and then disappear, leaving them stranded until morning unless they were able to find their way back in the dark. Another woman told me of how a child in her village broke out into sudden a fever. When the doctor came to examine the girl, the explanation he gave was that a spirit had come and stolen the child's organ. It is a common belief that the smells of burning candles or perfume mean an ancestral spirit is present. In the *South China Morning Post*, it was reported that a woman in Dau, Philippines, who becomes half monster at night, had been spotted flying around terrorizing people in bars and brothels.[9]

A majority of workers in the factories are young women who have left their villages and moved to the cities for work, bringing with them their cultural and religious beliefs. Many must work at night, a time when it is taboo for women to be on the streets, making it difficult to travel to work safely and without being harassed. In a society permeated by a belief in supernatural forces, are these spirits and demons metaphors for sociological demons that have permeated the subconscious mind?

site of the mind

psychological reparation

Studies done by psychiatrists and physicians on mass hysteria show that episodes typically affect small, tightly knit groups in enclosed settings such as schools, factories, convents, and orphanages.

> "Mass hysteria is characterized by the rapid spread of unexplained bodily functions with no organic basis. In such episodes, psychological distress is converted or channeled into physical symptoms. There are two common types: anxiety hysteria and motor hysteria. The former is of shorter duration and is triggered by the sudden perception of a threatening agent [...].Motor hysteria is prevalent in intolerable social situations such as strict school and religious settings where discipline is excessive. Symptoms include trance-like states, melodramatic acts of rebellion known as histrionics, and [...] 'psychomotor agitation in' (whereby pent-up anxiety built up over a long period results in disruptions to the nerves or neurons that send messages to the muscles, triggering temporary bouts of twitching, spasms and shaking). Motor hysteria appears gradually over time and usually takes weeks or months to subside."[10] "Many factors contribute to the formation and spread of collective delusions and hysterical illness: mass media, rumors, extraordinary anxiety or excitement; cultural beliefs and stereotypes; the social and political context; and reinforcing actions by authorities [...] or institutions of social control [...]. Episodes are also distinguished by the redefinition of mundane objects, events, and circumstances and reflect a rapidly spreading folk belief that contributes to an emerging definition of a situation."[11]

10 Bartholomew, Robert E. / Goode, Erich (2000): Mass Delusions and Hysterias, Highlights from the Past Millenium. In: *Skeptical Inquirer*, http://www.csicop.org/si/2000-0-5/delusions/htm [last access. 07/12/2001].

11 Bartholomew / Goode 2000.

According to Casper G. Schmidt in *The Journal of Psychohistory*,

"The most common pathway for unchanneled group tension, historically speaking, is recourse to action. Thus [...] human sacrifice, ritual scapegoating, cannibalism, and war throughout history [are regular occurrences], even though these rituals become more and more covert towards the present. The group actions need not necessarily be destructive, and reparative rituals such as baby booms are also found (usually as a guilt-motivated attempt at replacing those 'babies' that had been ritually killed off in fantasy during war)."[12] "Opposed to [...] group action, where the direction [...] of tension is pushed outward, there are also circumstances in which the aggression is turned inward. This gives rise to waves of psychological and psychosomatic disturbances that are called epidemic hysteria. These occur in group members of a lower status or in those who do not wield much power (predominantly women, children, laborers, prisoners, and other 'powerless' members of a group)."[13] "Just as with individuals, the delusions shared by groups are reparative mechanisms:

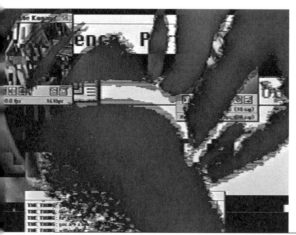

attempts at making sense out of [...] incoherent experiences, or out of a painful, poorly understood reality. [...] they come once the disturbance is already well under way. In most instances where the formation of delusions has been studied extensively [...], the person experiences a sudden and remarkable sense of relief once the delusion is formed. The confusion subsides."[14]

12 **Schmidt, Casper G.** (1984): The Group-Fantasy, Origins of AIDS. In: *The Journal of Psychohistory*, Summer 1984. http://www.virusmyth.net/aids/data/csfantasy.htm [last access: 01/28/2004].

13 **Schmidt** 1984.

14 **Schmidt** 1984.

15 **Schmidt** 1984.

16 **Hossfeld, Karen J.** (1990): Their Logic Against Them: Contradictions in Sex, Race and Class in Silicon Valley. In: *Women Workers and Global Restructuring*, Kathryn Ward, Ed., Ithaca / New York, 149.

17 **Hossfeld** 1990: 169.

18 **Hossfeld** 1990: 156.

19 **Hossfeld** 1990: 157.

Psychosomatic symptoms are solutions for anxieties of psychotic intensity. These fantasies are culture-specific in contents.

> "A [...] significant finding is that these epidemics follow the divisions of class, ethnic groups, and other cultural differences. [...] Thus, in an epidemic of hysteria in a Singapore factory, Malay workers were predominantly affected, while those of different ethnic groups who became affected were few and showed only mild [...] symptoms."[15]

site d: the factory floor

control and resistance

> "The bosses here have this type of reasoning like a seesaw. One day it's 'you're paid less because women are different than men', or 'immigrants need less to get by'. The next day it's 'you're all just workers here – no special treatment just because you're female or foreigners'. Well they think they're pretty clever with their doubletalk, and that we're just a bunch of dumb aliens. But it takes two to use a seesaw. What we're gradually figuring out here is *how to use their own logic against them.*" – Filipina circuit board assembler in Silicon Valley.[16]

Strategies of resistance have been reported as being used by both the management and immigrant women workers in the electronics industries in Silicon Valley. The workers are predominantly Asian but also come from Mexico and other Third World countries.

> "There is little incidence [...] of *formal* labor militancy among the [...] women [...] by either union participation or collectively planned mass actions such as strikes. Filing formal grievances is not common in these worker's [...] culture. Pacing of production to restrict output does occur, and there are occasional 'informal' incidences, such as spontaneous slowdowns and sabotage. But these actions are usually rare and small in scale. Definitions of workplace militancy and resistance vary [...] according to the observer's cultural background, but by their *own* definitions, the women do not frequently engage in traditional forms of labor militancy. There is, however, an important, although often subtle, arena in which the women do engage in struggle with management: the ideological battleground."[17]

> "Management frequently calls upon ideologies concerning sex and race, as well as class, to manipulate worker consciousness and to legitimate the hierarchical division of labor."[18]

> "I [Hossfeld] use the terms 'gender logic' and 'racial logic' to refer to strategies to promote gender and racial hierarchies."[19]

She states that:

> "From interviews with [...] managers and employers, it is evident that high-tech firms find immigrant women particularly appealing workers, not only because they are 'cheap' and considered easily 'expendable' but also because management can draw on and further exploit preexisting patriarchal and racist ideologies that have affected these women's consciousness and realities. In their dealings with the women, managers fragment multifaceted identities into falsely separated categories of 'worker,' 'ethnic,' 'woman.' The effect is to increase and play off the workers' vulnerabilities and splinter their consciousness."[20]

As one Portuguese worker states:

> "The boss tells me not to bring our 'women's problems' with us to work if we want to be treated equal. What does he mean by that? I am working here because of my 'women's problems' – because I am a woman. Working here creates my 'women's problems.' I need this job because I am a woman and have children to feed. And I'll probably get fired because I am a woman and need to spend more time with my children. I am only one person – and I bring my whole self to work with me. So what does he mean, don't bring my 'women's problems' here?"[21]

Just as employers and managers use racist, sexist, and class-based logic to manipulate and control workers, so do workers use this logic against management. Some women seem to draw strength from their multifaceted experiences and develop a unified consciousness with which to confront their oppressions.

> "A white-chip tester testified: It's pretty ironic because management seems to have this idea that male supervisors handle female workers better. You know, we're supposed to turn to mush whenever he's around and respect his authority or something. [...] This one guy thinks females are flighty and irresponsible because of our hormones – so we make sure to have as many hormone problems as we can. I'd say we each take hormone breaks several times a day."[22]

20 **Hossfeld** 1990: 157.

21 **Hossfeld** 1990: 168–169.

22 **Hossfeld** 1990: 171–172.

23 **Hossfeld** 1990:174–175.

24 **Hossfeld** 1990: 173–174.

25 **Hossfeld** 1990: 170.

26 **Hossfeld** 1990: 176.

"An [...] example of a large-scale demonstration [...] on the shop floor involved workers playing off supervisor's stereotypes regarding the superior work of Asians over Mexicans. The incident was precipitated when a young Mexicana, newly assigned to an assembly unit in which a new circuit board was being assembled, fell behind in her quota. The supervisor berated her with racial slurs about Mexicans' 'laziness' and 'stupidity' and told her to sit next to and 'watch the Orientals.' As a group, the Asian women she was stationed next to slowed down their production, thereby setting the average quota on the new boards at a slower than usual pace. The women were in fits of laughter after work because the supervisor had assumed that the speed set by the Asians was the fastest possible, since they were the 'best' workers."[23]

"Several workers have said they feigned a language barrier in order to avoid taking instructions; they have also called forth cultural taboos – both real and imaginary – to avoid undesirable situations. One [...] woman, who took a lot of kidding from her employer about [...] magic, insisted that she could not work the night shift because evil spirits were out then. Because she was a good worker, the employer let her switch to days. When I [Hossfeld] tried to establish whether she believed the evil spirits were real or imagined, the worker laughed and said: 'Does it matter? The result is the same: I can be at home at night with my kids.'"[24]

"[...] most of the women do not view their often elaborate efforts to manipulate their managers' behavior as forms of struggle. Rather, they think of their tactics 'just as a way to get by,' [...]."[25]

"For women and minority workers, the need for short-term gains and benefits and for the long-term equal treatment is a constant contradiction. For the majority of workers, short-term tactics are unlikely to result in long-term equality."[26]

Many of the women interviewed struck Hossfeld as potentially effective labor and community organizers. Yet almost none of them were interested in collective organizing, because of time limitations and family constraints and because of their lack of confidence in labor unions, the feminist movement, and community organizations. Many were simply too worn out from trying to make ends meet and caring for their families.

signs of change

A report done on two electronics firms in Malaysia show that as new technologies are introduced in the workplace, a transformation is occurring in management structures and in the women workers' own perceptions of

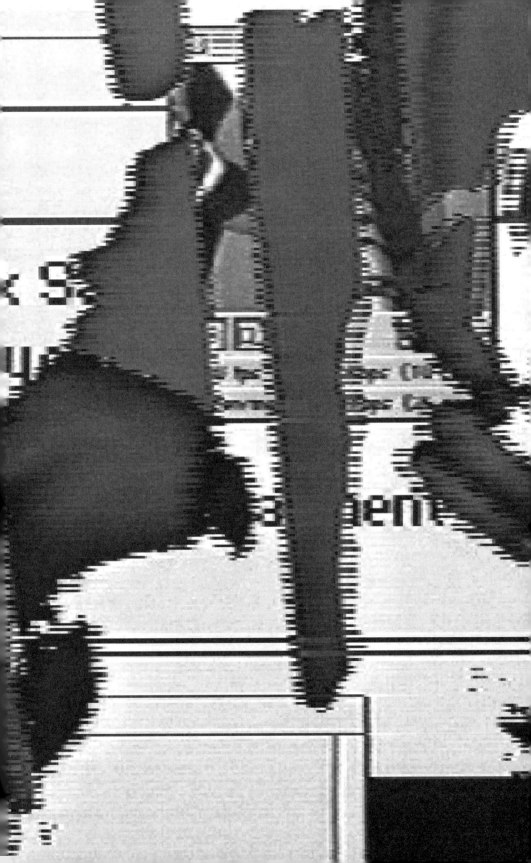

their labor.[27] Studies show that there is a tremendous concern now over the defects of manufacturing, to the extent, that in the case of one company, for example, a situation in which 100 units were defective out of the 1.3 billion produced was considered out of control. Product cycles have become increasingly shortened, leading to the extreme state of competitiveness among the electronics firms themselves. The measures for success in these firms are now being defined not only by being ahead in technology and minimizing defects but more importantly 1) a low labor turnover rate 2) lowered absenteeism 3) higher production output 4) reduction in supervisory or policing work-force and 5) management excellence. The organization of human resources would have to drastically be restructured to reflect this new state of competitiveness.

As more factories are turning to automated machines on all levels of production, shifts on the workfloor are taking place. Most importantly, the assembly process is becoming replaced by a means of collective production. Although a certain amount of positions are taken away while others are created and there is an increase in the surveillance of the workers production levels, a positive shift towards a decentralized knowledge base is occurring. Technology is now on the workfloor where the majority of positions are held by women rather than in the areas of production mainly held by men. Having a high turnover rate is now no longer bene-

---

27 Ng, Cecilia / Mohamad, Maznah (1997): Flexible Labor Regimes, New Technologies and Women's Labor: Case Studies of Two Electronic Firms in Malaysia. In: *AJWS*, vol. 3, no. 1.

28 Ng/Mohamad 1997: The value judgements made on these divisions of labor are problematic but in the workplace in terms of pay scale it is a positive change.

29 Chhachhi, Amrita (1998): Women's Work, Men's Work?: Shifting Identities in the Electronics Industry, AIT-GASAT ASIA CONFERENCE, August 4–7, 1998, http://gendevtech.ait.ac.th/gasat/papers/amritap.html [last access: 06/08/2002].

30 Chhachhi, Amrita (2000): *Women's Work, Men's Work?: Shifting Identities in the Electronics Industry*, New Delhi.

31 Chhachhi 2000.

32 Lingam, Lakshmi (1998): Women's Occupational and Reproductive Health: Research Evidences and Methodological Issues. Report of the Workshop. 23–25 February, 1998, http://www.hsph.harvard.edu/Organizations/health net/SAsia/suchana/0826/rh352.html [last access: 01/28/2004].

ficial to the employers due to high costs in production slow down when having to train new employees. Therefore, a sharing of information on the workfloor is now encouraged by the management among the women, with the more experienced women instructing the newer employees. Older more experienced women that would have once been replaced by the younger "more docile and nimble-fingered" women are now seen as a valuable source. Women performing manual labor which classified them before as "unskilled laborers" can now be classified as "skilled technicians" with their new technical training.[28] Many of the machines are run by several women at once making each person's individual role important to the group as a whole and not as easily replaceable once a level of production that easily meets the daily quota is established.

> "[T]he term 'flexibility' is increasingly being used by manufacturers and policy makers [...] and has been recommended by the World Bank,"[29] but not without suspicion. A flexible labor regime has supposedly replaced the Fordist regime where "consent of labor prevails, rather than its coercion into submission." Flexibility according to futurologists has become the metaphor for the technology age. A 'new economic order' is taking shape in which "flexible workers of flexible firms in flexible locations will be producing goods on a flexi-hour basis with the help of flexible manufacturing systems."[30]

But:

> "[t]he term 'flexibility' is widely contested. [...] The emergence of this term [...] is in many ways linked closely with the revival of neo-classical economics and the obsession with the 'free market.' The term is used loosely, has a variety of meanings and expresses different political positions, ranging from the neo-classical liberals who see a flexible labor force as evidence of a dynamic free market economy, to others who see it as leading to a dualism in the workforce and a new form of capitalist control – the Neo-Fordist response to the crisis of Fordism."[31]

But what significance do these discussions have for the women themselves when they still do not have equity in payscale, must work under physically and mentally unhealthy working conditions and who still carry the responsibility as primary caretakers in the domestic sphere?

As transnational corporations increasingly rely on Third World women as their mass producers, the 'new' international division of labor is increasingly based on gender, class, and nation.[32] The high-tech industry is at the forefront of these trends toward a globalized, 'gendered' labor division.[33] The rapid growth of and dependence on this labor force is expanding traditional notions of workplace resistance and control. Due to an increase in competitiveness and productivity, especially within the high-tech sector, capitalism as a system can no longer afford to thrive on sexist, racist, hierarchical structures. A genuine transformation must happen. Racist stereotyping, poor working conditions and coercive, despotic management structures must be replaced by gender equity, safe work environments and flexible, decentralized management structures. Some signs of change have slowly been happening through the introduction of new technologies into the manufacturing of high-tech goods. But until a full transformation occurs, these 'hysterical,' 'hallucinating' women will continue to wire the world while being forced to cope with insanely oppressive social and economic conditions.   <

33 **Hong, Evelyn** (2000): Women as Consumers and Producers in the World Market. In: *Third World Network*, http://www.twnsidc.org.sg/title/consu-cn.htm [last access: 01/28/2004]

BIBLIOGRAPHY

Print

Anonym. (1998): Winged Humanoid Creature Terrorizes Village. In: *Weekly World News*, 03/10/1998 Chhachhi, Amrita (2000): *Women's Work, Men's Work?: Shifting Identities in the Electronics Industry*, New Delhi Haraway, Donna (1991): A Cyborg Manifesto: Science, Technology, and Socialist-Feminism in the Late Twentieth Century. In: *Simians, Cyborgs, and Women: The Reinvention of Nature*, London Hossfeld, Karen J. (1990): Their Logic Against Them: Contradictions in Sex, Race and Class in Silicon Valley. In: *Women Workers and Global Restructuring*, Kathryn Ward, Ed., Ithaca / New York, 149-178 Ng, Cecilia / Mohamad, Maznah (1997): Flexible Labor Regimes, New Technologies and Women's Labor: Case Studies of Two Electronic Firms in Malaysia. In: AJWS, vol. 3, no. 1

Web

Bartholomew, Robert E. / Goode, Erich (2000): Mass Delusions and Hysterias, Highlights from the Past Millenium. In: *Skeptical Inquirer*, http://www.csicop.org/si/2000-0-5/delusions/htm [last access: 07/12/2001] Chhachhi, Amrita (1998): Women's Work, Men's Work?: Shifting Identities in the Electronics Industry, http://gendevtech.ait.ac.th/gasat/papers/amritap. html [last acess 06/08/2002] Hong, Evelyn (2000): Women as Consumers and Producers in the World Market. In: *Third World Network*, http://www. twnside.org.sg/title/consu-cn.htm [last access: 01/28/2004] Lingam, Lakshmi (1998): Women's Occupational and Reproductive Health: Research Evidences and Methodological Issues. Report of the Workshop. 23-25 February, 1998, http://www.hsph.harvard.edu/Organizations/healthnet/SAsia/ suchana/0826/rh352.html [last access: 01/28/2004] Seabrook, Jeremy / Figueroa, Hector / Luciente / Avakian, Bob (1999): Women in the Factories of the World. In: *The Revolutionary Worker Online*, no. 997, 03/07/1999, http://www.rwor.org/a/v20/990-99/997/workfem.htm [last access: 01/28/2004] Schmidt, Casper G. (1984): The Group-Fantasy, Origins of AIDS. In: *Journal of Psychohistory*, Summer 1984. http://www.virus myth.net/aids/data/csfantasy.htm [last access: 01/28/2004]

Illustration

All illustrations by Prema Murthy

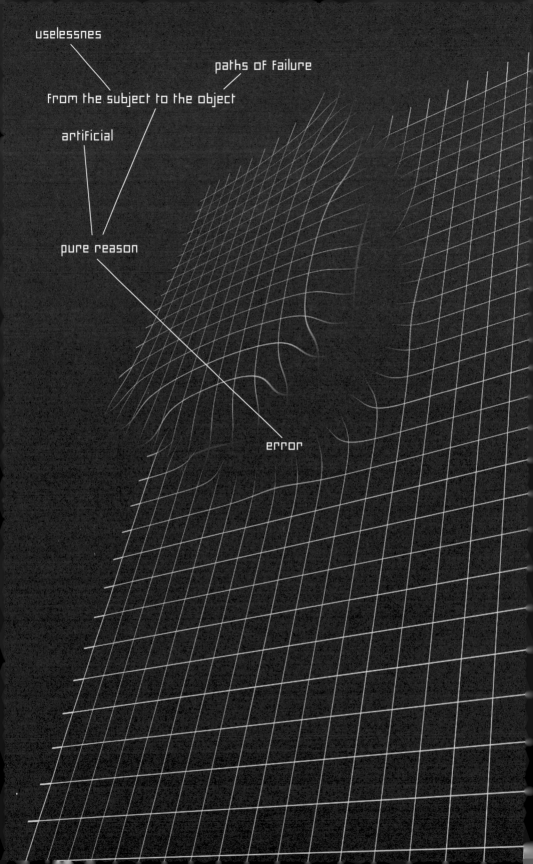

Monstrous Bodies and Subversive Errors

MARINA GRŽINIĆ

01. Monstrous bodies:
The Eastern Europe paradigm as a Woman

> I would like to start with a theoretical-political positioning of feminist theory and practice and subsequently deal with the relationship between philosophy and cyberfeminism. The idea of taking a conceptually specific stand is in order to identify and articulate philosophically a position specific to Eastern Europe. This desire does not grow out of the identity politics game as used by certain feminists to legitimize their right to colonize cyberspace; rather, it is a militant response to this constant process of fragmentation and particularization. I insist, moreover, on the repoliticization of the cyberworld by taking a stance that is based neither on a geographical space nor a location on the map of the 'New Europe' but is, as Edward Said would say, a concept.

It is important to emphasize that the cyberfeminists' posture is not, as it was during the legendary period of feminism in the 1960's (or even earlier, paralleling the period of modernism in art) a product of a natural and, in fact, existential position, but is a strictly artificial and conceptual position owing its existence to theory and not to the existential universe. This is what renders it so problematical; if it were existential it would be easy to deal with; but being purely theoretical, mediated and artificial, it now responds perfectly to, and subverts dramatically, the same circumstances that produced it.

My rethinking of the position of (post)feminism today is also a response to the frequent complaint that now is not the time to divide East and West (Europe), and that in the face of the current ideology of globalization, it is home that matters, as exemplified in the expression: "Neither East, nor West, home is the best!"

Apart from the ideological blindness behind such an attitude, which fails to see beyond the claustrophobic and totalitarian tendencies natural to any nationally-grounded, 'home'-rooted ideology, we have to ask again, where is this 'home' in which the spiritual and conceptual context is located, if indeed we can posit such a context?

I make this remark in the face of a barrage of writings, texts, and ideological positions spread by popular slogans such as the one above which endeavor to ignore the differences between East and West by focusing on a concept such as 'home,' as though there were any place on earth outside the sphere of the political, the social and the mediated! Or, to put it differently, 'home' in this context is perceived as an intimate and personal site in some way excluded from differentiation, and implying, wrongly, that there exists a 'core' whose features such as intimacy, or the feminine, can resist change.

Instead of describing myself as a cyberfeminist from Eastern Europe, I prefer a radical reversal of this Eastern European position or paradigm. I propose to redefine my own Eastern European position (or, if you prefer in Lyotardian terms: my Eastern European condition) as a (post)feminist, as a 'cyberfeminist paradigm.' Eastern Europe is to be seen as a Woman paradigm, in other words, as the female side in the process of sexual difference, whether grounding ourselves in the real or the cyberworld. This concept is a very precise one, as it indicates a repoliticization of the real and the cyberworld. It is rooted in a much deeper universal demand for identity, politics, strategy and tactics of action, theorization, emancipation and uselessness (to fight capitalism, we have to insist on a position that is equal to absolute uselessness, which is not productive at all for the capitalist machine). It can be perceived as the militant theorization, on entering the third millennium, of a particular position in the crucial debate regarding ways and modes and, last but not least, protocols for entering the (cyber)space of hopes, uselessness, theory, and terror.

To return to radical politics means to demand the universal in politics, and not to be squeezed into the narrow confines of a politics of constant exaggeration and of incessantly renewed identities and needs. This is crucial for an understanding of the changing position of the self and identity. What becomes apparent here is that the relation of the subject, along with her body, history, geography, space, etc., takes on in front of the computer console a kind of paradoxical communication which is not direct, but a communication with the excrescence behind her, mediated by the third gaze: that of the computing-machine. What is at stake here is the temporal loss of the subject's symbolic identity: *she* is forced to perceive that *she* is not what *she* thought herself to be. What does this mean? We find ourselves within all media, in all bodies, in all possible spaces at once. This calls into question some fundamental positions concerning art and culture. Operating from this new standpoint, from a new position of identity, other internal media and social processes are revealed to us. We are faced with leaving a historically defined position which imitated the natural world of our senses. With new media and technology we have the possibility of an artificial interface which is dominated by non-identity. Instead of producing a new identity, something much more radical is produced: *the total loss of identity*. The subject is forced to assume that s/he is not what s/he thought her/himself to be, but somebody-something else.

This somebody-something else that can be perceived as a body with geographical and organizational politics may also be attached to the rhetoric and logistics of space. We can be taken else-where and no-where.

Trinh T. Minh-ha has proposed a model for re-thinking Asian space and the so-called third world through the concept of the "inappropriate/d Other." This can also be seen as a possibly useful tool for developing specific concepts for reading the former Eastern European territory. It is time to find and to re-write paradigms of specific spaces, arts, and media productions in Eastern Europe. The whole of Eastern Europe functions like a symptom of the developed West's condition, especially in media or when using avant-garde media and art strategies. In examining the parallels between East/West, we can find in Eastern European media and artistic production significant examples of the perverted and/or symptomatic logic of Western media strategies and visual representation, employed in quite different ways. This can be shown, for example, in the use of pornographic representation, which is/was something that is not generally regarded as acceptable in the West because pornography is seen as part of the commercialization or consumerism of both the body and the media. In Eastern Europe, however, if we use pornography or pornographic visualization in the media as a political stance, a form of resistance to political conformity rather than sexual liberalization, then we get a completely inverted reading of what pornography represents.

To be more precise, the process of pornographic visualization was effected in Eastern Europe through the externalization of sexuality which had been adopted from the underground film tradition exemplified by Fassbinder, Rosa von Praunheim, Warhol, etc., whose films were shown in underground venues in the 1980's. The externalization of sexuality took the form of overtly staged pornography and gender confusion ('gender-bending') of gay, lesbian and transvestite sexual attitudes. It was a process that can be simply explained: the sexual and civil rights (!) stereotypes and prototypes were not only consumed in and by the underground, but immediately performed. In front of a VHS camera, in private rooms and bedrooms, an unparalleled political repositioning of the sexual and social could be acquired. In these works, the masquerade of re-appropriation ensured not only the simple question of the formation of the identity of the artists or of the underground community, but also the process of negotiation required to produce continually ambiguous and unbalanced situations and identities. The acquired hybrid and non-heterosexual positioning of sexuality, in the context of the remarkably impermeable gender boundaries of Communist Eastern Europe, was a way of overtly politicizing the sexual in Socialism and Communism, and fighting for civil rights.

With regard to the parallels between Eastern European space and Woman: just as Woman is not the "weaker part" of Man ("God's second mistake" – Nietzsche) so Eastern Europe is not simply the distorted mirror or, more accurately, the "ailing member" of the West. However, it is perceived as such – inasmuch as Western Europe wishes to see it as ailing, since for the West, Eastern Europe functions as a deceptive illusion of Western desire. The same can be said for Woman: She can be seen as the "weaker part" of the man, but that does not define her ontological status. Similarly, one can say of Eastern Europe that it may be a 'symptom' of the West's condition but that does not define its ontological status.

At the dawn of the third millennium, collective, simultaneous

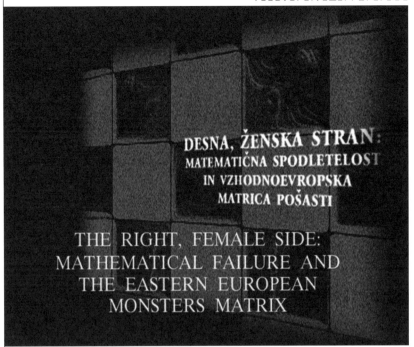

DESNA, ŽENSKA STRAN:
MATEMATIČNA SPODLETELOST
IN VZHODNOEVROPSKA
MATRICA POŠASTI

THE RIGHT, FEMALE SIDE:
MATHEMATICAL FAILURE AND
THE EASTERN EUROPEAN
MONSTERS MATRIX

processes of reception and communication in cyberspace have become a determining metaphor for the new media environment. What is happening on the Internet is increasingly seen and utilized as the 'new' public space. The Internet and the World Wide Web are becoming spaces which are not only parallel to the existing public one, but are increasingly becoming a substitute for it. So-called public opinion is being formulated via the Internet and is perhaps replacing any actual public opinion. First-hand information transmitted via email and then spread through the Web, without additional analysis and reflection, is sometimes enough to lead certain people to proclaim that they are also taking part in the media revolution because they are obtaining firsthand and 'eyewitness' information through the Net; although the community on the Net and its opinions are, in most cases, the sum total of read-and-forwarded messages and the information obtained therein.

An important issue concerning the Internet today, following the decade of the fall of the Berlin Wall, is to pinpoint who the old and the new actors are in the construction of this brave new world (which could be renamed the World Wide Web), and to identify and examine those groups who are concerned in developing a criticism of it. Generally speaking, I have identified two broad lines of critical thought which form positioning matrices in this debate.

The first emphasizes individuals or groups linked neither historically nor geographically, but who consciously take the position of the counter-culture. This position I name the "Scum of Society Matrix" – not as a mere critical label but to indicate that this matrix represents a condition of life and activism, a parasite dwelling within institutional and non-governmental structures. It refers principally to the position of the so-called critical Western European and North American participants – users and online community circuits on the WWW who form a kind of parasitic body trying to extract everything possible from the existing social structures. The 'Scum of Society Matrix' proposes a new, autonomous economy and new structures developed from the appropriation and restructuring of the so-called old ones.

As Peter Lamborn Wilson, alias Hakim Bey, stated in the lecture at the Nettime meeting "Beauty and the East" in Ljubljana in 1997, it seems that the second world has been erased and what is left is the first and third world. Instead of the second world, Bey argued, there is a big hole from which one jumps into the third. To extend the metaphor of the title of the Nettime conference with its reference to the fairy tale, I will call this hole and my second line of thought "The Matrix of Monsters." When it comes to the differences between East and West, it should be made clear that the actors from the black hole, i.e., the Eastern European web-users who are critical of the WWW, do not want to simply to mirror the first world's 'developed, capitalist societies,' but to articulate and interpret, and further, to adopt a distinctive position in this changed constellation.

'The Monsters' insist on pointing out a difference – a critical inherent difference, not simply a special classification method based on markers, such as apartheid, as Trinh T. Minh-ha suggests. The question of who is allowed to write about the history of art, culture, and politics in the area once known as Eastern Europe has to be posed along with the questions of how and when important political, cultural, and media events are marked. The following questions, indicative of moments of synthesis, are

---

1 Quotation from the essay by **Yvonne Volkart**: "'Stubborn Practices' in the Age of Information and Biotechnology," written as a part of her curatorial project *Tenacity: Cultural Practices in the Age of Information and Biotechnology*, presented at the Swiss Institute, New York, 2000 and at the Shedhalle, Zürich, 2000.

crucial, as formulated by Yvonne Volkart: "Which spaces do subjects and agents cross when they communicate? What do they call themselves? Are they subjects, cyborgs, monsters, nomads or simply hackers?"[1] We have to ask ourselves what space, which actors, whose agents and what subjects? The concepts of matrix, structure, position and constellation are to be thought of and perceived in a strictly theoretical and not existential way.

This attempt to define a new position of the subject has been meticulously covered, especially with regard to the potential means of organization on the Internet and in the real world. Donna Haraway invented the 'cyborg' to permit us to understand something much more important: that everybody can be reinvented as such; everybody can be in the position of the cyborg, in the position of 'the perfect excremental leftover.' Just as 'the proletariat' was at a certain point in time, the cyborg today is not something that is predefined, i.e., the features that differentiate the cyborg from the other are not objective, positively defined and understood. A positive definition of the cyborg does not exist in advance, but takes shape at the precise moment of its appearance; there exists no positive distinguishing feature. Positioning matches repoliticization. We can ask further: how does an 'excremental leftover' qualify for reinvention? My answer is that this reinvention must be perceived and understood in terms of meaning and positioning. The point is not that the cyberfeminist identity re-invents itself, but that this reinvention be re-articulated, re-read through theory.

I have stated that at the end of the millennium, the two matrices, the Western European 'Scum of Society Matrix' and the Eastern European 'Monsters' Matrix,' not only raise questions for reflection, but also highlight elements of political and analytical intersection that need to be discussed and articulated further and in a much more radical manner. Establishing the difference between East and West on historical premises only is extremely limiting, and I would like to proceed in a different way, albeit in a way not indifferent to history. I will attempt to explicate some generative principles behind the matrices and their complex functioning, and try also to explain why the Eastern Europe paradigm is to be seen as a 'Woman paradigm' or as the female side in the process of sexual differentiation, as a means of grounding ourselves in (cyber)space. The 'Monsters' Matrix' acts in comparison to the Western Matrix as a purely theoretical entity, and as such is fully permissible.

THESIS ONE: That East and West, despite our constantly redefining them, are not predicates (positively existing entities); which means that the label East or West, rather than increasing our knowledge of the subject, qualifies the mode of failure of our knowledge; and failure is assumed, according to Copjec, to be inherent.

Kant in the *Critique of Pure Reason* and the *Critique of Judgment* first made the distinction between the two ways in which reason falls into contradiction with itself. In both works he demonstrated that the failure of reason was not simple, but based upon an antinomic impasse through two separate routes: the first failure was mathematical; the second was dynamical. The first thing to note is that the two propositions that compose each side appear to have an antinomic relation to each other, i.e., they appear to contradict each other. Subsequently, in his *Seminar XX* entitled *Encore*, drawing upon the Kantian antinomic relations, Lacan defined the two formulae of sexuation (*Of Sexual Difference*) as two ways, or paths, of failure: the male and the female.

In her book *Read My Desire: Lacan against the Historicists*[2], which may be defined as a user's manual of Lacanism, Joan Copjec strongly

---

2 See **Copjec, Joan** (1994): *Read My Desire: Lacan Against the Historicists*, Cambridge (Mass.) / London.

emphasized these two antinomic ways as two ways of failure.

The antinomies and the formulae of sexuation are presented through a scheme that is clearly divided between the left and right sides. The left side of the scheme is designated as the male side, while the right side is female. The left, male side corresponds to the Kantian dynamical antinomies, and the right, female side, corresponds to the Kantian mathematical antinomies.

THESIS TWO: That the Eastern European 'Monsters' Matrix occupies, and is homologous with, the right, female side, and therefore represents the Kantian mathematical failure; while the Western European 'Scum of Society' Matrix is homologous with the left, male side, or the Kantian dynamical failure.

Dubious, you may ask: How is this possible? What permits such a homologous position?

Of crucial importance is the fact that Lacan, in his formulae of sexuation, employs the terms argument and function instead of subject and predicate (as they are referred to in the Kantian formulas). This substitution marks an important, and for us a critical, conceptual difference.

The principle of classification (between East and West, I mean) is no longer descriptive, i.e., it is not a matter of shared characteristics or of common substance. Copjec states, "Whether one falls into the class of males or females (and I would add, whether one falls into the 'Scum or the Monsters' failure matrix – M.G.) depends, rather, which enunciative position one assumes."

The antinomies should be read as positions on a Moebius strip, i.e., as a continuum of differences. There is an unmistakable asymmetry between the mathematical and the dynamical antinomies. Again, according to Copjec, on moving from one to the other, we seem to enter a completely different space.

THE RIGHT, FEMALE SIDE: MATHEMATICAL FAILURE and the Eastern European `Monsters Matrix`

I am not starting with the 'Monsters' just to get some sympathy. Contrary to the fairly common prejudice that psychoanalysis constructs the Woman as secondary – as a mere alteration of man – these formulae suggest, according to Copjec, that there is a kind of priority, an advantage of sorts on the right side.

This reading of the formulae is also consistent with the privileged position accorded the mathematical antinomies by Kant, who grants the mathematical synthesis a more immediate certitude than its dynamical counterpart. In Kant's analysis, it is the dynamical antinomies (the male side of the formula, or the Western European's 'Scum' Matrix in our reading) that appear in many ways secondary, a kind of resolution to the more complete impasse manifested by the mathematical conflict.[3] I will proceed in a very schematic way to reach my point.

What is a mathematical antinomy? First, every antinomy is composed of two propositions: thesis and antithesis. The mathematical antinomy we borrowed from Kant is occasioned by the attempt, generally speaking, to think the world. The thesis of the mathematical antinomy is this: the world has a beginning in time and is also limited in regard to space. The antithesis of the same mathematical antinomy is this: the world has no beginning and no limits in space but is, in relation both to time and space, infinite.

> "After examining both arguments, Kant concludes that while each successfully demonstrates the falsity of the other, neither is able to establish

3 Copjec 1994: 217.
4 Copjec 1994: 218.

convincingly its own truth. This conclusion creates a skeptical impasse, and the solution he arrives at is the following: rather than despairing over the fact that we cannot choose between the two alternatives, we must come to realization that we need not choose, since both alternatives are false. The thesis and antithesis, which initially appeared to constitute a contradictory opposition, turn out to be contraries."[4]

We might note that the structure of a contrary opposition that we find in a mathematical antinomy is demonstrated by the kind of joke Slavoj Zizek uses widely in his lectures:

"In your village there are no cannibals anymore.
When did you eat the last one?"

The form of the question does not allow the addressee to negate the accusation implicit in the question, but only to choose among contraries. Having demonstrated the impossibility of the existence of the world, Kant can then dismiss both the statements of thesis and antithesis. Kant's two statements regarding the solution of the first mathematical antinomy formally reduplicate those that Lacan gives for Woman, who, like the world, does not exist.

Lacan argues that a concept of Woman cannot be constructed because the task of fully unfolding her conditions cannot, in actuality, be carried out. Since we are finite beings, bound by space and time, our knowledge is subject to historical conditions.

And here we come to the most important point:

> "The existence of Woman is not only denied; it is also not condemnable as a normative and exclusionary notion; on the contrary, the Lacanian position argues that it is only by refusing to deny – or confirm – her existence that normative and exclusionary thinking can be avoided. That is, it is only by acknowledging that a concept of Woman cannot exist, that it is structurally impossible within the symbolic order, that each historical construction of her can be challenged. After all, nothing prohibits these historical constructions from asserting their universal truth; witness the historical assertion that a general, trans-historical category of Woman does not exist."[5]

It is crucial to see that Woman is the consequence, and not the cause, of the nonfunctioning of negation. She is the failure of the limit, not the cause of the failure.[6]

Now, following this rather crude and schematic cutting up of one part of the excellent chapter on the forms of sexuation in Copjec's book *Read My Desire: Lacan against the Historicists*, we must return to our 'Monsters Matrix ' – to accept the consequences of such a homologous position.

THESIS THREE: Similarly to Lacan's positing the nonexistence of Woman, we can speak of the nonexistence of the 'Matrix of Monsters.' If the 'Matrix of Monsters' does not exist, this is because it cannot be found. The 'Matrix of Monsters' cannot be constructed because the task of fully unfolding its conditions cannot, in actuality, be carried out. Our conception of the (Matrix of) 'Monsters' cannot run ahead of these limits and thus, we cannot construct a concept of the whole of the Matrix.[7]

The existence of the (Matrix of) 'Monsters' is not only denied; it is also not condemnable as a normative and exclusionary notion; on the contrary, the Lacanian position argues that it is only by refusing to deny – or confirm – its existence that normative and exclusionary thinking can be avoided. That is, it is only by acknowledging that a concept of the (Matrix of) 'Monsters' cannot exist, that it is structurally impossible within the symbolic order, that each historical construction of this Matrix can

---

5 Copjec 1994: 225.
6 Copjec 1994: 226.
7 Copjec 1994: 221.

be challenged. As long as it can be demonstrated that the world or the (Matrix of) 'Monsters' cannot form a whole, a universe, then the possibility of judging whether or not these phenomena or signifiers give us information about a reality independent of us vanishes.

It is crucial to see that the 'Matrix of Monsters,' to paraphrase Copjec, is the consequence, and not the cause, of the nonfunctioning of negation. It is the failure of the limit, not the cause of the failure.

THE LEFT, MALE SIDE: DYNAMICAL FAILURE and the Western European `Scum of Society Matrix`

Where the thesis and antithesis of the mathematical antinomies were both deemed to be false because both illegitimately asserted the existence of the world, the thesis and antithesis of the dynamical antinomies, the dynamical failure, are both deemed by Kant to be true. In the first case, the conflict between the two propositions was thought to be irresolvable (since they made contradictory claims about the same object); in the case of dynamical failure, the conflict is resolved by the assertion that the two statements do not contradict each other.

The thesis of the dynamical antinomy is, according to Kant, the following: Causality according to the laws of nature is not the only causality operating to originate the world. A causality of freedom is also necessary to account fully for these phenomena. The Kantian antithesis of the dynamical antinomy, or failure, is: that there is no such thing as freedom, but everything in the world happens solely according to the laws of nature.

Kant says that the antithesis in the dynamic antinomy is true, just as Lacan confirms the existence of the universe of men. Since the existence of the universe was regarded, in the case of Woman, as impossible because no limit could be found to the chain of signifiers, it would be logical to assume that the formation of the all on the male side, in fact, depends on the positing of a limit.

The shift from the female to the male side is a subtraction. The thesis and antithesis of the mathematical failure, according to Kant, said too much. On the dynamical side, this surplus is subtracted, and it is this subtraction that installs the limit. Which means that on this side it will always be a matter of saying too little. Incompleteness on the dynamic side, and inconsistency on the mathematical side.

Furthermore, according to Copjec, the question of existence that caused the conflict on the female side is silenced on the male side because it is, precisely, existence – or being – that is subtracted from the universe that is formed here. Kant taught us that if one were to say that a man existed, one would add absolutely nothing to this man, or to the concept of man. Thus we could argue that this concept lacks nothing. And yet, it does not include being, and is in this sense inadequate.

Again, the two failures or forms of sexuation according to Lacan consist of the following: the woman and the man are not to be treated symmetrically nor conceived as complements of each other. One category does not complete, or make up for what is lacking in, the other. While the universe of women is simply impossible, a universe of men is possible only on the condition that we except something from this universe. The universe of men is then an illusion based, according to Copjec, on a paradoxical prohibition: do not include everything in your all! The sexual relation fails for two reasons: it is impossible, and it is prohibited. And this is why we will never come up with a whole.

For an easy solution we could say that, like the Eastern European 'Monsters Matrix,' the Western European 'Scum of Society Matrix' does not exist. But there is no problem in locating it on the left side, homologous to the Lacanian sexuation table. Kant taught us that, if one were to say that the Western European 'Scum of Society Matrix' existed, one would add absolutely nothing to the concept of the Western European

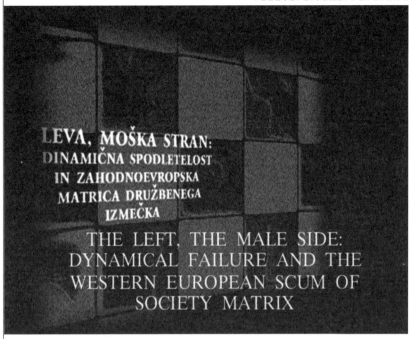

LEVA, MOŠKA STRAN:
DINAMIČNA SPODLETELOST
IN ZAHODNOEVROPSKA
MATRICA DRUŽBENEGA
IZMEČKA

THE LEFT, THE MALE SIDE:
DYNAMICAL FAILURE AND THE
WESTERN EUROPEAN SCUM OF
SOCIETY MATRIX

'Scum of Society Matrix.' Rather than defining a universe of men that is complemented by a universe of women, we can define, relying on Lacan, the Western European 'Scum of Society Matrix' (male side) as the prohibition against constructing a universe, and the Eastern European 'Monsters Matrix' (female side) as the impossibility of doing so.

Because of this implicit impossibility of constructing a universe, we have to constantly re-locate ourselves. This is why positioning and re-articulation means repoliticization.

02. A failure, an error, and a virus

It is not really a question of going to distant geopolitical spaces such as Africa, Asia, or even Eastern Europe, it is, rather, about the capitalization of ideas and concepts becoming territory in itself. Theory is such a territory, as is the Internet with the World Wide Web. These huge new territories, expanded and evolved on numerous servers, allow capital, the most internal vehicle of Capitalism at its purest, an even faster multiplication. Theory, art, and culture are huge archives, and it is the same with our bodies. That everything can be transformed into a territory for the expansion of capital is something that is fundamental to Capitalism. In this way the idea of territory itself changes – radically.

The year 2000 brought with it a completely different idea of how we think about territory. Territory as a pure geopolitical space is gone. Territory has become a much broader concept. Our intellectual concepts, our books, our works and, last but not least, all our archives are the new territories. Contributing concepts is, therefore, a gesture of expanding and broadening the concept of territory itself.

The second crucial change that has an effect on East and West, South and North is that in the 1980's, it was enough to be visible; at 2000 it is a question of re-articulation, and moreover, re-location, much more than pure visibility.

In today's world, photographic, electronic, and digital images are at the point of effective disintegration. Even with a very small PC we can manipulate any image. Photographic images especially are losing their credibility, as, for example in the process of judging world events. Images, and especially photography, have reached the point where their internal reality is questioned. This is not simply a question of truth or falsity. Questions of plausibility and implausibility override those concerning whether an image is simply true or false. The problem, therefore, no longer has to do with mental images and consciousness only, but with the paradoxical facticity of new media images, especially computer-generated photographic images.

If art poses, according to Scott Bukatman, the enigma of the body, then technique poses the enigma of art.

In such a context it is possible to establish an important connection between the image and the power structures that form and surround it and to approach the video or film image, etc., as part of a larger system of visual and representational communication. This approach is fundamentally concerned with the articulation of a representational politics. The politics of representation in terms of the video and media image is not something that is directly connected with everyday politics but it is connected in so far as the aesthetics of the image is always inscribed in a field of power. Power takes different forms; therefore, electronic and media images as a form of representation have different connections with different types of power.

Cyberspace treats material as a toxic agent. Materiality is extracted from cyberspace and reduced from object to abject – to a senseless,

8 I would like to express my gratitude for the English language editing of the present paper to Tina Horne and to Verena Kuni and Claudia Reiche for their engagement in the production, distribution and publishing of this essay.

obscene intervention (Julia Kristeva, Critical Art Ensemble and Pell). Something similar is happening with the body. It is possible to identify a process of estrangement: the body is a malfunctioning machine (Katarzyna Kozyra, Poland), or bodies are having love affairs between servers (Olia Lialina, Russia) waiting for a possible re-articulation. From an acrobat to an experimental engine, the body may take up any position, as exemplified by, in this order, Marina Abramovic (Yugoslavia/Netherlands), Vlasta Delimar (Croatia), Egle Rakauskaite (Lithuania) Sanja Ivekovic (Croatia). In the case of Marina Abramovic the body is a screen used for all sorts of changes including the complete masquerading of identity; Vlasta Delimar is the living work herself: she presents herself as the reservoir of the virus, reminding us of her potentiality waiting to become a reality. Egle Rakauskaite's work re-invents the potential cyborg (she connects her performers through their hair and not through the Internet); Sanja Ivekovic, on the other hand, develops a penultimate form of a cyborg, a modern Frankenstein.

The introduction of errors, failures, potential bodies, and viruses in perfect, simulated environments and the cyberworld can be viewed, therefore, as a means to developing new aesthetic and conceptual strategies, since the error as abject – an object of horror and disgust – cannot be integrated into the matrix. We can actually think about the error, in the words of Jacques Derrida, as a way of developing the logic of re-marking (re-marque). The logic of re-marking is similar to the function of the error or of the symptom, where what at first seemed an informative, general view of an event – a shot, so to speak, from a neutral, objective distance – suddenly turns out to be both threatening and embodied. The error is actually 'the thing' itself; it is the subject that is speaking, and tells more than the subject itself.

What characterizes the replacement of the depth of space by the depth of time is a splitting of viewpoint, the sharing of perception of the environment between the animate (the living subject), the inanimate (the object, the seeing machine) and, from now on, the abject (the error, mistake, failure). The vision(s) of this viewpoint, its visualizations, are what is already there in the eye of the camera(s), remaining in "a state of latent immediacy in the huge junk heap of the stuff of memory, wanting to reappear, inexorably, when the time comes" (Paul Virilio). To re-appropriate the place of this memory, of virtual memory, in the modern way means, therefore, not to leave any more traces (as virtual memory is no longer a function of the past, but of the future) but instead, to leave mistakes, errors, and failures!

The speed at which TV and radio information circulates (in terms of one-way distribution) has already been overtaken by the static speed of computer calculations; which means that the speed of internet connections becomes more and more important.

A failure, an error, a mistake is, therefore, the route leading to a transformation from the subject to the abject, which with its senseless, obscene intervention, can be perceived as the new (failed!) subject position.[8]   <

BIBLIOGRAPHY
Print

Copjec, Joan (1994): *Read My Desire: Lacan Against the Historicists*, Cambridge (Mass.) / London   Grzinic, Marina (2000): *Fiction Reconstructed. Eastern Europe, Post-socialism & Retro-Avantgarde*, Vienna 2000 [= Gržinić 2000a] Grzinic, Marina (2000): Exposure Time, the Aura, and Telerobotics. In: *The Robot in the Garden: Telerobotics and Telepistemology in the Age of the Internet*, Ken Goldberg, Ed., Cambridge (Mass.) [= Grzinic 2000b] Grzinic, Marina (2000): Strategies of Visualisation and the Aesthetics of Video in the New Europe. In: *Culture and Technology in the New Europe: Civic Discourse in Transformation in Post-Communist Nations*, Laura Lengel, Ed., London [= Grzinic 2000c] Gržinić, Marina / Eisenstein, Adele, Eds. (2000): *The Body Caught in the Intestines of the Computer & Beyond. Women's Strategies and /or Strategies by Women in Media, Art and Theory*, Ljubljana / Maribor Haraway, Donna (1992): The Promises of Monsters: A Regenerative Politics for Inappropriate/d Others. In: *Cultural Studies*, Lawrence Grossberg / Cary Nelson / Paula A. Treichler, Eds., New York / London Said, Edward (1978): *Orientalism. Western Conceptions of the Orient*, London

Web

Grzinic, Marina (2000): Spectralization of Space: The Virtual-Image and the Real-time Interval, see: *The Mars Patent*, http://www.mars-patent.org/projects/marina/marina1.html [last access 01/28/2004]

Illustration

All illustrations by Marina Grzinic

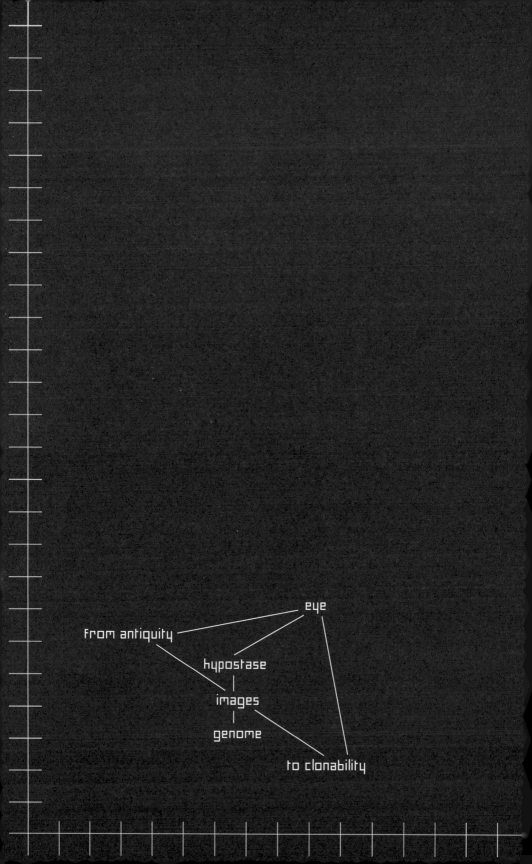

Remaking Eden:
On the Reproducibility of
Images and the Body
in the Age of Uirtual Reality
and Genetic Engineering

INGEBORG REICHLE

New images of human beings

> If one follows David Harvey's observation that advertising is the official art of capitalism[1], then it would appear worthwhile to take a look at advertisements for the laboratory equipment of genetic engineers, advertisements which frequently employ citations from the world of high Renaissance art. In the magazine *Nature*, Du Pont advertises with the *Mona Lisa's* smile: "Smile! Renaissance™..."[2] Above the text, da Vinci's *Mona Lisa* is presented à la Andy Warhol in multiple reproductions, i.e., as 'clones.'

YMC, another company, advertises with an alienated citation from Michelangelo's Vatican frescoes in the Sistine Chapel: *The Creation of Adam*.[3]

Smile! Renaissance™ non-rad DNA labeling kits give you reproducible results, not high backgrounds.

Are you repeating experiments just to reduce backgrounds? Then look into Renaissance™ non-radioactive DNA labeling and detection products from DuPont NEN®. And get low backgrounds and reproducible results the first time, and every time.

³²P EasyTides™ Chemiluminescence
24 hr at -80°C 30 min at room temp.

1.8 μg Molt-4 total RNA
was probed via Northern Blot
hybridization with
labeled GAPDH.

• Sensitive HRP-luminol systems for colony plaque lifts and Northern, Southern, and Western blots.
• Results in minutes.
• Guaranteed one-year shelf life.
• Backed by full protocol and comprehensive technical service.
• Now available: Random Primer Fluorescein dUTP Labeling Kit and Oligonucleotide 3' End Labeling kit (Fluorescein ddUTP).

DuPont gives you a choice of radioactive and now Renaissance non-radioactive labeling and detection products. For information, or orders call 1-800-551-2121. For information by fax, call 1-800-666-6527 and request number 9002.

DuPont NEN®

01 Du Pont "Smile! Renaissance™...", advertisement in *Nature* (1995)

1 **Harvey, David** (1992): *The Condition of Postmodernity*, Cambridge Mass., 63, see **Haraway, Donna** (1998): Deanimation: Maps and Portraits of Life itself. In: *Picturing Science – Producing Art*, Caroline A. Jones / Peter Galison, Eds., London / New York, 181–207.

2 The advertisement appeared in the magazine *Nature* (1995), vol. 373, no. 6509, 1.

3 *Nature* (1995), vol. 373, no. 6509, 8.

Walter Benjamin's thesis about the artwork's loss of aura in the age of its technical reproducibility[4] would seem to apply directly to these advertising images. At the beginning of his essay "The Work of Art in the Age of Mechanical Reproduction," Benjamin argued that works of art have in principle always been reproducible, as all works created by human beings are.[5] Benjamin coupled this diagnosis of the loss of aura with an emancipatory achievement: through its technical reproducibility, the artwork has for the first time in the history of humanity been liberated from its parasitic existence in ritual.[6] Future generations will presumably look back at our current age – an age in which the technical reproducibility of the human body through cloning has become possible in the laboratories of genetic engineers – and say something similar about the image of humans in

02 Andy Warhol, *Thirty Are Better Than One*, 1963 silkscreen print on acrylic paint on canvas, private collection, 279.4 x 240 cm

4 For arguments against Benjamin's thesis of the artwork's loss of aura in the age of its technical reproducibility, see **Tillim, Sidney** (1983): Benjamin Rediscovered: The Work of Art After the Age of Mechanical Reproduction. In: *Artforum*, vol. 21, no. 5, 65–73 and **Bredekamp, Horst** (1992): Der simulierte Benjamin. Mittelalterliche Bemerkungen zu seiner Aktualität. In: *Frankfurter Schule und Kunstgeschichte*, Andreas Berndt, Ed., Berlin, 117–140.

5 **Benjamin, Walter** (1991 [1936]): Das Kunstwerk im Zeitalter seiner technischen Reproduzierbarkeit. In: *Walter Benjamin, Abhandlungen, Gesammelte Schriften, vol. 1.2*, Rolf Tiedemann / Hermann Schweppenhäuser, Eds., Frankfurt am Main, 436–475. An English translation of the essay with the title 'The Work of Art in the Age of Mechanical Reproduction' can be found in: *Illuminations*, New York (1968), 217–251. The text first appeared 1936 in a French translation as an article in the *Zeitschrift für Sozialforschung* no. 5.

6 **Benjamin** 1991: 442.

which life has shriveled to mere commodity forms and the digital world has made the distinction between original and copy obsolete.

Over the past years, numerous art exhibitions[7] have focused on the *new images of human beings* which have arisen as a result of these new technical possibilities of reproducing the body – whether these be media reproduction in the computer-generated worlds of cyberspace, or medical reproduction in the form of simulation models, or biological reproduction in the test tubes in genetic engineers' laboratories.[9] The discussions here have moved between two poles, the one emphasizing the ostensibly impending option of escaping the burdensome physical body and existing weightless between bytes and bits, and the other focusing on the technological realization of this and the technical reproducibility of organic life.

The moment in which these new technologies directly converge is the rhetoric surrounding them, a rhetoric which stands in that problematic intellectual tradition that envisages human technology as potentially capable of creating a new nature, a second nature, and thereby implying the old motif of the technical re-instantiation of paradise,[10] in which

---

7 In the arts, particularly in media art, the body has become the venue of this questioning, as it is evident in the boom of exhibitions at the beginning of the 1990's focussing on body images and body perception. I name only a few exhibitions which possessed a clear theoretical conception: *Corporal Politics*, MIT List Visual Art Center, Cambridge Mass. 1992; *PostHuman*, Deichtorhallen, Hamburg, 1992; *Abject Art. Repulsion and Desire in American Art*, Whitney Museum of American Art, New York, 1993; *Real Sex, Real Real, Real Aids, Real Text*, Vienna / Graz / Salzburg / Klagenfurt, 1994; *Oh Boy, it's a Girl!*, Kunstverein München, 1994; *The Body, Le Corps*, Kunstmuseum Bielefeld, 1994.

8 *Ars Electronica* (1993) focussing on *Genetische Kunst – Künstliches Leben; GameGrrl. Abwerten biotechnologischer Annahmen*, Zurich / Munich (1994); *Frankensteins Kinder*, Zurich (1997); or *Tenacity: Cultural Practices in the Age of Information- and Biotechnology* (2000), New York / Zurich. On this, see **Kuni, Verena** (1998): Metamorphose im Zeitalter ihrer technischen Reproduzierbarkeit. In: *Raum und Körper in den Künsten der Nachkriegszeit*, Akademie der Künste, Ed., Amsterdam / Dresden, 201–217.

9 Two of the most important are the '*Visible Human Project*' and the '*Human Genome Project.*'

10 On the paradise tradition, see **Stöcklein, Ansgar** (1969): *Leitbilder der Technik. Biblische Tradition und technischer Fortschritt*, Munich, 36ff.

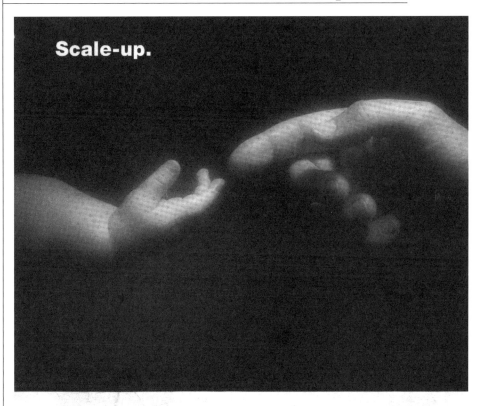

03 YMC "Scale-up", advertisment in *Nature* (1995)

there is neither transience and death, nor sex and sin. The medium in which information and communication technologies converge with the life sciences is the computer. Information and the life sciences are combined here into a new paradigm, for it is the computer which – as an instrument and as a medium – permits us to get a handle on genetic resources, that is, to analyze them more quickly, to interpret them and to visualize them. Here, we are dealing with a new communication basis *and* a new resource basis.

The creation of a bio-industrial nature

"We used to think our fate is in our stars. Now we know, in large measure, our fate is in our genes," declared James D. Watson, the first director of the *Human Genome Project*, a billion-dollar, internationally networked program established ten years ago with the goal of completely decoding human DNA. In early April of 2000, J. Craig Venter, an American geneticist

---

11 The article 'Why the future doesn't need us' by **Billy Joy**, one of the leading heads of the company Microsun Systems and the inventor of the programming language Java, appeared in the April edition 2000 of the magazine *Wired*. It caused a prolonged discussion about the consequences of genetic engineering, robotics and nanotechnology.

12 See **Rifkin, Jeremy** (1998): *The Biotech Century: Harnessing the Gene and Remaking the World*, London and **Flessner, Bernd**, Ed. (2000): *Nach dem Menschen. Der Mythos einer zweiten Schöpfung und das Entstehen einer posthumanan Kultur*, Freiburg im Breisgau.

13 See **Gottweis, Herbert** (1998): *Governing Molecules: The Discursive Politics of Genetic Engineering in Europe and the United States,* Cambridge Mass. / London, 153–163.

14 See **Fox Keller, Evelyn** (1995): *Refiguring Life: Metaphors of Twentieth-century Biology*, New York.

15 The processes of such abstract technologies, whose occur in microstructures invisible to the human eye, can only be represented as models and are thus dependent upon visualization. The biologist Donna Haraway refers to the cultural productions of DNA structure, as well as the fetishization of genes and their visualization in a specifically scientific-cultural context, see **Haraway** 1998: 181–187.

16 **Watson, James D. / Crick, Francis** (1953): The Structure of DNA. In: *Cold Spring Harbor Symposia on Quantitative Biology*, no. 18, 29–128.

17 **Toulmin, Stephen** (1953): *The Philosophy of Science: An Introduction*, London, 34.

and president of the Celera Genomic Company, announced to the Energy Committee of the United States Congress that the first human genome had been decoded. With this, a relatively small private company had – almost single-handedly – achieved the desired results more quickly than public research institutions. The technology of "shotgun" sequencing developed by Venter greatly accelerated the decoding of the human genome. The news of the *complete decoding* of human DNA triggered a new boom in biotechnology stocks, as well as numerous discussions about international patent law, about ethical concepts in the life sciences and ultimately about the future of human beings in general.[11]

Yet much more interesting than the race to decode the human genome is the fact that the classical separation of science and industry appears today to have become obsolete and that we are still in no position to estimate the consequences of this implosion. Genetic technologies and biotechnologies are regarded as contenders for *the* key technologies in the coming decades. The apostles of this biological revolution continue to promise that these technologies will set in motion nothing less than a second history of creation – this time an artificially created bio-industrial nature which is supposed to replace the original concept of evolution.[12] Since the 1950's, these apostles have described the future potentials of such technologies – initially of molecular biology and then of genetics – with the aid of the revolution metaphor.[13] At the beginning of the 1980's, bioinformatics, the most recent branch of genetics, was celebrated as the expression of a far-reaching upheaval and an historical break.[14] The fusion of the rapid developments of both information and computer technologies with the life sciences led to an enormous acceleration in research and to the use of advanced digital image technologies for the representation of new scientific models with their own aesthetic.[15] The genesis of the visualization of DNA makes clear how aesthetic representations have not only played a decisive role in the description of DNA structure, but that such aesthetic pre-figurations equally determined their discoverer. In 1953, the same year that James D. Watson and Francis Crick published a description of their model of the structure of DNA as a double helix,[16] the philosopher Stephen Toulmin argued that the discovery of new methods of representation lay at the center of all great discoveries in the natural sciences.[17] According to Toulmin, the criteria used to describe the analytic solution to a problem in the natural sciences always includes conceptions of beauty, harmony, simplicity, symmetry or consistency. Even the way in which a scientist seeks results, Toulmin argued, always involves choices among aesthetic notions – a process which does not deviate significantly from artistic practices.[18] In other words, models are made – they are not simply 'there' to be discovered. Just as structural models of DNA have undergone changes over the course of time, the concept of the gene has itself experienced a transformation. Curiously, the meaning of the concept 'gene' has been displaced – from an older perspective in which the gene eclipses the organism to the current understanding in which genes trigger dynamic processes within organisms.[19]

Today genetic technology makes possible functional interventions in essential life processes. Such technologies allow us to manipulate the reproduction cycle of nature as well as its ecological equilibrium. Above all, however, it has now become possible for humans to alter the genetic code – and with this to explode the boundaries of their own species.

Transgenic art

Geneticists today regard the idea of transplanting genes from one organism to another as harmless and unobjectionable. Transgenic animals and plants have become part of everyday life in the laboratory. Genetic engineers do not see anything monstrous nor supernatural about the con-

18 See **Root-Bernstein, Robert** (1996): Do We Have the Structure of DNA Right? Aesthetic Assumptions, Visual Conventions, and Unsolved Problems. In: *Art Journal, Contemporary Art and the Genetic Code*, vol. 55, no. 1, 47. See also the art-historian Judith Wechsler: **Wechsler, Judith**, Ed. (1978): *On Aesthetics in Science*, Cambridge Mass.; **Root-Bernstein, Robert** (1985): Visual Thinking: The Art of Imagining Reality. In: *Transactions of the American Philosophical Society*, no. 75, 50–67; and **Tauber, Alfred J.**, Ed. (1996): *The Elusive Synthesis: Aesthetics and Science*, Boston.

19 On this subject, see **Fox Keller, Evelyn** (1998): Das Gen und das Humangenomprojekt – zehn Jahre danach. In: Exh. Cat. *Genwelten, Kunst- und Ausstellungshalle der BRD*, Bonn, Petra Kruse, Ed., Cologne, 77–81. On the history of the reception of DNA models in genetic research in the context to gender relations in science, see also **Fox Keller, Evelyn** (1983): *A Feeling for the Organism – The Life and Work of Barbara McClintock*, San Francisco.

20 **Flusser, Vilém** (1988): Curies Children. In: *ArtForum*, vol. 16, no. 7, 9.

21 **Hoffmann, Peter Gerwin** (1987): Mikroben bei Kandinsky. In: *Animal Art, Steirischer Herbst*, Richard Kriesche, Ed., Graz, no page numbers.

22 **Davis, Joe** (1996): Microvenus. In: *Art Journal, Contemporary Art and the Genetic Code*, vol. 55, no. 1, 70–74.

cept of recombinant DNA and the idea connected with this of artificially creating a living being from two distinct beings. Genetic engineers and industrial investors – who have entered into a relationship of unprecedented intimacy – promise immeasurable gains from the future creations of human genetics and its medical applications (gene therapy), while playing down the inherent dangers of such technologies. The ideology of genetic determinism serves as the legitimation and the motor of a scientific-industrial branch which can boast double-digit growth rates and whose research findings are more immediately available on the stock market than in the relevant scholarly journals.

Even contemporary artists have taken up the procedures of gene technology and biotechnology in their own works and have transferred the functioning of the genetic laboratory, its instruments and scientific practices, into the aesthetic productions within art galleries. More than a decade ago, Vilém Flusser foresaw the contours of this artistic development and predicted that biotechnics would become an instrument of artists who someday might create wheat with the power of sight, photosynthetic horses, and

> "an enormous color symphony [...] in which the color of every living organism will complement the colors of every other organism" and would provide new artists with a "foundation for intellectual processes which have not existed up to now."[20]

A year earlier, the artist Peter Gerwin Hoffmann had presented his installation *Mikroben bei Kandinsky* for the first time in Graz, Austria. *Mikroben bei Kandinsky* consisted of bacterial cultures which Hoffmann had taken from a Kandinsky painting. Hoffman declared that with this procedure the dichotomy of art and nature had been transcended:

> "Gene technology has put [...] and end [to] [...] the polarity nature-art. The living organisms [...] that surround us [...] can only be understood and interpreted as works of art."[21]

Several years ago, the artist Joe Davis thematized attempts to introduce DNA as the carrier of non-biological information in his project *Microvenus*.[22] The media artist and theorist Eduardo Kac has moved along this interface between art and gene technology formulated by Flusser in his recent projects *GFP K-9* (1998), *Genesis* (1998/99) and *Bunny* (2000), thereby raising the debate about *transgenic* art as a new art form. These projects are supposed to use artistic means to investigate the cultural effects of the life sciences and their new possibilities for the transformation of life. However, the aesthetic of the artistic staging here drowns out the investigation of the laboratory as a site of the social processes of construction and as a social institution and a site of knowledge production.[23] Neither the practices nor the rhetoric of scientific debates about gene technology are analyzed in the exhibitions. Transgenic art appears, rather, to participate in a long tradition of art theory centered on the topos of the artist-engineer. However, in contrast to this topos, which referred via Newton's mechanics to the creation of 'living works,' transgenic art today is concerned with the actual creation of new organic life from aesthetic perspectives, a creation which is made possible through direct technological access to DNA, the carrier of genetic substance. In contrast to this, early geneticists such as Jacques Loeb understood themselves as engineer-artists. At the beginning of the 20th century Loeb was convinced that all life processes could ultimately be traced back to clear, simple and controllable connections. His vision was the development of a "biological engineering art" and a "technology of the living being." He did not want to

23 Cf. **Haraway, Donna** (1996): Anspruchsloser Zeuge @ Zweites Jahrtausend. FrauMann trifft OncoMouse. Leviathan und die vier Jots: Die Tatsachen verdrehen. In: *Vermittelte Weiblichkeit. Feministische Wissenschafts- und Gesellschaftstheorie*, Elvira Scheich, Ed., Hamburg, 347–389 und **Schultz, Susanne** Ed. (1996): Geld.beat.synthetik. Abwerten bio/technologischer Annahmen, Berlin / Amsterdam.

24 **Loeb, Jacques** (1911): *Das Leben*, Leipzig. See also **Pauly, Philip J.** (1987): *Controlling Life. Jacques Loeb and the Engineering Ideal in Biology*, New York / Oxford.

25 **Burnham, Jack** (1968): *Beyond Modern Sculpture: The Effects of Science and Technology on Sculpture of this Century*, New York, 376.

26 **Gesser, George** (1993): Notes on Genetic Art. In: *Leonardo*, vol. 26, no. 3, 210.

27 See **Kris, Ernst / Kurz, Otto** (1980): *Die Legende vom Künstler: Ein geschichtlicher Versuch*, Frankfurt am Main, 84.

28 See **Bredekamp, Horst** (1992): Der Mensch als 'zweiter Gott'. Motive der Wiederkehr eines kunsttheoretischen Topos im Zeitalter der Bildsimulation. In: *Interface I. Elektronische Medien und künstlerischen Kreativität*, Klaus Peter Dencker, Ed., Hamburg, 134–147.

29 See **Reiche, Claudia** (1998): 'Lebende Bilder' aus dem Computer. Konstruktionen ihrer Mediengeschichte". In: *BildKörper. Verwandlungen des Menschen zwischen Medium und Medizin*, Marianne Schuller / Claudia Reiche / Gunnar Schmidt, Eds., Hamburg, 123–165.

limit this re-forming of life to the world of plants and animals, but also wanted to derive from biology the criteria for the communal or social life of humans.[24]

The return of art-theoretical topoi

The desire to breathe life into created images as well as the attempt to create artificial life are the dreams of artists, which reach back into antiquity. The contemporary appropriation of such dreams, however, involves a number of alterations. Already in 1968, the art theorist Jack Burnham regarded the artists' dream of a Pygmalion created through a computer-generated world of images to be fulfilled:

> "As the Cybernetic Art of this generation grows more intelligent and sensitive, the Greek obsession with 'living' sculpture will take on an undreamt of reality."[25]

The artist George Gessert also sees this artists' dream to have been realized in the connection of art and genetics, and points, in addition to this, to the numerous similarities between traditional sculpture and transgentic art:

> "Genetic art involves many of the same choices that traditional painters and sculptors make, choices having to do with color, size, scale, form, texture and pattern. But at the same time, genetic art involves some very different considerations. Since it is alive, genetic art is constantly changing, at least on the surface. Some genetic art is self-replicating, much is seasonal and most is to some degree ecosystem-specific."[26]

Also inherent in this discourse is the notion of surpassing or exceeding nature, compensating for nature's lacks by bringing together the beauty of individual parts into *one* beautiful body through a combinatory art. In the 15th century, Leone Battista Alberti characterized artists' creations as those of "second Gods." This accords not only with the parable of the *"Deus artifex"* in the sense of an artistically active deity or a deity who supports artists, but also with that parable – recurring since the Renaissance – of the artist who creates his works like a god.[27] Over the centuries, the ancient dream of creating 'life itself' has produced a virtually infinite chain of simulation attempts: as the realization of a celibacy machine (*machine célibataire*), the attempt at autonomous male reproduction, a reproduction which does not require the child-bearing female body and which also implies phantasms of immortality. The tradition of this topos continues uninterruptedly in the computer-generated world of images;[28] and if, through the introduction of genetic algorithms, computer-generated image worlds appear to be alive,[29] this characterization seems all the more valid for transgenic art. If, in the simulation of life processes through images, only the logic of the *bios* is extracted from biology – or to formulate this differently, if the basic laws of biology are distilled from organic systems and introduced into technological systems such as the computer – then the logic of life has been separated from matter. In the rhetoric of the life sciences, the genome has been de-materialized into pure logos, that is, it has become liberated from the *materia* – which has negative connotations in terms of cultural history – and is torn out of *natura*. Through this, the genome becomes symbolically charged as an extract, as the "code of life," and thus becomes a symbol of the most diverse visions. However, the re-valuing of nature and culture here does not involve – as one might have expected – a transcendence of traditional valuations of the female sex/women as inferior. Once again the *materia*, which since antiquity has been equated with femininity, is strictly devalued in this figure of thought,[30] referring questions about the representation of gender in connection with reproduction technologies and thus their cultural and patriarchal implications.

The gender metamorphosis of cyberspace

The new technologies of telecommunication – first and foremost, the Internet and cyberspace – have also acquired a symbolic meaning in a way similar to that of the new technologies of reproduction. Cyberfeminists, in particular, have analyzed the gender metamorphosis of cyberspace with political and theoretical acuity – from the concept of the body in cyberspace up to the positioning of the female subject on the Internet.[31]

---

30 Becker-Schmidt, Regina (1996): Computer sapiens. Problemaufriß und sechs feministische Thesen zum Verhältnis von Wissenschaft, Technik und gesellschaftlicher Entwicklung. In: *Vermittelte Weiblichkeit. Feministische Wissenschafts- und Gesellschaftstheorie*, Elvira Scheich, Ed., Hamburg , 336ff.

31 Theorists such as Sherry Turkle, Anne Balsamo, Rosi Braidotti et al.

32 See Eerikäinen, Hannu (2000): Cyberspace – Cyborg – Cybersex. On the Topos of Disembodiment in the Cyber Discourse. In: *Nach dem Menschen. Der Mythos einer zweiten Schöpfung und das Entstehen einer posthumanan Kultur*, Bernd Flessner, Ed., Freiburg im Breisgau, 133–179.

33 Robins, Kevin (1996): *Into the Image. Culture and Politics in the Field of Vision*, London / New York, 13.

34 See Kris / Kurz 1980: 84ff.

The thesis which often forms the point of departure here is that current developments in media technologies significantly effect theoretical debates about embodiment and gender identity, and that technologies are always tied to images of the body and gender situated within an historically specific social matrix. One of the most powerful metaphors in the discourse about the new technologies is the disembodiment[32] of communication in new media practices.

The history of efforts to transcend the limits of the physical body does not begin with digitalization. In particular, the visual, sight-fixated tradition of Occidental history is implicated in this tendency to disembodiment. Since the Cartesian 17th century, the eye has assumed a life of its own, both discursively and technologically. It has become hypostatized, which also means that the body is denied and the material conditions of seeing and of creating images are suppressed. Descartes is regarded as the source of this strategy of disembodiment, which releases the gaze from all the limitations of human existence. From the *camera obscura* to cyberspace, this virtualization of seeing has been continually perfected, all the way up to the disembodied eye in the world of virtual reality.[33]

For a number of years, theorists have been concerned with the desire to leave behind one's physical body and to exist in a virtual body, i.e., the fusing together of human and machine and the 'dissolution' of the body as an ontological unit. Today we find ourselves in an advanced stage of development regarding such issues, a development which has been radicalized both by the historical avant-garde and its demand to transgress the boundaries between human and machine and by the dissemination of new technologies. The transgression of art and life or of human and machine was the explicit goal of the historical avant-garde of the 19th and 20th centuries, in particular of Italian futurism. In this projected symbiosis of human and machine, death was not regarded as something evil, but rather was recognized as the fulfillment and re-instantiation of a paradisiacal condition. The transformation of human beings into machines was supposed to secure not only their physical death, but, at the same time, their survival as well. With this vision of a technological re-instantiation of paradise, the futurists placed themselves in an intellectual tradition – as problematic as it is inexhaustible – which postulates human technology as able to mitigate original sin and thus refers to the old motif of the technological re-instantiation of paradise, passed on by artists who claim to be "second Gods."[34]

Disembodied communication practices

Today, networked computers make available worldwide a medium which enables communication between interlocutors who are spatially removed from one another and permits them to react simultaneously to each other. Isolated individuals in the new postmodern social order are pushed into a virtual proximity, making possible the revival of communication practices familiar in oral cultures. There is a particular vision connected with this: just as artificial intelligence attempts to realize spirit independent of the body, telematic communication establishes a reciprocal communication independent of the physical location or situatedness of the interlocutors. While the model for dialogical tele-presence can be found in the oral conversation, these two forms of communication are distinguished by the fact that the presence of the body is no longer a presupposition for the former. The written word already introduced a form of communication between interlocutors who were not physically present. However, this was only possible at the price of preventing direct interaction between self and other: written communication is a communication which necessarily forgoes this kind of interaction. And this is precisely what interactivity has been able to achieve: individuals who are not physically present can react to one another in their communication. This is considered to be the specific accomplishment of online-communication. The distinction between oral and telematic communication can thus be described as the distinction between physically-bound and physically-unbound forms of communication. While operating with symbols is indeed possible with traditional literary technologies, an interaction with symbolic artifacts is not. Computer-generated worlds make possible a new interactivity with symbolic structures. With this, however, the observer is not longer merely an observer, but rather becomes a participant in the computer-generated symbolic world of textual and imagistic spaces, a participant who can engage in telematic communication prac-

35 **Balsamo, Anne** (1993): The Virtual Body in Cyberspace. In: *Research in Philosophy and Technology*, vol. 13, 119–139.

36 **Müller, Jörg** (1996): *Virtuelle Körper. Aspekte sozialer Körperlichkeit im Cyberspace* (Schriftenreihe des WZB: Wissenschaftszentrum für Sozialforschung), Berlin, 96–105.

37 **Austin, John L.** (1962): *How to do Things with Words*, Oxford.

38 **Butler, Judith** (1997): *Excitable Speech. A Politics of the Performative*, London / New York.

tices, if his or her body has been transformed into a semiotic entity. This means that the entry or immersion into virtual reality is only possible through disembodiment.[35] The user must transform his or her body into a sign for the body, a transformation which often occurs with the assistance of 'bioapparatuses' such as datagloves, dataglasses and datasuits. Here, the term 'disembodiment' does not mean that the corporeality of the body has become obsolete, but rather that the body has been divided into a *physical body* which is situated in time and space and a *virtual body* which is present in the symbolic world only as a representation. The corporeality or physical situatedness of communicating individuals is transformed into staged or produced *digital bodies* in the sense of artificially created identities. The physical body – its movements and perspective within the virtual world as symbolic entity – continues to be present: the body must be 'present' here, precisely where it does not exist as a physical entity, in this case within a world of 'data.' Thus, disembodiment does not mean that the body disappears, but rather that the body is divided into a corporeal, spatio-temporally situated physical body and a virtual body existing only as an expression of data.[36] It is not that there are more people who act and communicate via the Internet, but rather that there are more representations – representations for which quite possibly there are no longer any natural references. These representations can be implicit in the sense that real head movements are synchronized with the perspective produced by the images, or they can be explicit in the sense that the body is represented as graphic representation – usually as a graphic hand – within the electronic image-space, i.e., real gestures are coordinated with the simulated hand so that the virtual hand is, in fact, able to act in the virtual world. Depersonalized communication in the Internet nullifies that 'performative dimension' of speech described by John L. Austin as "speech as action."[37] In her book *Excitable Speech*, Judith Butler takes up Austin's idea of the performative.[38] For Butler, performativity becomes not only the nucleus in the exercise of power in speech, but also the possibility for the subversion of that power. The fact that Butler takes up Austin's argument, but ultimately develops a different interpretation of performativity has to do with the different role which she attributes to the embodiment of speech. Butler concludes that speaking bodies can be transformed into data configurations and thereby nullify virtualization, which had constituted the characteristic feature of written or oral communication. The question arising from this is to what degree engendered practices of communication continue or disappear here.

Renaissance™

The fact that the advertisements cited at the beginning of the article play with the question of the technical reproducibility of images and bodies and that they employ citations from high Renaissance art should not be surprising given the current rhetoric of genetic engineering and its industrial uses, in particular its hearkening back to those artists' topoi from antiquity and the Renaissance described above. In the magazine *Nature*, Du Pont advertises with the *Mona Lisa's* smile. Above the text, we see images of da Vinci's *Mona Lisa* filling a grid of five *Mona Lisa's* across and six down, recalling Andy Warhol's larger-than-life photo-screen (in ink and polymer paint) from 1963 *Thirty Are Better Than One*, which consisted of multiple reproductions of the *Mona Lisa*. This alienation assumes the form of a pop art series à la Andy Warhol in the 1960's, which Baudrillard had already interpreted as the "subtle killing of the original."[39] YMC advertises with a citation from Michaelangelo's famous frescoes in the Sistine Chapel in Rome: *The Creation of Adam*. Here, however, it is not the power of God's hand which creates Adam, but rather that of a genetic engineer, which we see reaching out to the hand of a small child. In evoking the world of high Western art, these advertising images point to high cultural production. The *Mona Lisa* is a symbol of the culture of Western Humanism, and its creator Leonardo da Vinci[40] stands for a very particular type of artist, for scientific humanism and technical progress, just as the paintings of the Louvre stand for originality and authenticity. In the pre-digital world, a copy was always inferior to the original: even the best analogic technology could only produce an approximate duplicate. In the digital world, the question of the original

---

39 **Baudrillard, Jean** (1993): *Symbolic Exchange and Death*, London, 155.

40 Like almost no other artist, Leonardo da Vinci and his work have been appropriated by the life sciences and degraded within the context of corporate self-representation, advertising, science news illustrations, conference brochures and magazine covers. On this see **Haraway** 1998: 181–210.

41 **Haraway** 1998: 197.

42 **Richards, Catherine** (1993): Virtual Bodies. In: *Angles of Incidence. Video Reflections of Multimedia Artworks*, The Banff Centre for the Arts, 15–22, and **Hawthorne, Susan** (1999): Cyborgs, Virtual Bodies and Organic Bodies: Theoretical Feminist Responses. In: *CyberFeminism: Connectivity, Critique and Creativity*, Susan Hawthorne / Renate Klein, Eds., North Melbourne, 213–249.

becomes obsolete, since every copy – even thousands of copies – is just as good as the original.

In the practice of genetic cloning as well, there is no longer any object of reference. Original images and reproductions become indistinguishable, and the modernist opposition of copy and original – upon which most of the art market is ultimately based – is erased by the transnational postmodern power of genetic identification and replication in both bodies and laboratories.[41] Walter Benjamin's thesis of the artwork's loss of aura (today the human body's loss of aura) in an age of technical reproducibility appears particularly apt, as the separation between natural and artificial becomes obsolete.

The discussion of new technologies such as virtual reality, genetic engineering and robotics provides a forum for conflicting views on gender and body politics in postmodern societies. At the center of these conflicts are the postmodern subject and the definitions of gender and technology. The metaphorical images of the body in cyberspace are profoundly intertwined with the issue of technical speculation within a male-dominated society. Violent and sexist imagery are an integral part of contemporary discourses about new telecommunication technologies, discourses which cling to nineteenth-century notions of technology, sexual difference and gender roles in order to resist the transformations brought about by the new postmodern social order.

The predominant metaphors employed by genetic researchers stand unambiguously in the tradition of patriarchal models of thought. The discourses reflect the failure of traditional models of the human body to represent adequately the blurring and layering between cyborgs, the virtual body and the 'real' organic body.[42] However, although traditional concepts of the body are no longer adequate for these new technologies of reproduction and the old dichotomies have apparently become obsolete, binary constructions of gender continue to reappear as hierarchizing moments in the discourses about these technologies.   <

BIBLIOGRAPHY
Print

Austin, John L. (1962): *How to do Things with Words*, Oxford **Balsamo, Anne** (1993): The Virtual Body in Cyberspace. In: *Research in Philosophy and Technology*, vol. 13, 119–139 **Baudrillard, Jean** (1993): *Symbolic Exchange and Death*, London **Becker-Schmidt, Regina** (1996): Computer sapiens. Problemaufriß und sechs feministische Thesen zum Verhältnis von Wissenschaft, Technik und gesellschaftlicher Entwicklung. In: *Vermittelte Weiblichkeit. Feministische Wissenschafts- und Gesellschaftstheorie*, Elvira Scheich, Ed., Hamburg , 336ff. **Benjamin, Walter** (1936): L'Œuvre d'art à l'age de sa reproduction méchanisée. In: *Zeitschrift für Sozialforschung*, vol. 5, **Benjamin, Walter** (1968[1936]): The Work of Art in the Age of Mechanical Reproduction. In: *Illuminations*, New York, 217–251. **Benjamin, Walter** (1991[1936]): Das Kunstwerk im Zeitalter seiner technischen Reproduzierbarkeit. In: *Walter Benjamin, Abhandlungen, Gesammelte Schriften*, vol. 1.2, Rolf Tiedemann / Hermann Schweppenhäuser, Eds., Frankfurt am Main **Bredekamp, Horst** (1992): Der Mensch als 'zweiter Gott'. Motive der Wiederkehr eines kunsttheoretischen Topos im Zeitalter der Bildsimulation. In: *Interface I. Elektronische Medien und künstlerischen Kreativität*, Klaus Peter Dencker, Ed., Hamburg, 134–147 (=Bredekamp 1992a) **Bredekamp, Horst** (1992): Der simulierte Benjamin. Mittelalterliche Bemerkungen zu seiner Aktualität. In: *Frankfurter Schule und Kunstgeschichte*, Andreas Berndt, Ed., Berlin, 117–140 (=Bredekamp 1992b) **Burnham, Jack** (1968): *Beyond Modern Sculpture: The Effects of Science and Technology on Sculpture of this Century*, New York **Butler, Judith** (1997): *Excitable Speech. A Politics of the Performative*, London / New York **Davis, Joe** (1996): Microvenus. In: *Art Journal, Contemporary Art and the Genetic Code*, vol. 55, no. 1, 70–74 **Eerikäinen, Hannu** (2000): Cyberspace – Cyborg – Cybersex. On the Topos of Disembodiment in the Cyber Discourse. In: *Nach dem Menschen. Der Mythos einer zweiten Schöpfung und das Entstehen einer posthumanan Kultur*, Bernd Flessner, Ed., Freiburg im Breisgau, 133–179 **Flessner, Bernd**, Ed. (2000): *Nach dem Menschen. Der Mythos einer zweiten Schöpfung und das Entstehen einer posthumanan Kultur*, Freiburg im Breisgau **Flusser, Vilém** (1988): Curies Children. In: *Art Forum*, vol. 16, no. 7 **Fox Keller, Evelyn** (1983): *A Feeling for the Organism – The Life and Work of Barbara McClintock*, San Francisco **Fox Keller, Evelyn** (1995): *Refiguring Life: Metaphors of Twentieth-century Biology*, New York **Fox Keller, Evelyn** (1998): Das Gen und das Humangenomprojekt – zehn Jahre danach. In: Exh. Cat. *Genwelten, Kunst- und Ausstellungshalle der BRD*, Bonn, Petra Kruse, Ed., Cologne, 77–81

Gesser, George (1993): Notes on Genetic Art. In: *Leonardo*, vol. 26, no. 3, 210 **Gottweis, Herbert** (1998): *Governing Molecules: The Discursive Politics of Genetic Engineering in Europe and the United States*, Cambridge Mass. / London, 153–163 **Haraway, Donna** (1996): Anspruchsloser Zeuge @ Zweites Jahrtausend. FrauMann trifft OncoMouse. Leviathan und die vier Jots: Die Tatsachen verdrehen. In: *Vermittelte Weiblichkeit. Feministische Wissenschafts- und Gesellschaftstheorie*, Elvira Scheich, Ed., Hamburg, 347–389 **Haraway, Donna** (1998): Deanimation: Maps and Portraits of Life itself. In: *Picturing Science – Producing Art*, Caroline A. Jones / Peter Galison, Eds., London / New York, 181–207 **Harvey, David** (1992): *The Condition of Postmodernity*, Cambridge Mass. **Hawthorne, Susan** (1999): Cyborgs, Virtual Bodies and Organic Bodies: Theoretical Feminist Responses. In: *CyberFeminism: Connectivity, Critique and Creativity*, Susan Hawthorne / Renate Klein, Eds., North Melbourne, 213-249 **Hoffmann, Peter Gerwin** (1987): Mikroben bei Kandinsky. In: *Animal Art, Steirischer Herbst*, Richard Kriesche, Ed., Graz, no page numbers **Joy, Billy** (2000): Why the future doesn't need us. In: *Wired 4/2000* **Kris, Ernst / Kurz, Otto** (1980): *Die Legende vom Künstler: Ein geschichtlicher Versuch*, Frankfurt am Main **Kuni, Verena** (1998): Metamorphose im Zeitalter ihrer technischen Reproduzierbarkeit. In: *Raum und Körper in den Künsten der Nachkriegszeit*, Akademie der Künste, Ed., Amsterdam / Dresden, 201–217 **Loeb, Jacques** (1911): *Das Leben*, Leipzig **Müller, Jörg** (1996): *Virtuelle Körper. Aspekte sozialer Körperlichkeit im Cyberspace* (Schriftenreihe des WZB: Wissenschaftszentrum für Sozialforschung), Berlin , 96–105 **Pauly, Philip J.** (1987): *Controlling Life. Jacques Loeb and the Engineering Ideal in Biology*, New York / Oxford **Reiche, Claudia** (1998): 'Lebende Bilder' aus dem Computer. Konstruktionen ihrer Mediengeschichte". In: *BildKörper. Verwandlungen des Menschen zwischen Medium und Medizin*, Marianne Schuller / Claudia Reiche / Gunnar Schmidt, Eds., Hamburg, 123–165 **Richards, Catherine** (1993): Virtual Bodies. In: *Angles of Incidence. Video Reflections of Multimedia Artworks*, The Banff Centre for the Arts, 15–22 **Rifkin, Jeremy** (1998): *The Biotech Century: Harnessing the Gene and Remaking the World*, London **Robins, Kevin** (1996): *Into the Image. Culture and Politics in the Field of Vision*, London / New York **Root-Bernstein, Robert** (1985): Visual Thinking: The Art of Imagining Reality. In: *Transactions of the American Philosophical Society*, no. 75, 50–67 **Root-Bernstein, Robert** (1996): Do We Have the Structure of DNA Right? Aesthetic Assumptions, Visual

Conventions, and Unsolved Problems. In: *Art Journal, Contemporary Art and the Genetic Code*, vol. 55, no. 1 **Schultz, Susanne** Ed. (1996): *Geld.beat.synthetik. Abwerten bio/technologischer Annahmen*, Berlin / Amsterdam **Stöcklein, Ansgar** (1969): *Leitbilder der Technik. Biblische Tradition und technischer Fortschritt*, Munich, 36ff. **Tauber, Alfred J.**, Ed. (1996): *The Elusive Synthesis: Aesthetics and Science*, Boston **Tillim, Sidney** (1983): Benjamin Rediscovered: The Work of Art After the Age of Mechanical Reproduction. In: *Artforum*, vol. 21, no. 5, 65–73 **Toulmin, Stephen** (1953): *The Philosophy of Science: An Introduction*, London **Watson, James D.** / **Crick, Francis** (1953): The Structure of DNA. In: *Cold Spring Harbor Symposia on Quantitative Biology*, no. 18, 29–128 **Wechsler, Judith**, Ed. (1978): *On Aesthetics in Science*, Cambridge Mass.

Illustration

01 Du Pont advertisment "Smile! Renaissance™...", 1995. In: *Nature* (1995) vol. 373, no. 6509, 1

02 Andy Warhol, Thirty Are Better Than One, 1963. In: *Andy Warhol Retrospektive*, Kynaston McShine, Ed., Munich 1989, 237

03 YMC advertisment "Scale-up", 1995. In: *Nature* (1995) vol. 373, no. 6509, 8

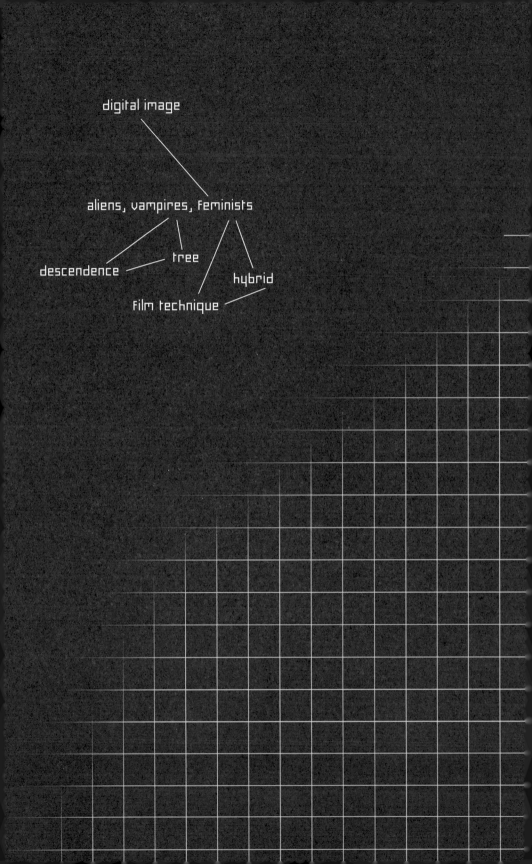

ANALOGUE TREES, GENETICS AND DIGITAL DIVING. PICTURES OF HUMAN AND ALIEN REPRODUCTION

ULRIKE BERGERMANN

01

> In the middle of the 19th century, the descent and origin of man were invented. The static diagrams of the "tree of evolution" (Haeckel), the "tree of life" or "nature" (Darwin[1]) came to represent the origin of the species: the descendence of man visible in the family of man. But, do "origin" and "family" belong together? In one single distinct picture? Not only is the regular, linear, ascending hierarchy[2], that shows mankind as the epitome of all life, surprising, but also the extent of relationship that characterises all life forms. The ideological logic of the tree is mirrored in racial discourse, while simultaneously introducing the concepts of relationship and kinship. In the history of biology it was assumed that all life started with single isolated individuals; in the 17th and 18th centuries the search for similarities and analogies was prominent

in comparative anatomy and physiology. In the 19th century, relationships were at the center of interest, and at about 1850 man became a "cousin of the apes."[3] The closer the observation, the more similar the species become. The "discovery" of the genome has brought the trend to its peak (as the 90% genetic matching of mankind and mouse shows[4]). The genetic code of all life forms is coded by the same four bases, only the combinations do vary[5]. Life forms appear dissimilar externally, however, internally they are genetically (invisibly) very similar. This visual irritation, and perhaps the horror of "the sameness" confronted the genetic researcher François Jacob while studying heterosexual reproduction. If the species are so similar, the individuals of a species must be even more similar.[6] This qualifies the difference between the masculine and feminine. Jacob, however, especially stresses this: he forms a "machine to produce the others," as only then could two gene pools be combined for the purpose of reproduction.[7] Thus, the old order saves its images in an age with new image-production processes. Non-microscopic films are also concerned with the relation of gender, vision, and knowledge.

1 In his letters and notebooks, Darwin sketched many such trees that were less symmetrical and static, but still functioned well, cf. **Topper, David** (1996): Towards an Epistemology of Scientific Illustration. In: *Picturing Knowledge. Historical and Philosophical Problems Concerning the Use of Art in Science*, Brian S. Baigrie, Ed., Toronto / Buffalo / London, 215–249, here 239: Darwin's third tree of nature diagram (ca. 1827–38).

2 Typical and controversial characteristics of a tree diagram are symmetry, regularity, predictivity, dimensionality, etc. Cf. **O'Hara, Robert J.** (1996): Representations of the Natural System in the Nineteenth Century. In: **Baigrie** 1996: 164–183, esp. 175 ff.

3 For further details about the history of biology, cf. **Jacob, François** (2000[1997]): *Die Maus, die Fliege und der Mensch. Über die moderne Genforschung*, Munich, french: La souris, la mouche et l'homme, Paris, here 117.

4 90% of our genes *have a counterpart* in that of mice. Beer yeast has 38% *identical* genes with those of humans, the worm a third, and 50–60% of the fruit fly, drosophilia. **Karow, Julia** (2000): Die Genome der 'Anderen'. Was haben wir mit Hefe, Würmern, Fliegen und Mäusen gemein? In: *Spektrum der Wissenschaft*, September 2000, 35.

5 **Jacob** 2000: 118 f.

6 "On average, one in every 500 nuclotide bases A, C, G and T differ from person to person." **Zaun, Harald** (2000): Stunde der Bioinformatik, in: *c't*,

RIPLEY'S REPRODUCTION

In 1997, Jeunet's *Alien Resurrection* pictured the female heroine Ellen Ripley in the fourth sequel of the Alien movies, but (apart from the fact that she obviously was played by Sigourney Weaver again) was it really her? Half of Ripley's DNA was of human, half of alien origin, we are told, and so the well-known plot about the fight between both species and the better mode of reproduction continues at a new site, in the deep interior of 'Ripley 4,' evolving around femininity, cloning and imaging. For the new being is said to be cloned, and Jacob's "machine to produce the other" is turned inside out here: the other, the Alien, is not the product of reproduction as in Jacob's heterosexual machine, but is part of it, right from the beginning.

This no longer fits into a tree diagram. Looking at Haeckel's engraving, you find the snakes, insects and reptiles (all contributing to the Alien's morphology) at the middle of the vertical timeline and mankind at the top, but no artificial beings, no clones or androids are included.[8] These, it seems, are not from earth but must come from somewhere out-

---

no. 20, 09/25/2000, 44, transl. Julia Macintosh-Schneider (J.M.S.).

7   **Jacob** 2000: 119, continues: "That is the paradox, on the one hand everything that appears different is very similar, on the other hand, everything that appears similar is in reality very different." – "Sexual reproduction is itself a machine for producing the other. 'Other' than the parents; other than all 'other' individuals of the species." 136. (J.M.S.) This sentence taken by itself is meaningless, it is a lame comparison. If all living-beings have a similar genetic code, men and women do, too. It only makes absurd sense from a naive perspective. What looks different externally, must be different internally, or respectively what looks similar externally is similar internally. If we want to follow this established paradox, we have to think further: men and women are separated by worlds, humans and animals live together … etc.

8   Even **Hans Moravec**, who in his first illustration to *Mind Children* (1988), his version of the tree of evolution, tried to include the coming species he predicted, did not succeed: The usual vertical time axis from four billion years ago to the present, from cells to plants, mollusks, fish, etc., has a second parallel column running in the opposite direction: at the bottom is the reproduction before DNA, followed by DNA, cells with nucleus, sexuality, polycelluar animals, brains, learning, tools, culture, amongst others, and at the crown at the outermost right corner: reproduction after DNA, indicating the breaking down of the scheme.

side. And so they do. But now we have to find new images for new life forms.[9] According to Jacob, a certain perversion is required here.

> "To be able to discover common features in the extreme diversity of life, requires much resourcefulness – you might also say perversion. There is much knowledge to be gained that contradicts appearances and intuition."[10]

Their perversion is here. Now that the body can be read, no longer just as part of an image (the tree) but as "writing" in a series of four letters, we have been given a new task: to invent new images to surround an abstract series of letters. When reproduction moves from its traditional method, through women's bodies and the heterosexual act, when the figures of the mother and alien become fused into one, and when technical reproduction changes radically, then the old analogue images must provide an answer.

If a digital copy is an identical artifact, and original and copy can no longer be differentiated, the order of the medium is threatened together with our orientation to reproductive cycles, the power of the author and the distributing institutions. In comparison, the production of genetically identical copies of life forms through cloning disrupts the linearity and hierarchy of generations and gender roles. It separates biological from social motherhood, evokes assembly line (re)production and technological feasibility madness, and the horror of the same (either as doppelganger or mass).

As Judith Roof states in *Reproductions of Reproduction*, the security of the symbolic order has to be upheld by the visual and metaphorical representations of reproduction in science and culture through all shifts in scientific knowledge about it – and that is a patriarchal order. This explains the centuries-old attribution of active and passive roles to

---

9 Although the tree metaphor still works in the opposite direction: contesting the material/information split, N. Katherine Hayles argues against the poverty of abstraction, using the multiplicity of trees: "The point [...] is to make clear how much had to be erased to arrive at such abstractions as bodiless information. Abstraction is of course an essential component in all theorizing, for no theory can account for the infinite multiplicity of or interactions with the real. But when we make moves that erase the world's multiplicity, we risk losing sight of *the variegated leaves, fractal branchings, and particular bark textures that make up the forest*." **Hayles, Katherine N.** (1999): *How We Became Posthuman. Virtual Bodies in Cybernetics, Literature, and Informatics*, Chicago / London, 12. My italics.

10 **Jacob** 2000: 8 f. (J.M.S.).

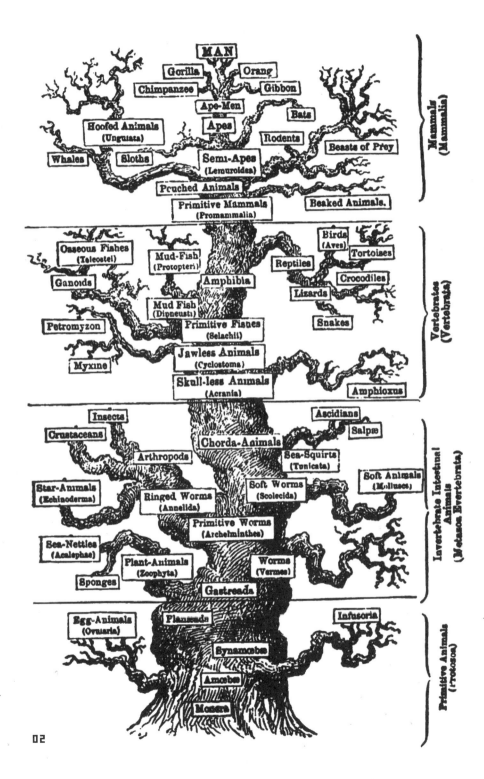

MAN

Gorilla   Orang
Chimpanzee   Gibbon
Ape-Men   Bats
Apes
Hoofed Animals   Rodents
(Ungulata)
Whales   Sloths   Beasts of Prey
Semi-Apes
(Lemuroidea)
Pouched Animals
Primitive Mammals   Beaked Animals.
(Promammalia)

Mammals (Mammalia)

Birds
(Aves)
Osseous Fishes   Tortoises
(Teleostei)   Mud-Fish
(Protopteri)   Reptiles
Ganoids   Crocodiles
Amphibia   Lizards
Mud Fish
(Dipneusti)
Petromyzon   Primitive Fishes   Snakes
(Selachii)
Jawless Animals
Myxine   (Cyclostoma)
Skull-less Animals
(Acrania)   Amphioxus

Vertebrates (Vertebrata)

Insects   Ascidians
Crustaceans   Salpæ
Chorda-Animals
Arthropods   Sea-Squirts
(Tunicata)
Star-Animals   Soft Animals
(Echinoderma)   Ringed Worms   Soft Worms   (Molluscs)
(Annelida)   (Scolecida)
Sea-Nettles   Primitive Worms
(Acalephae)   (Archelminthes)
Sponges   Plant-Animals   Worms
(Zoophyta)   (Vermes)
Gastreada

Invertebrate Intestinal Animals (Metazon Evertebrata)

Egg-Animals   Planaeada   Infusoria
(Ovularia)
Synamoebæ
Amoeba
Monera

Primitive Animals (Protozoa)

02

sperm and egg.[11] Now that the focused elements of reproduction are microscopically small and genes determine discourse, we must find new images guaranteed by the old order, such as the continuation of the egg/sperm roles in the relation of cell nucleus to cytoplasm.[12] The narrative and ideological structures remain, only a few new figures appear on the stage. According to Roof, aliens, vampires and feminists have always indicated a threat to the reproduction of this order.[13] Additionally, these figures each appeared with a new medium.[14] What the vampire was for industrialization, the emancipated woman for the service soci-

---

11 Jacob 2000 sketches out the idea of active and passive roles for egg and sperm during fertilization on 63 ff. Cf. **Laqueur, Thomas** (1990 [1996]): *Making Sex*, German: *Auf den Leib geschrieben. Die Inszenierung der Geschlechter von der Antike bis Freud*, Munich, transl. H. Jochen Bußmann, 166 et passim. Judith Roof writes: "Sperm tales: As visual technologies improve and smaller and smaller vistas can be distinctly displayed, the narrative of human reproduction shifts from its macroscopic frame of romance and avian/apiarian fable to an increasingly microscopic, epic narrative of travel and penetration. As the frame of reference shrinks, the scale of seminal accomplishment expands and the sperm's figuration shifts from the metaphysical (little critter, for example) to the synecdochically paternal (the father's genetic material). Reproduction's courtship narrative – an egg and a sperm blissfully uniting – imagines a coming together of tiny elements that simply substitute for human players in an invisible imaginary field." **Roof, Judith** (1996): *Reproductions of Reproduction. Imaging Symbolic Change*, New York / London, 3.

12 **Fox Keller, Evelyn** (1995): *Refiguring Life. Metaphors of Twentieth-Century Biology*, New York, 18, 23, 28, 30, 34, 101; the gene becomes the metaphor for scientific discipline, the nation and finally gender: "Finally, there is another metaphoric reference of nucleus and cytoplasm, surely the most conspicuous of all, and that is to be found in sexual reproduction. By tradition as well as by biological experience, at least until World War II nucleus and cytoplasm were also tropes for male and female. Until the emergence of bacterial genetics in the mid-1940s, all research in genetics and embryology, both in Europe and the United States, focused on organisms that pass through embryonic stages of development; for these organisms, a persistent asymmetry is evident in male and female contributions to fertilization. The female gamete, the egg, is vastly larger than the male gamete, the sperm. The difference is the cytoplasm, deriving from the maternal parent (a no-man's-

ety and the alien for the computer/net, the cyberfeminist promises to become for the digital image era.

MOTHERHOOD: THE FINAL FRONTIER
In 1979, Ridley Scott's alien was simply the enemy. The parasitic, cruel, and metamorphosing monster had nothing in common with the human astronauts (and a scene alluding to a sexual interest in Ripley was not realized[15]). That was to change. In one of the best-known scenes in James Cameron's *Aliens* (1986), when Ripley and the foundling Newt meet eye-to-eye with

land indeed); by contrast, the sperm cell is almost pure nucleus. It is thus hardly surprising to find that in the conventional discourse about nucleus and cytoplasm, cytoplasm is routinely taken to be synonymous with egg. Furthermore – by an all too familiar twist of logic – the nucleus was often taken as a stand-in for sperm. Theodor Boveri argued for the need to recognize at least some function for the cytoplasm on the ground of 'the absurdity of the idea that it would be possible to bring a sperm to develop my means of an artificial culture medium' […] debates […] reflect older debates about the relative importance (or activity) of maternal and paternal contributions to reproduction, where the overwhelming historical tendency has been to attribute activity […] to the male contribution while relegating the female contribution to the role of passive, facilitating environment. In Platonic terms, the egg represented the body and the nucleus the activating soul. […] I suggest that in these associations surely lies part of the background both for the force of the assumption of gene action and perhaps even its gradual fading away form the status of self-evident truth. More specifically, I suggest that such associations bear quite directly on the historic discounting of maternal effects." 38–40.

13 **Roof** 1996: 3, 10, passim.

14 **Roof** 1996: 13, analyses this as an overcompensation for an order that is giving way. Aliens and vampires have in common "their usurpation of human order through unauthorized and extra patriarchal reproductions." They are only overcome by strong fathers (van Helsing) or heroic mothers (Ripley).

15 **Thomson, David** (1998): *The Alien Quartet*, London, quotes Sigourney Weaver, putting the audience in the alien's position: "You're almost seeing me through the alien's eyes. […] There were so many different endings. One of them was that the alien would surprise me and I would run into the closet where I'd take off my suit and put on another. So there would have been a

the alien queen among her eggs. Two concepts of motherhood confront each other: the human mother-by-choice and the mechanical egg-from-assembly-line-principle alien.[16] The one protector by choice and affection, the other protector by instinct. The phallic machine gun and flame-thrower against the cold mechanics and slime.[17] If the human species survives (and the girl, Newt, represents this view), it is only through the abandonment of biological-mechanical reproduction principles. From a progressive viewpoint, Ripley releases the image of women from her bond to instinctive, automatic reproduction. According to Penley, the bonding of reproduction to the visible image of women, however, remains reactionary.[18] No matter what, here a singular mother-daughter relationship juxtaposes the mass production of the identical, a relationship of the similar and one of interchangeability/identity (attributes that will play a role again in the characterization of digital technology). The boundaries become blurred during the following two *Alien* sequels. In David Fincher's *Alien3* (1992), Ripley is pregnant, expecting an alien queen and commits suicide at the moment of birth. In Jean-Pierre Jeunet's *Alien Resurrection* (1997), a mixed being, half human and half alien, is cloned from the genetic remains. The clone, in the form of Ripley, bears an alien queen.

In this *Alien* sequel, Ripley once more destroys a room and all its contents with a flame-thrower and machine gun. The egg cave in *Aliens* becomes the laboratory in which Ripley was cloned and in which she discovers her malformed predecessors. Just like in a medical chamber of horrors, monstrous forms are enclosed in enormous jars filled with fluid.

---

moment when the alien would see me between suits and be fascinated. Because the alien isn't evil. It's just following its natural instincts to reproduce through whatever living things are around it.", 57 f.

16 See **Doane, Mary Ann** (1999): Technophilia. Technology, Representation and the Feminine. In: *Cybersexualities. A Reader on Feminist Theory, Cyborgs and Cyberspace*, Jenny Wolmark, Ed., Edinburgh, 26, "The alien itself, in its horrifying otherness, also evokes the maternal." The queen as mother-machine laying eggs as on a conveyer belt: an "awesome excess of reproduction."

17 This needs to be relativized. Ripley's choice can indeed be called instinctive (according to the film script, Newt replaces the deserted biological daughter) and the alien is described as "nature gone wild." The adult alien does, however, have technological characteristics: the metallic shimmer, it looks

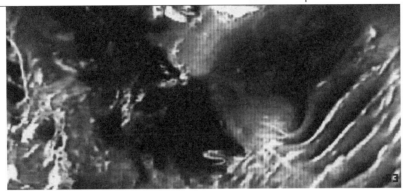

Only experiment no. 7 is lying on an operation table. Deformed and cabled, she begs Ripley to kill her. The deformed, but identical face of no. 7 evokes 'human' mimicry, pity, self-realization and horror for the first time in no. 8, and she fulfils her 'sister's' final wish. The woman who gives Ripley the gun is an android. Two non-human women (one half alien the other half robot) turn against mechanical reproduction techniques: they destroy the cloning laboratory, fight the aliens, thus saving the humans on the earth from them. They embody the principles of solidarity and responsibility. Where previously social confronted biological motherhood, affection and choice automatism, as personified in the human Ripley and the faceless alien evolutionary program, two decades later the phallic weapon directs itself against the alien character of the human reproduction technique of cloning. But this time, Ripley cannot destroy the hostile other with the same weapon she used against the alien in the previous sequels, because she carries it within her. Not in the same

---

like it has been constructed from individual components, its jaws look like hinges, its bodily fluids are like lubrication, it lays its eggs mechanically as if on a conveyor belt, etc., cf. **Brauerhoch, Annette** (1996): *Die gute und die böse Mutter. Kino zwischen Melodram und Horror*, Marburg, 169.

18 "*Aliens* reintroduces the issue of sexual difference, but not in order to offer a newer, more modern configuration of that difference. Rather, by focusing on Ripley alone […], the question of the couple is supplanted by the problem of the woman as a mother. What we get finally is a conservative moral lesson about maternity, futuristic or otherwise: mothers will be mothers, and they will always be women." **Penley, Constance** (1991): Time Travel, Primal Scene, and the Critical Dystopia. In: *Close Encounters. Film, Feminism, and Science Fiction*, Constance Penley / Elisabeth Lyon / Lynn Spigel / Janet Bergstrom, Eds., Minneapolis / Oxford, 73.

way as the embryo in *Alien3*, but more fundamentally in every cell in her body. And worse, it is not that she carries it in her, but she is it herself. The future of the human species lies only in the moral superiority of the human/feminine parts over the alien deep inside the heroine Ripley. Her interior has not yet been seen though a microscope and has no existing model, and thus evades the traditional Hollywood techniques of psychological visualization. If cloning is successful, why are there not innumerable Ripleys? Why do all feature films that include cloned humans show either individual figures or a limited, qualitative differentiable number of individuals (mostly beautiful women created by men)?[19] Mass (re)production plays on similarities to vampirism but never acts it out. Instead, the beings 1–8 depict an evolutionary process: they are the dead branches on a tree with a new crown. A linear development from monster to superhuman. And all this played by real actors: cloning is a process to know about, but not to be visualized in image technology.

ALIEN: THE AFTER-BURN
If the metamorphosis of the alien embodies the principles of reproduction (its mechanical facet combined with monstrosity, torture and Darwinism), how the alien is not visualized embodies a production of film techniques.

Every production technique has something to do with reproduction. We believe pictures depict and repeat the optical composition of an object in a transformed version. The (re)productive moment inherent in each depiction becomes evident in photography and film, which both produce nearly automatically many positive "clones" from an original negative.[20] If the medium is itself a machine that produces pictures by imitating the original and reproducing theoretically unlimited numbers

---

19 Cloning also takes place in *Species* (directed by Roger Donaldson, US 1995), and *The Fifth Element* (Luc Besson, US 1997): blonde attractive women are produced from human and extraterrestrial DNA. As an interbreeding technique, cloning appears more attractive as a tool for identical repetition. *Antz* and *A Bug's Life* are fully digitalized animated films that show nearly identical insect-beings. They contain the horror, however, through the action and heroes. Both use huge amounts of computer performance to differentiate between individual insects in the mass.

20 It is not surprising that **Walter Benjamin** gave the film medium special status in his 'Kunstwerk' essay: (1974 [1936]): Das Kunstwerk im Zeitalter seiner

and distributing them, then the film is also a reproduction machine. As Telotte writes:

> "[...] film is itself one of those machines – indeed, for most of this century, the preeminent one – whose 'power to produce replicas and reproductions' has 'altered our culture' in ways we are only beginning to assess."[21]

The quasi-mechanical alien that appears in identical copies is primarily characterized by its invisibility. The director Ridley Scott explains his decision to drastically cut the screen appearances of the alien with:

> "The most important thing in a film of this type is not what you see, but the effect of what you think you saw. It's like a sort of after-burn – that's the reason why I decided to limit the creature's appearances."[22]

The after-burn that is branded on the retina is also the psychological basis of film awareness/perception (that from only about 16 frames per second manages to produce an illusion of movement). The alien takes the place of the after-burn effect, not that of presence in the picture, and so stands for the principle of film itself.

The pre-digital alien was hidden from sight as the difference between the film frames that only becomes visible during technical interference. The "alien" is not one, but many. It is never completely seen, and when seen it is only briefly, mostly in the dark, continually in movement and shrouded in mist. Harvey R. Greenberg characterizes the "anatomy of the monster" as the impossibility of creating a coherent form from the parts of the body that are only seen for a split second. If not for the final sequence of *Alien*, we would never have been able to imagine its 'whole.'

> "Fully ninety percent of the Alien footage consists of close-ups of its head and jaws [...]" – "The entire creature appears for the first and last time in the shuttlecraft, but the viewer's sight is obscured by flashing strobes within the ship, and by the dazzling engine exhaust outside. Scott

technischen Reproduzierbarkeit. In: *Walter Benjamin, Gesammelte Schriften, Band I.2, Abhandlungen, Werkausgabe*, Rolf Tiedemann / Hermann Schweppenhäuser, Eds., Frankfurt/M.

21 Telotte, J. P. (1999): *A Distant Technology. Science Fiction Film and the Machine Age*, Hanover / London, 1 f. Feminist film theory has already made a beginning, cf. **Bergermann, Ulrike** (2000): Amorphe Maschinen. Unbekannte Frauen Objekte und andere Differenzen im Science-Fiction. In: *UFOs. Objekte des Ungewissen*, Helene von Oldenburg, Ed., Oldenburg.

22 Quoted. in: **Flynn, John L.** (1995): *Dissecting Aliens. Terror in Space*, London, 31. My italics.

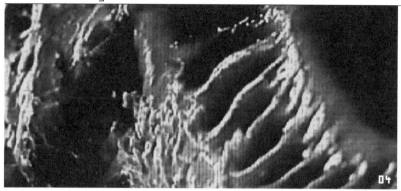

thus compels the viewer to piece together an impression of the monster
based on tantalizing fragments, fleshed out by the potent nuances of subjective fantasy, surely the scariest beast of all [...]."[23]

Bernhard Siegert adds to this:

"The film sequence disintegrates its form (and if the final scene, which
was only included to comply with Hollywood's policy of the imaginary,
had been excluded, no one would have had an image of it). Additionally,
there is the lighting that cuts out even more of the scene, narrow bars of light
as if looking through blinds, only let fractions of the alien be seen." [24]

Here the script and film industry, camera and montage make the film what
it is. The frequent use of flickering lights is interpreted by Siegert as the
(re)emergence of the most basic film technology which is based on the
stroboscopic illusion of perception:

"Strobe light announces the presence of the alien by splitting its continual
movement into discrete phases. When the strobe light effect, on which
the production of continual movement in film is based, also appears in

---

23 **Greenberg, Harvey R.** (1991): Reimagining the Gargoyle: Psychoanalytic
Notes on *Alien*. In: *Close Encounters. Film, Feminism, and Science Fiction*,
Constance Penley / Elisabeth Lyon / Lynn Spigel / Janet Bergstrom, Eds.,
Minneapolis / Oxford, 89.

24 **Siegert** continues: "Ridley Scott's film is not only about exploding the
image, dissecting the body, it also includes it. The alien appears six times
(and excluding the final sequence) each lasts between half a second and two
seconds." **Siegert, Bernhard** (1999): ALIENS. Zum Trauma des nicht-Konvergenten in Literatur, Mathematik und technischen Medien. In: *Kommunikation, Medien, Macht*, Rudolf Maresch / Niels Werber, Eds., Frankfurt/M., 194,
(J.M.S.). Thanks go to Andrea Sick for bringing this to my notice.

25 **Siegert** 1999: 197.

the film, it creates an auto-reference of the film to the scene, in which the film creates continuity by the jerky turning further of discontinuous individual images. The alien is the other of the continuum."[25]

In other words: The difference between the individual images of the film strip is not resolved in the representation of the alien[26], but is repeated. The changeable, flickering, threatening, multiplying, devouring, always feared and reproducing creature is part of the film in its old-fashioned form. At the beginning of the 20th century, Georges Méliès used a stop-motion trick to change men into women and women into men and thus demonstrated *film techniques* through their effects – the directors of *Alien* produced a repetition of the technique on the *image level*.

The strobe light is in all sequels. *Alien Resurrection* is the first sequel to feature entirely computer-generated aliens.

"You can only show one part of the alien at a time to enable the puppets and costumes to work. If you want to show a complete alien, you can only do it with a computer-generated figure. Once you have the alien in a computer, you can do almost anything with it,"

says Tom Woodruff, designer and player of alien figures.[27] Can the optically complete, new digital alien, direct its own production as well as the old flickering one?

Digital image processing appears in the narrative level of cloning as well as in the new old metaphoric of 'flow.'

DIGITAL FLUIDITY

In 1979, *Alien* was the first film to use a computer-processing. A sequence showed a spaceship that could have been produced using traditional ani-

---

26 In Fritz Lang's *Metropolis* (GER 1925) this is different. Instead of changing a man into a woman in steps, the conversion process is shown in full: the awakening masculine creator, the conversion of the robot Hel into the false Maria, performed using light, mechanics, electricity and chemistry – all materials of film techniques. Rotwang, as the mad director, promised to show the awakening process in full, to make the difference between the images visible – which is, of course, impossible. The robot is burnt as a witch, Maria brings peace between capital and workers in Frede. Motherless humanity conquers wild black technology.

27 Quoted in: **Murdock, Andrew / Aberly, Rachel** (1997): *The Making of Alien™ – Die Wiedergeburt, Offizielles Souvenirmagazin der Twentieth Century Fox*, Munich, transl. Brigitte Saar, 24, (J.M.S.).

mation methods (albeit more slowly and expensively).[28] *Alien3* did not feature computer-generated aliens – computer graphics were only used in post-production to generate shadows on the walls.[29] (Even in its motifs the new technology is used in the same way as the early characterization of the old , when it was said that it only shows shadows of life.) In view of the new possibilities, suddenly an ethics or reality was proclaimed: the effects

"were real and designed. They were Giger's [the designer's] art, transformed by film, and not the electronic engineering that was to come. In that sense, the *Alien* films do not cheat; they create their world for the camera – and are thus a little old-fashioned."[30]

More than anyone, James Cameron wanted to film without animation techniques and post-production, but wanted to film the puppets (rod- and cable-actuated) "live."[31] As the alien, Cameron said, he needed "a

---

28 **Baker, Robin** (1993): Computer Technology and Special Effects in Contemporary Cinema. In: *Future Visions. New Technologies of the Screen*, Philip Hayward / Tana Wollen, Eds., 33: "It is quite difficult to establish just where and when the first computer-generated sequence was used in a movie, but *Alien* (U.S., 1979) directed by Ridley Scott, was certainly among the first to use computer-generated images within the main body of the movie as opposed to the title sequence." The spaceship in space in Alien "could well have been produced by traditional techniques," using digital techniques, however, made it cheaper and quicker. Ibid. 34.

29 **Osteried, Peter** (1999): *Alien Aliens Alien3 Alien Die Wiedergeburt – Filmgalerie, Nr. 3, Sonderheft*, Hille, October, 49.

30 **Thomson** 1998: 54.

31 **Shay, Don** (1997): Aliens: This Time It's War. In: *Bill Norton, Alien™ – The Special Effects*, Don Shay, Ed., London, first published in *Cinefex Magazine*, 81 f. With 'floor effects' (smoke, steam) there was "more flexibility with puppets we could shoot 'live' on a miniature set."

32 According to Cameron, the film script demanded: "[...] fairly quick action-turns and spins and rapid strides – the sort of moves that in stop-motion would cause so much displacement per frame that the arms and legs would end up strobing." **Shay** 1997: 82. To prevent this effect in the shots, high-speed camera movements were necessary for the puppets' movements, "shooting at high-speed to smooth out the moves and create a believable sense of mass"; however, high-speed was necessary to compensate the slow motion shooting (120 frames per seconds), 88.

33 "What makes an effect 'special'? Everything in a film is an 'effect' – some-

real and believable character," and this demanded a live set as well as the avoidance of the strobe effect during the stop-motion trick.[32] Old-fashioned reality models are based on strobe effects and, in the era of digital images, its tricks suddenly appear real. In early reviews of the genre it was said that science fiction places a special before its effects, to naturalize the previous techniques and to claim them as reality.[33]

The first *Alien* figures were static – not created with a view to movement and animation.[34] It was proudly reported *Alien Resurrection* that Woodruff was so good a dancer and actor that many scenes of him in an alien *suit* could be filmed analogously instead of using computer aliens.[35] Finally, in 1997, the same year the first sheep was cloned in Scotland[36], the first completely computer-generated aliens were created[37] and they could "luckily act without any limitations."[38] The relative scenes show

thing fabricated, made. No shots compose or photograph themselves."
Stern, Michael (1990): Making Culture into Nature, In: *Alien Zone. Cultural Theory and Contemporary Science Fiction Cinema*, Annette Kuhn, Ed., London / New York, 66–72, here 67. Cf. also Sobchack, Vivian (1987): *Screening Space. The American Science Fiction Film, 2.* enhanced edition New Brunswick / New Jersey / London, 259 f.: "[…] the privileged punctuation of *cinematic* effects (taken as 'normal' and therefore transparent) by clearly marked *electronic* effects is not an instance of cinema celebrating itself and its 'own' technology. […] a conservative attempt to *contain* this new technology […] Rather, these moments attest to a cinema attempting to protect its representational function against domination by a radically *other* mode of representation." And she continues with reference to digital images: "The hyperreality of electronic simulation, then, authenticates and conserves the 'reality' of cinematic representation […]." Ibd. 261. Cf. **Barclay, Steven** (2000): *The Motion Picture Image: From Film to Digital*, Boston / Oxford et al., 35 f.: It is a common protest: digital imagery is not real. But no picture is.

34 See **Murdock / Aberly** 1997: 24.

35 **Murdock / Aberly** 1997: 24 f. Also **Osteried** 1999: 68.

36 The film crew was surprised by this news. The official souvenir magazine of Twentieth Century Fox says: "In February 1997, a group of Scottish researchers led by Dr. Ian Wilmut managed to clone a lamb from the DNA of an adult sheep for the first time. Science fiction has become reality." The film's script writer Whedon immediately began calling himself Nostradamus. **Murdock / Aberly** 1997: 29.

37 **Murdock / Aberly** 1997: 25.

38 Ibid.

how aliens hunt their human prey underwater – and that aliens are piti-lessly superior to humans. Their style of swimming was developed by Sigourney Weaver and was supposed to demonstrate the relationship of the alien to Ripley 4. Sigourney Weaver researched lizard and alligator movements according to the morphology quoted in the tree of life.

That CGIs should be used in the underwater scenes is perhaps for rea-sons of practicability and is, at least metaphorically, plausible: the digital being adapts better to new images/habitats (even if it is emotionally highly-charged, as water is considered the source of all life).[39] The digital alien, however, also reminds us of Siegert's modeling. The mechanically created being demonstrates fluidity of movement. It is no longer found in the flickering between the images, but in the diffuse light underwater. This offers soft transitions corresponding to the "flowing stream." This alien is no longer "the other in continuum," the continual film movement is not "dissected into discrete phases."

Now there is a second type of image that connects the alien to image generation: matter in motion.

MATRIX INSTEAD OF LINEAGE/ROOTS
At the beginning of *Alien Resurrection* (with the title credits – the source of the story[40]), the screen is filled with unstructured tissue moved by the

39 The cloning experiments in the laboratory also float in water (or a similar fluid) and are attacked with fire and machine gun. In *Sphere* from the same year, all action is underwater and countless jelly fish were produced digitally, cf. *Sphere* (US 1998) Director: Barry Levinson.

40 Apart from the institutional and personal components and conditions of films, since the 1940s film motifs have been used almost like overtures. This is not just in retrospect, as can be illustrated in Hitchcock's *Vertigo*: Saul Bass produces a "spiral form that a 19th century physicist had drawn for scientific purposes by letting a pendel move over paper. Hitchcock repeats the spiral form in some scenes – which was not originally planned. It predicts the flow of events into which the protagonist moves deeper and deeper through the plot. **Zumpe, Angela** (1997): Vorspiel. In: *PAGE* 11/1997, 38, (J.M.S.). Many thanks to Gabriele Bergermann for bringing this to my notice.

41 Camera movement between inanimate objects in order to "animate" them has a long history in film. A prominent example is the opening scene in Riefenstahl's *Olympia*.

42 Thanks to Bev Alcock for the inspiration!

05

camera lens and camera movement. Individual elements, an eye, teeth, etc., indicate at least partially human tissue. Later, in retrospect, we can draw the conclusion: it is the greatest possible proximity a non-microscopic camera can have to that which embodies the unification of human and alien.

What does not become clear is who moved what. Even if the camera perspective cannot be recognized (are we seeing the image from above, below or the front?) we are used to the movement, the camera pans. Even to the distorting effect as if looking through a wide-angle and fish-eye lens in a close-up. Here, the effects are combined with a change in the image itself, making what moves indistinguishable: the camera as the supposed eye of the spectator (we have learned to identify our eye with the camera) or the watched? Does it produce blisters or is this bulge an effect of the lens distortion? Does the opening move after the camera has glided past it (incidentally in our direction of reading; the unknown refers back to cultural techniques), or is it immovable, i.e., not living?[41] It can be assumed that the optical analogue camera and digital image processing meet here. It would be easy to imagine (because it connects to the use of technology) a boundary between objective and tissue. When a movement is performed by the camera and another by digital image processing, the objective retains its traditional distance to what is shown while the new technology moves within it. Perhaps, however, the camera movement is simulated and orientation typical of the old medium has become obsolete.

Usually, the infinite expanse of the universe would have filled the background during a flight through solar systems and galaxies. *Space, the final frontier*[42] has been superseded, emptiness replaced by matter, for the alien is no longer, like truth, "somewhere out there," but somewhere in there.

As Judith Butler reconstructs, matter (*matrix/hyle*) is marked in the history of philosophy, originally by its potential.[43] No longer the tree, and not yet the furniture, this is the Greek *hyle:*

> "wood that already has been cut from trees, instrumentalized and instrumentalizable, artifactual, on the way to being put to use. *Materia* in Latin denotes the stuff out of which things are made, not only the timber for houses and ships but whatever serves as nourishment for infants."[44]

Thus, material and its pre-figuration from which the material should develop, cannot be significantly differentiated, as an opposition of "female principle material" and a "male principle form" would suggest.[45] "This link between matter, origin, and significance suggests the indissolubility of classical Greek notions of materiality and signification. That which matters about an object is its matter."[46] If such a connection can be set in an image, the credits are a successful approximation. Like "material" (*materia* and *hyle*), you can observe "neither a simple, brute positivity or referent nor a blank surface or slate awaiting an external signification, but is always in some sense temporalized,"[47] but the matrix of the (his)story. "The matrix is an originating and formative principle which inaugurates and informs a development of some organism or object."[48]

---

43 **Butler, Judith** (1993): *Bodies that Matter. On the Discursive Limits of 'Sex'*, New York / London, esp. 27–55.

44 **Butler** 1993: 31 f., continues: "Insofar as matter appears in these cases to be invested with a certain capacity to originate and to compose that for which it also supplies the principle of intelligibility, then matter is clearly defined by a certain power of creation and rationality that is for the most part divested from the more modern empirical deployments of the term. To speak within these classical contexts of *bodies that matter* is not an ideal pun, for to be material means to materialize, where the principle of that materialization is precisely what 'matters' about the body, its very intelligibility. In this sense, to know the significance of something is to know how and why it matters, where 'to matter' means at once 'to materialize' and 'to mean'."

45 Ibid. "The matrix is an originating and formative principle which inaugurates and informs a development of some organism or object. Hence, for Aristotle, 'matter is potentiality [*dynameos*], form actuality.' In reproduction, women are said to contribute the matter; men, the form."

46 Ibid. "In Greek, *hyle* is the wood or timber out of which various cultural constructions are made, but also a principle of origin, development, and teleology which is at once causal and explanatory."

47 Ibid. "This is true for Marx as well, when 'matter' is understood as a principle

That it is matter that makes it matter and cannot be featured in a Hollywood plot and is the fate of a genre that from all inherent possibilities of the Greek "wood" (*hyle*) always re-makes the old tree.

DIGITAL MATRIX

Such a fate is also contained in many descriptions of new digital techniques that, as so often when a new medium is introduced, initially anthropomorphize, psychologicalize and sometimes genderize. It is said that digital media imitate or plagiarize the old. By mixing different medial genres it threatens the bounds of known genres and traditions. For Timothy Binkley, Professor at the School of Visual Arts in New York , this "behavior" of digital technology becomes the ceremonial courting of a lady. Apart from the usual manner of speaking about the "virginal hard-disk"[49] he attributes the new technology with the "female social character": "she" is merciful, obedient, yielding, devote, flexible, adaptable and accommodating. The "removal" of structure from matter, as in his description of digitalisation, creates only abstraction, the senselessness of which does not support the human (artistic) intuition without material basis.[50]

---

of *transformation*, presuming and inducing a future."

48 Ibid.

49 Binkley, Timothy (1993): Refiguring Culture. In: *Future Visions. New Technologies of The Screen*, Philip Hayward / Tana Wollen, Eds., London, 96 "A digital medium is not virgin territory, but needs to be formatted first before it can receive messages from a communicator. No imprint is pressed; rather a lattice is filled. A digital medium is prepared to receive information not by smoothing it into an undifferentiated continuum, but rather by imposing on it an essential grid that delineates receptacles for data."

50 According to Binkley, the analogue media paradigm is determined by an *imprinting process*: storage is the transcription of one physical configuration into another. Printing, embossing and stamping – analogue images imprint themselves permanently in a material and are never completely reversible. Photography is also in this sense the writing of light that stores a mimetic relation to the depicted in a continual form. Digital media do not transcribe, they convert, dissect a continual impulse into segments that are ordered to a number of numbers in a raster: "But when a digital video system converts lights into numbers, it strips the structure of a physical event away from its underlying substance and turns the incoming signal into a pure abstraction, a file of numbers untethered to any intrinsic material alliance." ibid. 98.

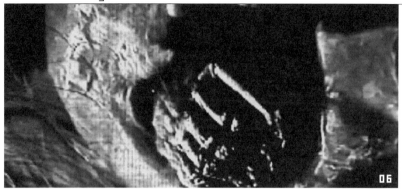

06

Attributes of the computer include arcane (secretive, elite), arbitrary, invisible, inviolable symbols that replace the actual track of events – matter succumbs to an *alien process*.[51] What began as a song of praise for the classical arts, however, veers around:

> "It takes strength and skill to chip a block of stone into a beautiful bust, and once cleaved, elementary laws of physics prevent the stone from becoming whole again. Digital media, on the other hand, are graciously forgiving and will obediently retract any regretted action. But this indulgence carries its own problems and perils."[52]

The replacement of the aggressive chisel by the pliable plot is not without problems, but still more resilient. "Each cipher gently occupies its assigned seat with quiet assurance but then agreeably leaves when asked to make room for another cast of characters"[53]; "despite their submissiveness, digital data tend to possess more resilience."[54] Another player in the

51 Ibid. "A digital medium stores numbers without tying them to a unit of measurement. Digital video turns a quantity of light into nothing but a quantity, a bare token that stands only for a number and not for a certain amount of matter or energy measured according to a conventional unit. The process converts an image into a collection of numbers that can be abstractly manipulated using mathematical techniques, a process completely alien to analogue media."

52 Ibid. 100.

53 Ibid. 97.

54 Ibid. 101.

55 **Gross, Sabine** (1994): *Lese-Zeichen. Kognition, Medium und Materialität im Leseprozeß*, Darmstadt, 55, (J.M.S.).

56 **Binkley** 1993: 120; "Some of the philosophical unease about entrenched dualism is discovering a kind of avatar in computers, which are beginning to support growing doubts about disparities between mind and matter." –

transfer, or to be more precise, elapsing era of the analogue and digital is the attribution. Sabine Gross's observation of the analogue/digital principles points out that these are initially defined by the context, which may also be said about gender identity:

> "The concepts of digital and analogue are not absolute, but depend on context and defined conventionally. One and the same character, be it a graphics one, colour tone or shading, can be understood as digital or analogue. The relative status is not a feature of the character, but is attributed by interpretation. Also the relative difference in digital and analogue decoding must be learnt."[55]

Naturally we have learned to read, learned to differentiate between masculine and feminine, analogue and digital, in contexts that change quicker than we can think. *Alien 5* will help us to re-situate reproduction modes like the concepts analogue, digital, masculine and feminine. Some, however, do not let themselves be helped. Binkley closes with a reconciliation between *mind* and *matter*: especially the computer no longer supports this duality.[56] It is a duality that he himself, in retrospect, introduced for analogue media (that left its mark in matter) and that he now further describes with changed, but nevertheless, old roles. Roof claims a similar cultural angst of the digital (where Haraway's cyborg had proclaimed the savoring of the blurring of boundaries) as "fear of systemic take-over in the field of reproduction itself"[57], even if the old gender roles would close the new breaks. The transformation of the old media formats she sees as being performed in the figure of aliens[58]: they go

---

> "If digital reproduction is the more promising form – is it then female connotated? Is it the more true, safe [...] reproduction that should be characterised as feminine? If so, then the design is the opposite of the alien whose perfect Darwinism is awful – and fitted out with the opposite of feminine: cold, slimy [...]."

57 "Anxieties about the digital – about the subtle infiltration and reorganisation of the Symbolic itself – manifest not only in the compensatory salvations of paternity plots or characterization of DNA as unreliable, but, as we have seen, also register as a fear of systemic takeover in the field of reproduction itself." **Roof** 1996: 178.

58 "Aliens who invade and twist human forms also enact the drama of a Symbolic shift played out with the rise of the digital. While the paternal gloss is strictly the son's affair, the specter of the alien comes with vestiges of feminine threat; this is as true for the 1980s Aliens films as it is for the 1995

through a process of metamorphosis and threaten to change humans (perhaps into their wombs). The relative image processing is digital: morphing.

The computer calculates transitions between images, fills the phases between poses as moving images, changes a vase into a ball and vice-versa. Where one image dot replaces another, a melting, moving, or merging can be simulated step-by-step. As this occurs between digitized images, they are more easily manipulated than an analogue film image can be replaced by another object. The continuity reached, the merging of images would be nearly immeasurable, if it were not reduced to the individual film image.[59] The T-1000 in *Terminator 2* that could take on both animate and non-animate forms just by touching them, was the first to exhibit the violence of the order of fluids; the mimetic as armor.[60] In contrast, Roof describes the pre-digital *Alien* as one that does not conceal its genesis from individual images.[61] Morphing is also a technique to deny a basic differential structure[62], in the attempt "to replace the arching generalizations of analogy with the fullness of a complete range of pixellated facts that occupy every gap while producing new gaps, or a kind of counter-simulacra"[63], whereby the digital is characterized not by a smooth transition, but by discontinuity.[64] But, also the digital alien that appeared on the screen/scene a year after Roof's book would hardly contribute to the current figure. The new star of the scene of angst, lust, and

---

Species.", ibid – "In films that provide symptomatic moments of reproductive anxiety – the overt threat to paternal order of the *Terminator* series and the unauthorized reproductions of vampires and aliens – one of the most threatening moments is the possibility of transformation. The *Terminator* threatens a larger transformation from human to machine culture. Vampires transform into various shapes[…]," ibid. 183.

59 "In other words, digital imaging is capable of masking its own lack of gradation by producing images of seamless transition that could only otherwise be captured on film through animation (a more primitive form of stepped sequence) of by filming an actual metamorphosis.", ibid.

60 "Imaged through digital technology, it [T-1000] threatens human patriarchy with a post-digital machine order. [as well as the alien in *Species*] The T-1000 belongs to the order of the liquid.", ibid. 84.

61 "But the difference between the Alien's threat and the T-1000's menace […] is that the Alien presents a specifically stepped, metonymical version of reproduction, while the T-1000 […] present that metonymy masked by a metaphor of seamless transition. The digital has covered its tracks, or cov-

medial reference is called DNA. It could have entered the stage any time since the 1950s between womanhood/femininity and image transition/morphing. Since the decoding of the human genome it has become particularly interesting. "DNA exemplifies the site where the code meets the material, where analogy becomes reality. DNA is the model matrix," writes Roof[65] – if this matrix, though, becomes readable[66], the balance moves to the point where code becomes matter, because DNA is still "the model matrix." The potentiality of this matrix, however, seems to be exposed to the access of the decoder/cloner. The cyberfeminist era of the digital image is concerned with the decoding of images, their creation and the policies that imply new selection possibilities. Where the code encounters matter, the encoding and the cell encounter an individual and social organism.

DNA also belongs to the invisible repertoire of *Alien* films: it is not in the image, but still structures it. Using classic narrative methods, we discover the origins of the new Ripley and alien. With this knowledge the images are seen in a new light, as if they were manipulated, as if Weaver were not human and the alien were not exactly depicted as in the previous sequels. The "real" place of manipulation (that is unexpected) is not labeled; which alien is computer-generated and which is not, can only be guessed.

---

ered the tracks of the villains through whom its threat is projected.", ibid. 84.

62 "While morphing can be realized on-screen as a way of hiding a series of contiguous differences, the imaginary transformations enacted by morphing's successive alterations are, in turn, actually performed on a more physical phenotypical level.", ibid. 184.

63 As Roof writes in relation to Baudrillard: "Baudrillard rejects the map's abstraction for images generated without precedent, or 'simulacra'," ibid. 189.

64 "The digital itself [...] is characterized by gaps – the pause, space, discontinuity between one value and the next. The emergence of the digital and metonymy as an order, then, provides multiple possibilities for interruption, digression, mutation, and redirection.", ibid.

65 Ibid.

66 About the writing, book and also metaphoric of genetics, cf. **Kay, Lily E.** (2000): *Who Wrote the Book of Life? A History of the Genetic Code*, Stanford – cf. also **Hayles, Katherine N.** (1999): *How We Became Posthuman. Virtual Bodies in Cybernetics, Literature, and Informatics*, Chicago / London, 110, about Pattee's thoughts on how molecules become oral messages.

Flowing not only accompanies the application of morphing and metaphors about "femininity," but also the expression of "information." From the beginning, according to criticism, this expression is disembodied. According to Hayles, Norbert Wiener and Claude Shannon had

> "conceptualized information as an entity distinct form the substrates carrying it. From this formulation, it was a small step to think of information as a kind of bodiless fluid that could flow between different substrates without loss of meaning or form."[67]

This flowing cannot be thought of without a material basis and so, "how *information lost its body*, that is, how it came to be conceptualized as an entity separate from the material forms in which it is thought to be embedded"[68] needs to be imagined. This is an enterprise that Haraway supports in the mission against false aliens: "a powerful prophylactic against our most likely alien abduction scenario – to be raptured out of the bodies that matter in the lust for information."[69] In this case, however, the expression "matter" is robbed of its informedness to enable it to be confronted by "abstraction," which Hayles refers to as the loss of embodiment – as if such a unit existed before the concept of information was discovered/inverted.   <

TRANSLATION: **Julia Macintosh-Schneider**

---

67 **Hayles** 1999: xi.

68 Feedback loops also imply idea of flow within the subject and between subject and environment.

69 **Haraway** on the back cover of **Hayles** 1999.

BIBLIOGRAPHY
Print

Baker, Robin (1993): Computer Technology and Special Effects in Contemporary Cinema. In: *Future Visions. New Technologies of the Screen*, Philip Hayward / Tana Wollen, Eds., 31–45 **Barclay, Steven** (2000): *The Motion Picture Image: From Film to Digital*, Boston / Oxford et al. **Benjamin, Walter** (1974 [1936]): Das Kunstwerk im Zeitalter seiner technischen Reproduzierbarkeit. In: *Walter Benjamin, Gesammelte Schriften, Band I.2, Abhandlungen, Werkausgabe*, Rolf Tiedemann / Hermann Schweppenhäuser, Eds., Frankfurt/M., 471–508 **Bergermann, Ulrike** (2000): Amorphe Maschinen. Unbekannte Frauen Objekte und andere Differenzen im Science-Fiction. In: *UFOs. Objekte des Ungewissen*, Helene von Oldenburg, Ed., Oldenburg, 9–21 **Binkley, Timothy** (1993): Refiguring Culture. In: *Future Visions. New Technologies of The Screen*, Philip Hayward / Tana Wollen, Eds., London, 92–122 **Brauerhoch, Annette** (1996): *Die gute und die böse Mutter. Kino zwischen Melodram und Horror*, Marburg **Butler, Judith** (1993): *Bodies that Matter. On the Discursive Limits of 'Sex'*, New York / London **Continenza, Barbara** (1999): *Darwin, Ein Leben für die Evolutionsbiologie*, Heidelberg, first published Milan 1998, transl. Michael Spang **Creed, Barbara** (1990): Alien and the Monstrous-Feminine. In: *Alien Zone. Cultural Theory and Contemporary Science Fiction Cinema*, Annette Kuhn, Ed., London / New York, 128–141 (=Creed 1990a) **Creed, Barbara** (1990): Gynesis, Postmodernism and the Science Fiction. In: *Alien Zone. Cultural Theory and Contemporary Science Fiction Cinema*, Annette Kuhn, Ed., London / New York, 214–218 (=Creed 1990b) **Condit, Celeste** (1999): The Materiality of Coding. Rhetoric, Genetics, and the Matter of Life. In: *Rhetorical Bodies*, Jack Selzer / Sharon Crowley, Eds., Madison (Wisconsin) / London, 326–356 **Dadoun, Roger** (1991): Metropolis: Mother-City – 'Mittler' – Hitler. In: *Close Encounters. Film, Feminism, and Science Fiction*, Constance Penley / Elisabeth Lyon / Lynn Spigel / Janet Bergstrom, Eds., Minneapolis / Oxford, 133–159 **Dawkins, Richard** (1976): *The Selfish Gene*, Oxford **Dijck, José van** (1998): *Imagenation. Popular Images of Genetics*, New York **Doane, Mary Ann** (1999): Technophilia. Technology, Representation and the Feminine. In: *Cybersexualities. A Reader on Feminist Theory, Cyborgs and Cyberspace*, Jenny Wolmark, Ed., Edinburgh, 20–33 [first published 1990 in: *Body/Politics. Women and the Discourses of Sciences*, M. Jacobus / E. Fox Keller / S. Shuttleworth, Eds., New York / London, 163–176] **Fischer, Ernst Peter**, Ed. (1994): Erwin Schrödinger, What is Life?, Cambridge, 9–25 **Fischer, Lucy** (1997): *Cinematernity. Film, Motherhood, Genre*, Princeton **Flynn, John L.**

(1995): *Dissecting Aliens. Terror in Space*, London **Kaplan, E. Ann** (1992): *Motherhood and Representation. The Mother in Popular Culture and Melodrama*, London / New York **Fox Keller, Evelyn** (1995): *Refiguring Life. Metaphors of Twentieth-Century Biology*, New York **Fox Keller, Evelyn** (2000): *The Century of the Gene*, Harvard **Greenberg, Harvey R**. (1991): Reimagining the Gargoyle: Psychoanalytic Notes on Alien. In: *Close Encounters. Film, Feminism, and Science Fiction*, Constance Penley / Elisabeth Lyon / Lynn Spigel / Janet Bergstrom, Eds., Minneapolis / Oxford, 83–104 **Gross, Sabine** (1994): *Lese-Zeichen. Kognition, Medium und Materialität im Leseprozeß*, Darmstadt **Haraway, Donna J**. (1995): Foreword. Cyborgs and Symbionts: Living Together in the New World Order. In: *The Cyborg Handbook*, Chris Hables Gray / with the assistance of Heidi J. Figueroa-Sarriera / Steven Mentor, New York / London, xi-xx **Haraway, Donna J**. (1997): *Modest_Witness@ Second_Millenium.Female_Man©_Meets_OncoMouse™, Feminism and Technoscience*, New York / London **Hayles, Katherine N**. (1999): *How We Became Posthuman. Virtual Bodies in Cybernetics, Literature, and Informatics*, Chicago / London **Jacob, François** (2000[1997]): *Die Maus, die Fliege und der Mensch. Über die moderne Genforschung*, Munich, french: *La souris, la mouche et l'homme*, Paris **Kay, Lily E**. (2000): *Who Wrote the Book of Life? A History of the Genetic Code*, Stanford **Hayward, Philip / Wollen, Tana** (1993): Introduction. Surpassing the Real. In: *Future Visions. New Technologies of The Screen*, Philip Hayward / Tana Wollen, Eds., London, 1–9 **Karow, Julia** (2000): Die Genome der 'Anderen'. Was haben wir mit Hefe, Würmern, Fliegen und Mäusen gemein? In: *Spektrum der Wissenschaft*, September 2000 **Kavanagh, James H**. (1990): Feminism, Humanism and Science in Alien (1980). In: *Alien Zone. Cultural Theory and Contemporary Science Fiction Cinema*, Annette Kuhn, Ed., London / New York, 73–81 **Laqueur, Thomas** (1990 [1996]): Making Sex, German: *Auf den Leib geschrieben. Die Inszenierung der Geschlechter von der Antike bis Freud*, Munich, transl. H. Jochen Bußmann **Moravec, Hans** (1988): *Mind Children. The Future of Robot and Human Intelligence*, Cambridge (Mass.) **Murdock, Andrew / Aberly, Rachel** (1997): *The Making of Alien™ – Die Wiedergeburt, Offizielles Souvenirmagazin der Twentieth Century Fox*, Munich, transl. Brigitte Saar **Neale, Steve** (1990): 'You've Got To Be Fucking Kidding!' Knowledge, Belief and Judgement in Science Fiction. In: *Alien Zone. Cultural Theory and Contemporary Science Fiction Cinema*, Annette Kuhn, Ed., London / New York, 160–168 **Newton, Judith** (1990):

Feminism and Anxiety in Alien. In: *Alien Zone. Cultural Theory and Contemporary Science Fiction Cinema*, Annette Kuhn, Ed., London / New York, 82–87 **O'Hara, Robert J**. (1996): Representations of the Natural System in the Nineteenth Century. In: *Picturing Knowledge. Historical and Philosophical Problems Concerning the Use of Art in Science*, Brian S. Baigrie, Ed., Toronto / Buffalo / London, 164–183 **Osteried, Peter** (1999): *Alien Aliens Alien3 Alien Die Wiedergeburt – Filmgalerie, Nr. 3, Sonderheft*, Hille, October **Penley, Constance** (1991): Time Travel, Primal Scene, and the Critical Dystopia. In: *Close Encounters. Film, Feminism, and Science Fiction*, Constance Penley / Elisabeth Lyon / Lynn Spigel / Janet Bergstrom, Eds., Minneapolis / Oxford, 63–80 (=Penley 1991a) **Penley, Constance** (1991): Introduction. In: *Close Encounters. Film, Feminism, and Science Fiction*, Constance Penley / Elisabeth Lyon / Lynn Spigel / Janet Bergstrom, Eds., Minneapolis / Oxford, vii-xi (=Penley 1991b) **Roof, Judith** (1996): *Reproductions of Reproduction. Imaging Symbolic Change*, New York / London **Ruse, Michael** (1996): Are Pictures Really Necessary? The Case of Sewall Wright's 'Adaptive Landscapes'. In: *Picturing Knowledge. Historical and Philosophical Problems Concerning the Use of Art in Science*, Brian S. Baigrie, Ed., Toronto / Buffalo / London, 303–337 **Siegert, Bernhard** (1999): ALIENS. Zum Trauma des nicht-Konvergenten in Literatur, Mathematik und technischen Medien. In: *Kommunikation, Medien, Macht*, Rudolf Maresch / Niels Werber, Eds., Frankfurt/M., 192–219 **Shay, Don** (1997): Aliens: This Time It's War. In: *Bill Norton, Alien™ – The Special Effects*, Don Shay, Ed., London 44–107, first published in *Cinefex Magazine* **Sobchack, Vivian** (1987): *Screening Space. The American Science Fiction Film*, 2nd enhanced edition New Brunswick / New Jersey / London [first published in 1980 under the title *The Limits of Infinity: The American Science Fiction Film*; 1987 enhanced with one chapter] **Sobchack, Vivian** (1991): Child/Alien/Father: Patriarchal Crisis and Generic Exchange. In: *Close Encounters. Film, Feminism, and Science Fiction*, Constance Penley / Elisabeth Lyon / Lynn Spigel / Janet Bergstrom, Eds., Minneapolis / Oxford, 3–30 **Sobchack, Vivian** (1996): The Virginity of Astronauts: Sex and the Science-Fiction-Film. In: *Alien Zone. Cultural Theory and Contemporary Science Fiction Cinema*, Annette Kuhn, Ed., London / New York, 103–115 **Spallone, Pat** (1997): Technologies of Reproduction: Why Women's Issues Make a Difference. In: *Science and the Construction of Women*, Mary Maynard, Ed., London / Bristol, 126–141 **Stern, Michael** (1990): Making Culture into Nature, In: *Alien Zone. Cultural Theory and Contemporary Science Fiction Cinema*, Annette

Kuhn, Ed., London / New York, 66–72 **Telotte, J. P.** (1999): *A Distant Technology. Science Fiction Film and the Machine Age*, Hanover / London **Thomson, David** (1998): *The Alien Quartet*, London **Topper, David** (1996): Towards an Epistemology of Scientific Illustration In: *Picturing Knowledge. Historical and Philosophical Problems Concerning the Use of Art in Science*, Brian S. Baigrie, Ed., Toronto / Buffalo / London, 215–249 **Wright, Gene** (1983): *The Science Fiction Image. The Illustrated Encyclopedia of Science Fiction in Film, Television, Radio and the Theater*, London **Zaun, Harald** (2000): Stunde der Bioinformatik, in: *c't*, no. 20, 09/25/2000 **Zumpe, Angela** (1997): Vorspiel. In: *PAGE* 11/1997, 38–42

Film | **A Bug's Life** (US 1998) 1'34", Animated Film, Production: Pixar Animation Studios, Walt Disney Pictures / Darla K. Anderson, Kevin Reher, Director: John Lasseter, Andrew Stanton, Screenwriters: John Lasseter, Andrew Stanton, Joe Ranft, Don McEnery et al., Performers (voices): Dave Foley, Kevin Spacey, Julia Louis-Dreyfus, Hayden Panettiere, Phyllis Diller et al., Music: Randy Newman

Antz (US 1998) 1'23", Animated Film, Production: DreamWorks SKG , Pacific Data Images / Brad Lewis et al., Director: Eric Darnell, Tim Johnson, Screenwriters: Todd Alcott, Chris Weitz, Paul Weitz, Chris Miller, Performers (voices): Woody Allen, Dan Aykroyd, Anne Bancroft, Jane Curtin, Danny Glover, Gene Hackman, Jennifer Lopez et al., Editor: Stan Webb, Music: Gavin Greenaway et al.

Alien (US 1979) 1'56", Production: 20th Century Fox, Brandywine Productions Ltd. / Gordon Carroll et al., Director: Ridley Scott, Screenwriters: David Giler, Walter Hill, Dan O'Bannon, Ronald Shusett et al., Performers: Tom Skerritt, Sigourney Weaver, Veronica Cartwright, Harry Dean Stanton, John Hurt et al., Cinematography: Derek Vanlint, Editors: Terry Rawlings, Peter Weatherley, Music: Jerry Goldsmith

Aliens (US 1986) 2'15", Production: 20th Century Fox, Brandywine Productions Ltd. / Gale Anne Hurd et al., Director: James Cameron, Screnwriters: James Cameron, David Giler, Walter Hill, Performers: Sigourney Weaver, Michael Biehn, Paul Reiser, Lance Henriksen, Carrie Henn, Bill Paxton et al., Cinematography: Adrian Biddle, Editor: Ray Lovejoy, Music: James Horner

Alien3 (US 1992) 1'50", Production: 20th Century Fox, Brandywine Productions Ltd / Gordon Carroll et al., Director: David Fincher, Screenwriters: Vincent Ward, Larry Ferguson et al., Performers: Sigourney Weaver, Charles Dutton, Charles Dance, Paul McGann, Brian Glover, Ralph Brown, Daniel

Webb, Christopher John Fields, Holt McCallany, Danielle Edmond et al., Cinematography: Alex Thomson, Editor: Terry Rawlings, Music: Elliot Goldenthal

Alien Resurrection (US 1997) 1'49'', Production: 20th Century Fox, Brandywine Productions Ltd. / Bill Badalato et al., Director: Jean-Pierre Jeunet, Screenwriters: Dan O'Bannon, Ronald Shusett, Joss Whedon, Performers: Sigourney Weaver, Winona Ryder, Dominique Pinon, Ron Perlman, Gary Dourdan, Michael Wincott et al., Cinematography: Darius Khondji, Editor: Hervé Schneid, Music: John Frizzell

Metropolis (GER 1926) 2', Production: UfA, Director: Fritz Lang, Screenwriters: Fritz Lang, Thea von Harbou, Performers: Alfred Abel, Gustav Fröhlich, Rudolf Klein-Rogge, Brigitte Helm, Fritz Rasp et al., Cinematography: Karl Freund, Gunther Rittau,

Olympia 1. Teil – Fest der Völker (GER 1938) 1'55'', Production: International Olympic Committee, Olympia Film, Tobis Filmkunst / Leni Riefenstahl, Director: Leni Riefenstahl, Screenwriter: Leni Riefenstahl, Cinematography: Wilfried Basse, Werner Bundhausen, Leo De Lafrue, Walter Frentz, Hans Karl Gottschalk, Willy Hameister, Walter Hege, Carl Junghans, Albert Kling, Ernst Kunstmann, Guzzi Lantschner, Otto Lantschner, Kurt Neubert, Erich Nitzschmann, Hans Scheib, Hugo O. Schulze, Károly Vass, Willy Zielke, Andor von Barsy, Franz von Friedl, Heinz von Jaworsky, Hugo von Kaweczynski, Alexander von Lagorio, Editors: Leni Riefenstahl, Erna Peters, Music: Walter Gronostay, Herbert Windt

Species (US 1995) 1'48'', Production: Metro Goldwyn Mayer / Dennis Feldman, Frank Mancuso Jr., Director: Roger Donaldson, Screenwriter: Dennis Feldman, Performers: Ben Kingsley, Michael Madsen, Alfred Molina, Forest Whitaker, Marg Helgenberger, Natasha Henstridge, Michelle Williams et al., Cinematography: Andrzej Bartkowiak, Editor: Conrad Buff, Music: Christopher Young

Sphere (US 1998), 2'12'', Production: Baltimore Pictures, Constant c Productions, Punch Productions / Michael Crichton, Barry Levinson et al., Director: Barry Levinson, Screenwriters: Michael Crichton, Kurt Wimmer, Stephen Hauser, Paul Attanasio, Performers: Dustin Hoffman, Sharon Stone, Samuel L. Jackson, Peter Coyote, Liev Schreiber, Queen Latifah et al., Cinematography: Adam Greenber, Editor: Stu Linder, Music: Elliot Goldenthal

The Terminator (US 1984) 1'48'', Production: Cinema 84, Euro Film Fund, Hemdale Film Corporation, Pacific Western / Gale Anne Hurd, Director: James Cameron, Screenwriters: James Cameron, Gale Anne Hurd et al., Performers: Arnold Schwarzenegger, Michael Biehn, Linda Hamilton, Paul Winfield, Lance

Henriksen et al., Cinematography: Adam Greenberg, Editor: Mark Goldblatt, Music: Joe Dolce, Brad Fiedel, Tane McClure

Terminator 2: Judgment Day (US/FR 1991) 2'15'', Production: Carolco Pictures, Le Studio Canal+ [fr], Lightstorm Entertainment, Pacific Western / James Cameron, Mario Cassar et al., Director: James Cameron, Screenwriters: James Cameron, William Wisher Jr., Performers: Arnold Schwarzenegger, Linda Hamilton, Edward Furlong, Robert Patrick, Earl Boen, Joe Morton et al., Cinematography: Adam Greenberg, Editors: Conrad Buff, Mark Goldblatt, Richard A. Harris, Music: Brad Fiedel et al.

The Fifth Element (FR 1997) 2'17'', Production: Gaumont / Patrice Ledoux et al., Director: Luc Besson, Screnwriter: Luc Besson, Robert Mark Kamen, Performers: Bruce Willis, Gary Oldman, Ian Holm, Milla Jovovich, Chris Tucker, Luke Perry, Brion James et al., Cinematography: Thierry Arbogast, Editor: Sylvie Landra, Music: Eric Serra

Vertigo (US 1958) 2'8'', Production: Alfred J. Hitchcock Productions, Paramount Pictures, Director: Alfred Hitchcock, Screenwriter: Samuel A. Taylor, Alec Coppel et al., Performers: James Stewart, Kim Novak, Barbara Bel Geddes, Tom Helmore, Henry Jones et al., Cinematography: Robert Burks, Editor: George Tomasini, Music: Bernard Herrmann

Illustration

01,03–06 Screenshots, Opening sequence of: *Alien Resurrection* (US 1997)

02 The Tree of Life, by Ernst Haeckel (1902), taken from: **Robin, Harry** (1992): *The Scientific Image. From Cave to Computer*, New York, 161

androgyn alien

violent

sexual organs

jouissance

CHRISTINA GOESTL

IF CYBERFEMINISM IS A MONSTER ... THEN CLITORIS VISIBILITY = TRUE

http://www.clitoressa.net/clitoris

The Clitoris is an impressive super organ.
(Rendering of the clitoris based on the anatomical findings of the Australian urologist Helen O'Connell, 1998)

onanie

onami   onadi

onadumi

onaidi   onaimi

onadudi

onaimia   onaidia

onaididumi

onaimidumi

onadumiidi

onadumidudi

onaoft

onanie. poly*special, postpunk approach.

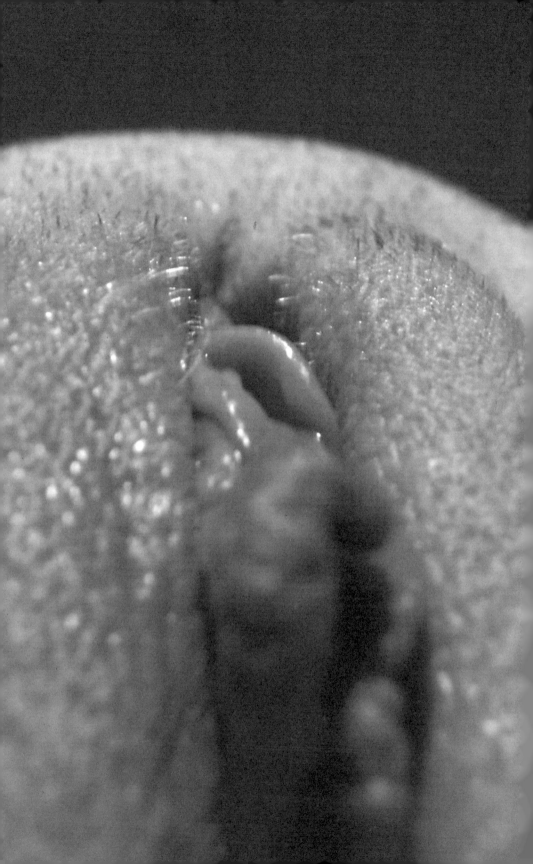

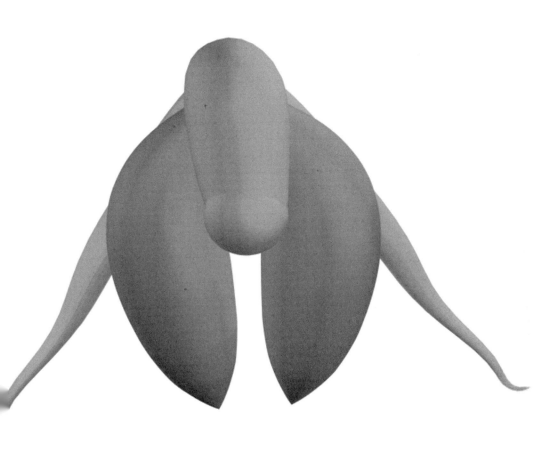

Clitoris Locator, clitorally speaking.
< Visual exploration of the Clitoris in full size.

Glans Clitoris. Clitoris Body. Clitoris Arms (or legs or wings). Clitoris Bulbs.

Erect Clitoris. Glans and Body swell and harden.

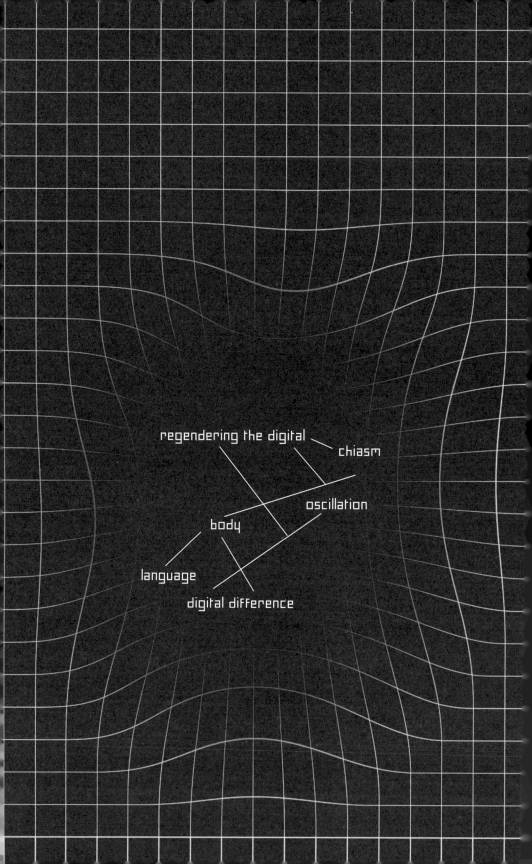

regendering the digital

chiasm

oscillation

body

language

digital difference

ELISABETH STROWICK

Cyberfeminist Rhetoric, or The Digital Act and Interfaced Bodies

The Performative Regendering of the Digital

> What is the subject of a cyberfeminist rhetoric? Or to put it in other words: How can digital media be applied in a feminist theory and politics of the performative[1] thus stressing the structural *binding* of language/code and body in the performativity of the gendered body? In her study of Austin's theory of the speech act that influenced Butler's consideration of the performativity of the gendered body, Shoshana Felman characterizes the performative act as the articulation of

the *chiastic* relation of language and body, i.e., a relationship of failed intersection "consisting at once of incongruity and of inseparability."[2] It is the "inherent incongruity of the speaking body"[3] articulated in the performative act that makes this a scandalous act that not only topples the metaphysical opposition of mind and body, language and matter[4], but furthermore also crosses the idea of the precedence of the subject over the act and the phantom of intentional availability that is bound to it. To formulate the relationship between language and body as *chiastic* does not mean reducing the body to a medium of linguistic utterance, but allows speech itself to appear as a bodily action in which the body persists not in a mode of presence, but as the "excess of utterance over the statement."[5] The feminist theory of the performative emphasizes the scandal of the *medium* that does not only suspend the idea of the body as a pre-symbolic entity, but also reads language in its corporeality/materiality – which has always been gendered. In short: The performative act articulates the materiality of the medium.

Starting with these theoretical reflections, the following statements question the performance of the digital media and the corporeal concepts bound to them, and conceptions of materiality. What possibilities of rethinking materiality in a cyberfeminist theory of the performative are

1 Cf. **Felman, Shoshana** (1983): *The Literary Speech Act. Don Juan with J.L. Austin, or Seduction in Two Languages*, Ithaca / New York; **Butler, Judith** (1997): *Excitable Speech. A Politics of the Performative*, New York / London.

2 **Felman** 1983: 96.

3 Ibid. 115.

4 Cf. ibid. 94.

5 Ibid. 78.

6 "Asymmetrical articulation of presence and absence, of 0 and 1, [...] chiastic construction of appearing and disappearing" (transl. Claudia Reiche – C.R.), **Tholen, Georg Christoph** (1994): Platzverweis. Unmögliche Zwischen-spiele von Mensch und Maschine. In: *Computer als Medium*, Norbert Bolz / Friedrich A. Kittler / Georg Christoph Tholen, Eds., Munich, 134.

7 **Felman** 1983: 148.

8 Chiasm: 1. rhetorical: the crossing of equivalent parts of a sentence in equivalent phrases named after the Greek X (Chi); 2. philosophical historical: Figure of thought that joins opposites to a unit (Heraclit, Plato, Aristotle, Hegel); 3. in deconstructivism: Accentuating the chiastic inversion of inherent fundamental asymmetries that marks the impossibility of reversing a rhetorical

opened by the digital act given that it repeats the digital difference as the fundamental "asymmetrische Artikulation von Anwesenheit und Abwesenheit, von 0 und 1, [...] chiastische Konstruktion des Auftauchens und Verschwindens"[6]? Which *"new type of materialism"*[7] comes into play with digital information? In the sense of a cyberfeminist politics of the performative, the digital act marks the crossing through of a gendered material/immaterial duality in favor of the re-articulation of the material as a question about the *gender difference* in its digital performance, i.e., the intersection of the body and the gendered code. Does the *interface* in this context describe the intertwining of body and code, of matter and matrix? And what would such a *chiastic*[8] structure of the interface mean in the context of the digital media and the conceptions of gendered bodies bound to them? What does it mean to consider the mediality of the digital as a crossing process, the articulation of the boundary as a relationship and thus as the (gender) difference beyond an oppositional logic? And how can the digital code 0/1 – the medial crossing of gender code and the digital body – be read as a question of gender difference?[9] Which X perfor(m)ates the digital difference 0/1? For what else could be contained in a cyberfeminist rhetoric if not this X of the digital act – in the sense of Ulrike Bergermann's cyberfeminist manifesto: *do x*?[10]

---

displacement and thus to neutralize it (de Man); asymmetrical shift of the chiasm through its medial link back to the "Medium jeder möglichen Teilung" ["medium of every possible division" C.R.], **Derrida, Jacques** (1995): *Dissemination*, Vienna, 143, whereby it becomes a figure that is simultaneously constructed and deconstructed by its own totality (Derrida); 4. in the deconstructivist-feminist theory of the performative (Felman, Butler): representation of a paradoxical relationship between language and the body in their mutual priority and inability to overtake each other. For more details, cf. **Gasché, Rodolphe** (1998): Über chiastische Umkehrbarkeit. In: *Die paradoxe Metapher,* Anselm Haverkamp, Ed., Frankfurt am Main, 437–455. My discussion uses the deconstructivist-feminist reception of chiasm as the articulation of a radically asymmetrical difference.

9 About the digital difference as a gender difference, cf. **Reiche, Claudia** (1998): Feminism is digital. In: *First Cyberfeminist International, 20.-28. September 1997 Kassel*, Cornelia Sollfrank / Old Boys Network, Eds., Hamburg, 24–32.

10 **Bergermann, Ulrike** (1998): do x. Manifesto no. 372. In: **Sollfrank/Old Boys Network** 1998: 8f.

Digital Act: How to do X with 0/1?[11]

The question of *How to do X with 0/1?* is aimed at the reading of the digital difference[12] as a gender difference in the sense of the performance of the digital. My train of thought about the digital act follows the psychoanalytical-deconstructivist reception of Austin (Felman, Derrida[13]) that presents the performative act as bound to the iteration of the sign as an act of repetition, i.e., structurally as an act of failing. Although Austin presents the possibility of failure/infelicity as a characteristic of the performative utterance, he excludes it in his theory of the speech act which he directs at the happy performative and the intention of the speaker. In contrast to this, Felman's psychoanalytical reception of the speech-act theory stresses the failure/infelicity of the act as shown in the misfire ("Fehlhandlung"[14]) as the determining moment of the performative, making this into a crossing through of intentionality and sense, and within this to an articulation of desire/gender difference. Lacan characterizes the slip/failure as the very articulation of the sexual in every (speech) act and the basic structure of the sexual act:

> "Freud's so-called sexuality consists in noting that everything having to do with sex is always a failure. [...] *Failure (misfire) itself can be defined as what is sexual in every human act.* That is why there are so many *actes manqués*. Freud indicated perfectly clearly that an *acte manqué* always has to do with sex. The *acte manqué par excellence* is precisely the sexual act. [...] And that is what people are always talking about."[15]

---

11 This subtitle can be understood as the program of a cyberfeminist politics of the performative quotes/crosses the title *How to do things with Words* by **John L. Austin** (1962), Cambridge and 'do x' by **Ulrike Bergermann**.

12 Cf. **Tholen, Georg Christoph** (1997): Digitale Differenz. Zur Phantasmatik und Topik des Medialen. In: *HyperKult. Geschichte, Theorie und Kontext digitaler Medien*, Martin Warnke / Wolfgang Coy / G. Christoph Tholen, Eds., Basel, 99–118.

13 Cf. **Derrida, Jacques** (2000): *Limited Inc*, Evanston.

14 **Freud, Sigmund** (1969): Vorlesungen zur Einführung in die Psychoanalyse. In: *Studienausgabe, Bd. I*, Alexander Mitscherlich / Angela Richards / James Strachey, Eds., Frankfurt am Main, 58.

15 **Lacan, Jacques**, *Le Symptôme*, 19, quoted in: **Felman** 1983: 110.

16 Cf. **Felman** 1983: 110f.

17 Cf. **Lacan, Jacques** (1991): *The Seminar Book II (The Ego in Freud's Theory and in the Technique of Psychoanalysis 1954–1955)*, New York / London, 294–326, (Psychoanalysis and Cybernetics, or on the Nature of Language).

In this context, Shoshana Felman indicates that the actual scandal of the performative as articulated in failure is not that all speech is of a sexual nature, but that the sexual act is a linguistic act, a speech act.[16] An essentialist understanding of the gender difference has thus been irrevocably crossed through. The erotic performative as sexual, i.e., failed act, is not used to bridge the gender difference but is apt to repeat it in its unavailability.

But, based on the deconstructivist-psychoanalytic performative, how can the digital difference be imagined in its performance? The digital act – as a failed sexual act? And what does such a failure mean for the digital difference as a gender difference? Which gender performances/multiplications/crossings does the digital difference inaugurate? In which way does the difference 0/1 creep performatively into the binary gender-code? What happens to the digital when it is read in its performance, i.e., as gendered body?

In his seminar session on *Psychoanalysis and Cybernetics*[17], Lacan illustrates cybernetics and the digital difference 0/1 using the different states of a door – for Lacan "the symbol *par excellence*" which he also uses in his signifier-theory formulation of the gender difference. (In *The Agency of the Letter*, however, there are *two* doors – more exactly two toilet doors – both of which are closed. But more about this later.) What fails in the psychoanalytic-cybernetic door – and this is the crucial trick of the door/significant – is the duality/symmetry of either-or, which is a basis for binary logic and the concept of gender connected to it (*either* open *or* closed, present *or* absent, 0 *or* 1, yes *or* no, female *or* male):

> "A door must, it is true, be either open or shut. But they aren't equivalent. [...] There is an asymmetry between the opening and the closing – if the opening of the door controls access, when closed, it closes the circuit. The door is a real symbol, the symbol *par excellence*, that symbol in which man's passing through the cross it sketches, intersecting access and closure, can always be recognized. Once it has become possible to fold the two characteristics together, to construct an enclosure, that is to say an circuit, so that something passes when it is closed, and doesn't when it is open, that is when the science of the conjuncture passes into the realm of realisation of cybernetics. [...] Note that what's important about this is the relation as such of access and closure. Once the door is open, it closes. When it is closed, it opens. A door isn't either open or shut, it must be either open and then shut, and then opened and then shut. Thanks to the electric circuit, and to the induction circuit connected on to it, that is to say, what is called feedback, it's sufficient for the door to close for it to be

returned by an electro-magnet to an open state and that is its closure again, and its opening again. In this way what is called an oscillation is produced. This oscillation is the scansion. And the scansion is the basis upon which one can inscribe indefinitely the ordered action through employing a series of montages which will be nothing more than child's play."[18]

The door – the signifier – brings the digital difference into play, not in the sense of binary logic, i.e., a symmetrical either/or, but as the articulation of a radical non-equivalence of states. These are crossed in their alternating/*feedback* and the difference contained in them eludes any oppositional structure. The door does not embody the opposition of two states, but marks a difference that cannot be represented in any opposition, that precedes an either-or, is above it, is performatively unhinging it. The alternating crossing that according to Lacan is performed in the differential play of zeroes and ones that functions through blank spaces, i.e., the significant difference between 0 and 1, cannot be coded in binary form. In this respect the digital character string attests to the structure of the symbolic, i.e., the structure of language that functions entirely through differences, the blank spaces of which defy not only any referential logic but also subordinate semantics to syntax.

"In other words, within this perspective, syntax exists before semantics. Cybernetics is a science of syntax, and it is in a good position to help us perceive that the exact sciences do nothing other than tie the real to a syntax."[19]

But what does such a deconstruction of the digital difference mean for a cyberfeminist rhetoric or respectively a politics of the performative? What does it mean for cyber-engendered bodies that the digital difference is not thought of as binary-opposed but as an alternating crossing, or more exactly: the 0 only as the 0 of a 1, the 1 as the 1 of a 0? For such an alternating asymmetrical presence and absence, as *fort/da* game "whose aim, in its alternation, is simply that of being the *fort* of a *da*, and

18 **Lacan** 1991: 301f.

19 Ibid. 305.

20 **Lacan, Jacques** (1998): *The Seminar Book XI (The Four Fundamental Concepts of Psychoanalysis)*, New York / London, 62f.

21 About failure, cf. **Reiche, Claudia** (2000): Tödliche Muster mit Aussetzern. Mutationen des Wissens und der Geschlechter in Jon Amiel's 'Copycat'. In: *Serialität: Reihen und Netze*, Elke Bippus / Andrea Sick, Eds., (CD-ROM), Bremen.

the *da* of a *fort*"[20], and that Lacan alludes to as a "child's play," is what the act of shutting/opening a door refers to.

If we consider the digital (door) act more exactly, it can be indeed read as a failed act.[21] The act of opening closes the door and closing opens the door: each closing is crossed by an opening. Opening and closing interrupt each other in asymmetrical alternation. The digital act is an act of (inter)crossing, in itself a failed sexual act. The rhythmic crossing/oscillation performs as a *feedback*, i.e., as a repetition. Each cybernetic act is an act of repetition, an act of *feedback* and thus already removed from itself, divided, an act of difference.[22] With *feedback* as the fundamental principle, cybernetics suspends the logic of identity. Correspondingly, the cybernetical concept of *Botschaft* [message] is not identity-logical semantic but one that functions as a syntactical repetitive force.

In which way does the digital act articulate the gender difference? For as rhythm/failure it can be read as a gendered act. With the alternating crossing of 0 and 1 the gender difference does not appear as symmetrically binary, but as a fundamentally asymmetrical act/chiasm. At this point, Lacan's other doors begin to become interesting: the two doors in *The Agency of the Letter* that illustrate the gender difference as the difference of signifiers, and thus the difference of signifiers as gendered difference. There are two closed toilet doors, which means that the place that signifier and gendered body cross is a lavatory *[Ab-ort]*. Lacan's door illustration is situated in the context of his reformulation of Saussure's sign theory. To mark the differential structure of the signifier, Lacan does not choose one tree, but *two* identical doors with the signs "Gentlemen" *[Hommes]* and "Ladies" *[Dames]* that are thus immediately recognizable as toilet doors.

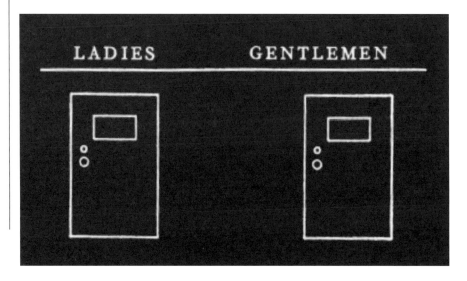

In the same context, Lacan tells the story of two children, a brother and sister, sitting opposite one another on a train that is entering a station.

> "A train arrives at a station. A little boy and a little girl, brother and sister, are seated in a compartment face to face next to the window through which the buildings along the station platform can be seen passing as the train pulls to a stop. 'Look', says the brother, 'we're at Ladies!', 'Idiot!' replies his sister, 'Can't you see we're at Gentlemen'."[23]

The signs on the toilet doors seem to align the signifier's difference/the symbolic with a binary-opposed genderedness [Hommes/Dames] which would make it questionable not only from the point of view of a feminist theory of the performative, but also in view of the radical differential structure of the signifier – the heterogeneity of the signifier is definitely not heterosexuality. Does Lacan's reformulating of the signifier have to submit to the reproach of being a symptomatic reproduction of the heterosexual matrix?[24] Is the symptom of the Lacanian text heterosexuality? 'Symptomatic' as in the fixing of semantic effect in the sense of a metaphor[25] that obstructs the irreducible belatedness of the meaning, its constitution and slipping by the differential play of the signifier. In view

---

22 About repetition, cf. **Deleuze, Gilles** (1992): *Differenz und Wiederholung*, Munich; and **Strowick, Elisabeth** (1999): *Passagen der Wiederholung.*
Kierkegaard – Lacan – Freud, Stuttgart / Weimar; and **Strowick, Elisabeth**
(2000): Wiederholung und Performativität. Rhetorik des Seriellen. In: Bippus/
Sick 2000; **Strowick, Elisabeth** (2001): Singularität des Aktes. Zur Perfor-
manz des Lesens. In: *Singularitäten. Literatur – Wissenschaft – Verantwortung*,
Marianne Schuller / Elisabeth Strowick, Eds., Freiburg i. Br., 59–72.

23 **Lacan, Jacques** (1977): The Agency of the Letter in the Unconscious or
Reason since Freud. In: *Écrits. A Selection*, transl. Alan Sheridan, New York /
London, 152.

24 Such criticism is explicitly understood as not denying the phallic structuring of
desire and its entanglement in the power discourse, but rather as a question of
possible actions for shifting the symbolic matrix, cf. also **Butler, Judith**
(1993): *Bodies that matter. On the discursive limits of "sex"*, New York / London,
73, 84–91.

25 "For the symptom is a metaphor" (**Lacan** 1977: 175).

26 "This form of the chiasm, of the X, interests me a great deal, not as the symbol of the unknown, but because there is in it [...] a kind of fork [...] that is,
moreover, unequal, one of the points extending its range further than the
other", **Derrida, Jacques** (1987): *Positions*, Chicago / London, 70.

of the differential structure of the signifier, the gender identity accorded by the two toilet doors appears exceedingly feeble. The positions they give to the genders proves to be a deceptive stabilisation/fixing of the sexual difference that, as the story of the siblings shows, leads to irreconcilable dissent. In this connection, from the perspective of the boy they are in 'Ladies,' while that of the girl is that they are in 'Gentlemen.' The mistake about their own position is here at least a double one: 1. The failure to appreciate the relativity of one's own perspective that makes the conflict irreconcilable, 2. The failure to appreciate that both quarrelling parties are in the wrong place: The boy in 'Ladies' and the girl in 'Gents.' – Are in Lacan's signifier-theoretical reformulating of the gender difference any moments represented that infiltrate the pre-programmed dilemma found in a heterosexual setting? In other words: Where is the symmetrical crossing X based in the pictorial and narrative interrupted and exposed to the asymmetrical difference of the chiasm?[26]

The decisive difference, here, is the bar that as paradoxical-double movement both simultaneously produces and obstructs meaning, letting gender duality be read as signifier effect, and refers to a gender difference beyond binary gender categories. In this sense, Samuel Weber does not connect the gender difference of the signifier to the opposition of two passable doors, but to the bar as a *Ab-Ort* [non-place].

> "[...] the first thing that has to be taken into account is that 'the rails' [...] materialize the bar of the Saussurean algorithm [...] The subject here is literally borne by the bar separating the signifier from the signified; its place is on the rails that simultaneously derail. The quarrel between the little girl, who claims to have arrived in 'Gentlemen,' and the little boy, for whom the place can only be called 'Ladies,' is impossible to arbitrate, at least as long as the question at issue – the relationship of the sexes – remains couched in the binary structure of an alternative: *either* 'gentlemen,' *or* 'ladies,' each ostensibly in its proper *place*. It is therefore no accident that the place described in Lacan's illustrative figure is a toilet [*Abort*], a place that is never entirely 'proper,' and to which access is generally more or less regulated. In Lacan's figure, the doors seem to be closed. We can, therefore, never be entirely certain about what stands behind it all, and for Lacan, this is probably the most important aspect of the story."[27]

The crucial moment for the constitution of the gender difference are the rails that carry the entire story and that continue to de-rail the meaning it takes in the battle of the sexes. The meaning that the siblings are arguing about is constituted in the movement of the train along the rails. The rails function as an interface through which the positions of the children cross with the station toilet doors representing the signifiers of the genders (ladies, gentlemen), i.e., that meet in a mode of failure – Tholen speaks of a "kreuzverkehrte[n] Blick" ["crosswisely reversed gaze"][28]. The contested meaning is an effect of the metaphor that moves along the rails undermining the meaning itself. The interface represents the *Ab-Ort* [non-place] of the metaphor: the paradoxical double movement of constitution and deconstruction of the gender positions.

Using the rails/bar as an interface brings a gender difference into play that simultaneously undermines the gender dualism 0/1 as depicted in narrative as a symptomatic effect of meaning while producing it. As a difference, the bar bars meaning, suspending it, embedding it in the slipped/failed act, thereby becoming the articulation of desire. The gender difference of the signifier is not articulated on the level of meaning, but in its performative crossing through, as an act failed in itself. Thus, the meeting/crossing of the children and the gender positions – necessarily

27 **Weber, Samuel M.** (1991): *Return to Freud. Jacques Lacan's Dislocation of Psychoanalysis*, Cambridge, 43.

28 "Der kreuzverkehrte Blick der Kinder bestätigt […] das chiastische Kreuz der Differenz, das die Geschlechter trennt, und zwar notgedrungen in der Form eines nicht enden wollenden, imaginär rivalisierenden Streits, der die konfliktuöse Urszene darstellen soll, welche wiederum […] vom je narzißtischen Standpunkt der Kinder ich-gerecht zurechtgebogen und umgedeutet sein will." ["The crosswisely reversed gaze of the children confirms […] the chiastic cross of difference, that separates the sexes, actually perforce in its form as a never ending, imaginarily competitive argument, that shall represent the conflictuous primal scene, which in itself has to be bent and interpreted by the indivdually narcisstic point of view of the children according to the demands of their egos.", C.R.], **Tholen, Georg Christoph** (2001): Der Ort des Abwesenden. Konturen des Differenz-Denkens bei Derrida, Lacan und Levinas. In: Schuller/Strowick 2001: 171.

29 "Crosswisely reversed gaze", C.R..

30 **Austin, John L.** (1962): *How to do things with Words*, Cambridge, 22.

31 Ibid. 22.

32 **Parker, Andrew / Sedgwick, Eve Kosofsky**, Eds. (1995): *Performativity and Performance*, New York / London, 5.

33 Cf. **Sedgwick, Eve Kosofsky** (1993): Queer Performativity. Henry James's The Art of the Novel. In: *GLQ. A Journal of Lesbian and Gay Studies 1.1*, 1–16.

through the interface – can only be considered as a failure. The "*kreuzverkehrte Blick*"[29] does not result in a symmetrical cross, as might be expected in the phantasm of heterosexuality, but is undermined by the bar as a moment of radical loss of meaning and opened to a chiastic asymmetry. Formulating the gender difference as a chiastic difference does not aim at the crossing of the two symmetrical poles 0 and 1, but at its unstoppable de-railing in a multiplying difference as described in Lacan's *Psychoanalysis and Cybernetics*. If one wanted to turn to Lacan's cybernetic doors with their rhythmic crossing once more, it would be best placed exactly at the *Ab-Ort* [non-place] of the bar, the interface that articulates the gender difference as chiasm.

As a chiastically failed sexual act the digital act allows a further gender-theoretical reading. In as far as the act 0/1 does not occur as straight X, but as an act of the multiplication of difference, it can be hardly referred to as anything else but queer: It is known that Austin excludes literary speech acts and acts of repetition (e.g., quotation) from his theory. As a "*parasitic*"[30] utilization of the normal use of speech they fall under "the doctrine of the *etiolations* of language."[31] In their introduction to *Performativity and Performance*, Andrew Parker and Eve Kosofsky Sedgwick refer to the semantic field of "etiolation" as the sign of the artificial, unnatural and abnormal that reaches from the botanical discourse to the gender discourse, namely from the homophobic discourse of the late 19th century in England. Consequently, according to Parker and Sedgwick, "the performative has […] been from its inception already infected with queerness."[32] "Queer performativity"[33] (Sedgwick) performs the etiolation of the naturalistic concepts of gender identity. Etiolation operates as the performative dissemination of the genders, and, as Austin notes, the whole as a matter of language, or as a digital act as could be added from a cyberfeminist point of view.

Thus, *to do X with 0/1*, means to perform/repeat the digital act as a *queer* act, i.e., as an act undermining the dualistic pattern of thought as can be found in abundance in discourses about digital media (e.g., information/material, body/code, human/machine, speech/action, real/virtual), and articulates the digital difference as a chiastic gender-difference. Instead of being a reason to question the traditional body and gender concepts and the logic of representation and reference, are the technical possibilities of the digital media actually going to lead to nothing more than a unimaginative discursive reproduction of metaphysical oppositions and reactionary fantasies of redemption?

MatrX

To think of the digital difference in terms of the performative, as I am attempting with the term 'digital act,' makes the reformulation of the relationship between digital code or digital information and materiality both possible and necessary. How is this relationship expressed in information technology and media theory? What displacements are made in the constellation with the feminist reception of the performative (Felman, Butler) that can be distinguished by the fact that it does not question the body and materiality as opposed to speech but poses the question in sign theory terms? In what respect is the term of the digital act suitable to recycle the (not gender neutral) term of materiality in the discourses about digital media, without reproducing the duality materiality/information? Can the digital act be conceived as an interface that, in a double move, refers the concept of 'digital information' to the materiality of the code and an ontological concept of material to the digital difference? Which shifts do 'materiality' and 'digital code' or 'information' undergo during their crossing in the digital act? And, to refer back to the discourse of the previous section that attempted to read the digital difference in terms of a chiastic difference: To what extent does the X of the digital difference with the binary logic of 0 and 1 also cross through a material/

---

34 Cf. **Felman** 1983: 147f.

35 "Embodiment has been systematically downplayed or erased in the cybernetic construction of the posthuman in ways that have not occurred in other critiques of the liberal humanist subject, especially in feminist and postcolonial theories.", **Hayles, N. Katherine** (1999): *How We Became Posthuman. Virtual Bodies in Cybernetics, Literature, and Informatics*, Chicago / London, 4.

36 Cf. **Hayles** 1999: xi.

37 Ibid. 12.

38 Ibid. 12.

39 Ibid. 13.

40 Cf. **Derrida, Jacques** (1991): Die différance. In: *Postmoderne und Dekonstruktion. Texte französischer Philosophen der Gegenwart*, Peter Engelmann, Ed., Stuttgart, 76–113.

41 Thus Tholen talks of "Zäsuren oder Bruch-Stellen einer bilderlosen, intermedialen Dazwischenkunft des Medialen" ["caesuras or breaks of the medium's pictureless and inter-medial interference", C.R.], **Tholen** 1997: 103, and also of a "a-präsente techné, die uneinholbar und vorgängig bleibt, weil so erst – von diesem ab-gründigen Ort aus – das Feld differentieller Technik- und Medienverhältnisse spurengesichert werden kann" ["non-presentic techné that remains

information dualism? Can the performance of the digital (to do X with 0/1) be read as the intervention of a "new type of materialism"[34] in the digital matrix? The matrix – a matter X, i.e., a materiality, that connects to the differentiality of linguistic/digital sign? This section, the title of which binds 'matrix' and 'matter X,' is aimed at a cyberfeminist questioning of the concept of matter in the context of the performance of the digital.

Real Virtuality or, Difference that Matters

The topic of the immateriality of information has tradition. Katherine Hayles sketches its historical development in *How We Became Posthuman* and refers to the parallels between the metaphysical and posthuman material/immaterial duality (body/spirit, material/information) that hierarchically subordinates the body/material to the immaterial (spirit, information).[35] The dualistic separation of information and material has already come into effect in Wiener's and Shannon's definitions of 'information'[36] and is further developed in concepts of the virtual. By claiming parallel representations of RL (Real Life) and VR (Virtual Reality), these promise the separation and liberation of information from the ballast of the body which frequently also appears as disabled. Hayles replies by setting up the irreducible mediality/materiality of information against the posthuman "materiality/information separation"[37] that lends itself to the idea of "bodiless information"[38]:

> "[…] for information to exist, it must *always* be instantiated in a medium, whether that medium is the page from the Bell Laboratories Journal on which Shannon's equations are printed, the computer-generated topological maps used by the Human Genome Project, or the cathode ray tube on which virtual worlds are imaged. The point is not only that abstracting information from a material base is an imaginary act but also, and more fundamentally, that conceiving of information as a thing separate from the medium instantiating it is a prior imaginary act that constructs a holistic phenomenon as an information/matter duality."[39]

The "information/matter duality" goes hand in hand with the forgetting of mediality. In view of Hayles' stressed medial containment of information, a matter/information duality can no longer be upheld. Mediality, however, implies a materiality of information that cannot be positioned in an opposed schemata, but in a deconstructive reading connected to a difference over and above this schemata: the difference/*différance*[40] that is aimed at in Tholen's reformulation of the medial/techné[41] as one that first of all opens the possibility of presence while simultaneously evading it. What type of materiality comes into play with the retrait/*différance* of mediality? The 'materialistic' character of the *différance* Derrida formulates, too:

> "[...] if and in the extent to which, matter in this general economy designates [...] radical alternity (I will specify: in relation to philosophical oppositions), then what I write can be considered 'materialist'."[42]

Thus, to connect the materiality of the digital to the presence of the code 0/1 would be a mistake. Rather just the "mediale Zäsur"[43]/failed crossing of the digital difference 0/1 should be considered as a material occurrence, the digital matrix as materiality of the *différance*/matter X, materiality of the digital act.

When Norbert Wiener characterizes 'information' with the words: "information is information, not matter or energy. No materialism which does not admit this can survive at the present day"[44] he continues to write metaphysical matter/immaterial dualism. In deconstructive reading, however, Wiener's information-technological understanding of 'matter' implies the material infiltration of information. Where information technology confronts the concept of matter with information as its non-obtainable 'other' and displaces it, the concept of information (with all its tendency towards the self-asserting tautology: "information is information") for its part does not escape this displacement. Irreducibly bound to

---

inaccessible and predecessing, because only coming from this unreasonable site, thus the field of technical and media-relations – as based on the principle of difference – can undergo its securing of evidence", C.R.], ibid. 110.

42 **Derrida** 1987: 64.

43 "Medium's caesura", C.R., **Tholen** 1997: 104.

44 **Wiener, Norbert** (1948): *Cybernetics; or, Control and Communication in the Animal and the Machine*, Cambridge, 132.

45 **Tholen** 1997: 103.

46 **Hayles** 1999: 13.

47 Ibid. 13f.; cf. ibid. 192–212 (The Materiality of Informatics).

48 My criticism should not be misunderstood as a general judgement of the 'science fiction' genre. In which ways science fiction films avoid, in regards to the production of digital technology, the traditional discursive patterns, e.g., gender concepts, are shown, for example, in the work of **Ulrike Bergermann**, cf. Analogue Trees, Genetics, and Digital Diving. Pictures of Human and Alien Reproductions (in this volume); Hollywood Reproductions. Mothers,

the "Dazwischenkunft des Medialen" ["medium's interference"][45] information appears in a chiastic intersection with matter, whereby not only a
pre-linguistic/pre-informational understanding of matter, but also the idea
of immaterial information has always been considered to be crossed by an
embodied code. Contrary to the material/immaterial duality the digital act
means the scandal of materiality of information, the chiastic crossing/mutual
priority of matter and information. Hayles formulates such a crossing in a
similar manner in her "strategic definition of 'virtuality'"[46]:

> *"Virtuality is the cultural perception that material objects are interpenetrated
> by information patterns.* The definition plays off the duality at the heart of
> the condition of virtuality – materiality on the one hand, information on
> the other. Normally virtuality is associated with computer simulations
> that put the body into a feedback loop with a computer-generated image.
> [...] Virtual reality technologies are fascinating because they make visually
> immediate the perception that a world of information exists parallel to
> the 'real' world [...] Hence the definition's strategic quality, strategic
> because it seeks to connect virtual technologies with the sense, pervasive
> in the late twentieth century, that all material objects are interpenetrated
> by flows of information, from DNA code to the global reach of the
> World Wide Web."[47]

Hayles's definition enables virtuality to figure as a form of medial doubling
that does not claim parallels between two worlds – RL (real life) and VR
(virtual reality) – but rather binds reality to a process of perception that is
fundamentally medially structured. Medially qualified, each reality is virtual and thus in itself doubled/failed in the way that concepts of parallel,
or analogue reality collapse. So, although media-theoretical discourse
propagates VR as a liberation from materiality and body, it paradoxically
is in effect nothing more than a denial of virtuality, in as much as this
reality – bound to the performance of medium/perception – can be considered as doubled/virtual in itself. Thus, from a discourse-analytical
point of view it appears remarkable that the fact that with the boom in
the concept of 'virtuality' experiences in the contexts of the new media, it
is frequently accompanied by an abolishment of a virtual dimension of
the medial. Within the framework of a post-structuralist understanding of
language, this dimension should be considered as a doubling structure of
the media that is suitable to re-signify concepts such as reality, materiality, representation, etc. and thus to liberate the digital media from its discursive function of guardian of the ontological simplicity of the world.

    According to Hayles's definition of virtuality, and in the sense of a cyberfeminist politics of the performative, the digital act is, precisely, *virtual*, in as much as it performatively repeats the 'interpenetration' of material and information. In other words, it articulates both relationship as a simultaneous failure and inseparability. The digital act is not performed as the transition of a hypostatic 'real body' (RL) into a 'virtual corporeality' (VR), i.e., as an act of overcoming the mortality of the body – a phantasm that cannot hide its eschatological source and one that science fiction films do not become tired of reproducing[48] – but persists as a flickering *interface* that crosses the sign-bond of the body with the corporeality of the code.

Matrix of Absence – Matter X

Hayles criticizes the description of digital information in the modus of a difference that is described in Freud's '*Fort-Da-Spiel.*'[49] In the game's repetitive articulation of the phonetic difference 'o – a' Lacan finds the formulation of the signifier's difference. Opposing Lacan's "floating signifiers" Hayles conceives of a "flickering signifier" which does not define the differential structure of the signifier in the logic of presence and absence, but as pattern and randomness.[50] Hayles' criticism of Lacan's concept of the signifier, however, does not avoid a simplification of the psychoanalytical formulated '*Fort-Da*'/absence-presence relationship. The difference of the signifier which "in its alternation[,] is simply that of being the *fort* of a *da*, and the *da* of a *fort*,"[51] does not find its application in the symmetrical opposition of a present 'there' [fort] and a present

---

Clones, and Aliens (forthcoming). In: *Representations of the Body*, Insa Härtel / Sigrid Schade, Eds., Opladen.

49 ['gone-here-game' C.R.] Cf. **Freud, Sigmund** (1975): Jenseits des Lustprinzips. In: *Studienausgabe, Bd. III*, Alexander Mitscherlich / Angela Richards / James Strachey, Eds., Frankfurt am Main, 224ff.

50 Cf. **Hayles** 1999: 30f.

51 **Lacan** 1998: 62f.

52 This does not mean that the psychoanalytical theory of the signifier in the context of digital media could not be modified in the sense that **Claudia Reiche** does, based on Hayles: "Das medial Neue ist hier die Leichtigkeit der Verschiebung auf allen Ebenen – eine Flüchtigkeit, Flüssigkeit des Signifizierten in rest- und spurloser Verschiebbarkeit als neue Qualität, als angewandtes und sich potentiell verselbständigendes Prinzip stellenwertiger Verschiebung." ["The media-specific novelty is the ease of tranfers on every plane – a volatility and

'here' [da], but as the articulation of a scansion, fundamentally asymmetrical difference. The absence that repeats the articulation of the difference 'o – a' as basically failed and cannot be ordered to one of the sides ('o' *or* 'a'), has its *Ab-Ort* [non-place] in the scandalous crossing/multiplying difference there/here, which avoids a logical opposition of presence and absence. According to a reading of the 'Fort-Da-Spiel'/the signifier's difference as scandalous crossing of 0 and 1, the criticism of the transference of the signifier theory of psychoanalysis to the digital media cannot be made on the level that Hayles does it,[52] by positioning the (floating) signifier in the print-technological sense/logic of presence as a "single marker"[53]/"ink mark on a page"[54] while the digitally flickering signifier escapes this logic. The "internal play of difference"[55] as well as the "flexible chain of markers bound together by the arbitrary relations specified by the relevant codes"[56] that Hayles brings into play with the digital media and her concept of the "flickering signifier" are exactly the features with which Lacan characterizes the play of the signifiers. And, thus, together with the reading of Lacan undertaken here, the functioning of pattern/randomness Hayles chooses to describe digital information cannot be seen as one that replaces the difference of *fort/da*, but one that enacts it. The model of pattern/randomness is fundamental for Lacan's concept of the symbolic as well as the compulsion of repetition. Lacan's concept of repetition reformulates the relationship of pattern and randomness in a way approximating Hayles' definition of information, illustrated using the concept of mutation.[57]

---

fluidity of the signified in a complete and traceless transference as a new quality, as an applied principle of place value shifting – potentially becoming independent.", C.R.], **Reiche** 2000.

53 **Hayles** 1999: 30f.

54 Ibid. 30f.

55 Ibid. 30f.

56 Ibid. 30f.

57 "Identifying information with both pattern and randomness proved to be a powerful paradox, leading to the realization that in some instances, an infusion of noise into a system can cause it to reorganize at a higher level of complexity. Within such a system, patterns and randomness are bound together in a complex dialectic that makes them not so much opposites as complements or supplements to one another." **Hayles** 1999: 25; cf. also ibid. 33.

The *fort/da* game makes it clear that the signifier's difference ('o – a', 0/1) or the digital act as an act of repetition in respect to a specific materiality is a material occurrence. The differential articulation of the signifier repeats nothing more than the leaving/absence of the mother [*mater*], so to say a materiality *in absentia* that – in retrospect according to the game of the signifiers – has always affected the signifiers. In cyberfeminism the *fort/da* game lends a reading to the digital difference in respect of its *extime* materiality. The digital act articulates the materiality of the digital medium/the digital matrix as matter X/matter *in absentia* that does not allow itself to be positioned in opposition to information, but as crossed chiastically with the code: a matter of difference/a difference that matters.

The question of materiality is anything but gender-neutral. The etymology of material, which is derived from the *Lat.* 'matter'/'matrix' bears witness to a discursive proximity of material and maternity/femininity. As Judith Butler emphasises in *Bodies That Matter* "the history of matter is in part determined by the negotiation of sexual difference."[58] The construction of an irreducible and pre-discourse matter/materiality of the gendered body appears as a discursive strategy that "ontologizes and fixes" a "problematic gendered matrix."[59] The determining subject for a feminist politics of the performative is in this respect "not the materiality of sex, but the sex of materiality,"[60] in other words, the question "how a gen-

---

58 **Butler** 1993: 29.

59 Ibid. 29.

60 Ibid. 49.

61 Ibid. 32.

62 "The act, an enigmatic and problematic production of the speaking body, destroys from its inception the metaphysical dichotomy between the domain of the 'mental' and the domain of the 'physical,' breaks down the opposition between body and spirit, between matter and language.", **Felman** 1983: 94 "[…] it is precisely here that Austin's originality lies, for through the new concept of 'language act' he explodes both the opposition and the separation between matter (or body) and language: matter, like the act, without being reducible to language, is no longer entirely separable from it, either.", ibid. 147f. Cf. also **Butler** 1993: 67ff.

63 "Thus we are dealing, in the Austinian discovery (as, moreover, in the Freudian discovery), with the institution of nothing less then a new type of materialism. […] Austinian materialism is a materialism of the residue, that is, literally, of the trivial: a materialism of the speaking body", **Felman** 1983: 147f.

dered matrix is at work in the constitution of materiality."[61]

The crossing of materiality and symbolic matrix, or, more exactly: the materiality of the gendered body and the sexuality of the symbolic matrix, is theorized in the feminist concept of the performative act as an articulation of the chiastic intertwining of 'matter' and 'language'[62]. For Felman the performative is connected to the question of "a new type of materialism,"[63] i.e., to a materialism that not only subverts each ontology, but also, inasmuch as it is related to the differentiated structure of the in-itself-failed act, enters into a re-signifying of gender difference.

Insofar as the crossing of 'matter' and 'language' raises the question not only of the material signifier processes but also of the materiality of language, the cyberfeminist question concerning the gendered materiality of the digital code can be posed. The digital act articulates the materiality of the digital medium/digital matrix as matter X. Which digital gender constructions are bound to matrX? Which possibilities for a regendering of discursive materiality concepts are opened, if materiality is structurally bound to the digital *queer* act? According to this the digital matrix cannot be associated with an concept of femininity that is traditionally positioned outside the code, but shows itself as a matter of difference, reproduction not of the heterosexual matrix but a *queer* engendering/ multiplication of gender that performs the repetition of difference/failure of the code. Digital matrix installs materiality/maternity on the code level; not as the identical reproduction of digital information but as the mutation of the matrix that suspends materiality as a naturalistic concept and refers to the *queer* act of paradox genders – in the sense of the 'Call for Papers' for *Cyberfeminism. Next Protocols*, which reads:

> "Like IF, the basic element of programming languages for case differentiation and ramification – 'Cyberfeminism' indicates an operation. The feed-back loop: 'IF X THEN A ELSE B' sets an unpredictable future for the machine's actions. Who would seriously trust such autonomous operations? Since the war-decision programming of the 1940s, almost everybody (preferably without knowing) trusts IF-THEN commands as a means to prophesy the immediate future. Reported errors will already have predicted the unknown message, as a message is the transmission of certain calculable probabilities. Metaphorically (and incorrectly) spoken, a feminist bet could engage in the finding of some less predictable errors – one step beyond coding – in order to trigger a change in the immediate future of the machine's universe. Making a mess of the message? Count differently? Change the alphabet? Calculate faster? Rearm the hardware

to devices capable of all of the first four rules of arithmetic? Transmit viruses? Put the data of your genetic fingerprint in an Artificial Life environment to parody literary origin myths? Live new or ambiguous genders?"[64]

Interfaced Bodies. Surface-Act

The question of a digital body concept is raised by the formulation of the crossing of body and code by the performative reading of digital media which I have attempted to develop in the concept of the 'digital act.' From the viewpoint of a cyberfeminist politics of the performative, the usual pattern whereby media acts as a prosthesis of the human body whose metaphysical constitution remains untouched, is without doubt inappropriate.[65] Instead a concept of the body should be discussed as it is implied by the digital act as an interface of body and code. Felman's writings on the performative act characterize the speaking body through its

64 Call for Papers: *Cyberfeminism. Next Protocols*, **Claudia Reiche / Verena Kuni** / (Old Boys Network) , Eds., published in the mailing lists 'Faces', 'Nettime' etc. from 9/1999, in this volume.

65 About the criticism of the media-theoretical prostheses discourse cf. **Tholen** 1994; **Tholen** 1997; **Fogle, Douglas** (1996): Virtuelle Hysterische. Körper als Medium und das Interface. In: *Die Wiederkehr des Anderen (Interventionen 5)*, Jörg Huber / Alois Martin Müller, Eds., Basel, Frankfurt am Main, Zürich, 245–263.

66 Cf. **Tholen** 1997: 99f.

67 "Caesura or break of the medium's pictureless and inter-medial interference", C.R., ibid. 103.

68 **Tholen** 1994: 112.

69 **Freud, Sigmund** (1964): The Ego and the Id. In: *The Standard Edition of the Complete Psychological Works of Sigmund Freud*, Vol. XIX, James Strachey, Ed., transl. J. Strachey, London, 26.

70 Cf. **Strowick, Elisabeth** (2000): Körper von Evidenz. Zur Performativität hysterischer Geschlechter. In: *Hysterie und Wahnsinn*, Silke Leopold / Agnes Speck, Eds., Heidelberg, 144–171.

71 My argument is reasoned on the fundaments of Judith Butler's reformulation of the "morphological imaginary", cf. **Butler** 1993: 57–119. About the imaginary, cf. also: **Tholen, Georg Christoph** (1999): Der blinde Fleck des Sehens: Über das raumzeitliche Geflecht des Imaginären. In: *Konstruktionen Sichtbarkeiten (Interventionen 8)*, Jörg Huber / Martin Heller, Eds., Vienna / New York, 191–214.

own inherent incongruity. How is the "inherent incongruity of the speaking body" represented in reference to the digital medium? The digital act – it may be said – articulates the body as an *interfaced body* which does not refer to a pragmatic fitting of human and machine, but as radical insecurity of categories.[66]

The concept of digital corporeality, formulated as interfaced body by the digital act, not only does not support the dichotomy of human-machine, but opens a paradoxical differential space. As "Zäsur[] oder Bruch-Stelle[] einer bilderlosen, intermedialen Dazwischenkunft des Medialen"[67] the interface crosses the logic of representation. The *interfaced body* – the interface in its engendered corporeality – is simultaneously surface and gap ["Kluft"[68]]. The expression 'surface' introduced here is not a binary opposition to 'depth' as in the traditional space concept, but is conceived from psychoanalytical and feminist body concepts (Freud, Lacan, Butler). These enable the structural crossing of surface and performative act, thus criticizing metaphysical body categories such as 'depth' and 'introspection.' Thus, Freud in *The Ego and the Id* develops the 'Ego' as corporeal and the body as surface: "The ego is first and foremost a bodily ego; it is merely a surface entity, but is itself the projection of a surface."[69] Such a superficial corporeality of the 'Ego' can also be encountered in Lacan's *The Mirror Stage*. The mirror image/body image is used to form the 'Ego'-function, i.e., as performative. The 'Ego'-formation is an image act that is performed through a surface/evidence, in as much as the body image forms the 'Ego' as corporeal, i.e., the body, or bodily evidence can be read as the body performative. Evidence is not representation, but performance that continues writing bodily concepts/produces bodies.[70]

Developing from the psychoanalytical-feminist theories of the performative and imaginary[71] the digital act can be read as an articulation of digital corporeality in its paradoxical facets; as a superficial act. The performative surface structure of the interfaced body cannot be reduced to a logic-of-presence concept of visibility, but persists as a flickering/paradoxical imagery that, by performatively paralyzing the visibility paradigm, refers images to their media-constituent conditions. Maybe it is nothing more than this flickering that makes digital imagery so evident.   <

TRANSLATION: **Julia Macintosh-Schneider**

BIBLIOGRAPHY

Print

Austin, John L. (1962): *How to do things with Words*, Cambridge **Berger-mann, Ulrike** (1998): do x. Manifesto no. 372. In: *First Cyberfeminist International,20.-28. September 1997, Kassel,* Cornelia Sollfrank / Old Boys Network, Eds. 8f. **Bergermann, Ulrike** (2002): Analogue Trees, Genetics, and Digital Diving. Pictures of Human and Alien Reproductions (in this volume) (=Bergermann 2002a); **Bergermann, Ulrike** (2002): Hollywood Reproductions. Mothers, Clones, and Aliens (forthcoming). In: *Representations of the Body*, Insa Härtel / Sigrid Schade, Eds., Opladen (=Bergermann 2002b) **Bippus, Elke / Sick, Andrea**, Eds. (2000): *Serialität: Reihen und Netze*, (CD-ROM), Bremen **Butler, Judith** (1997): *Excitable Speech. A Politics of the Performative*, New York / London **Deleuze, Gilles** (1992): *Differenz und Wiederholung*, Munich **Derrida, Jacques** (1987): *Positions*, Chicago / London **Derrida, Jacques** (1991): Die différance. In: *Postmoderne und Dekonstruktion. Texte französischer Philosophen der Gegenwart*, Peter Engelmann, Ed., Stuttgart, 76–113 **Derrida, Jacques** (1995): *Dissemination*, Vienna **Derrida, Jacques** (2000): *Limited Inc*, Evanston **Felman, Shoshana** (1983): *The Literary Speech Act. Don Juan with J.L. Austin, or Seduction in Two Languages*, Ithaca / New York **Fogle, Douglas** (1996): Virtuelle Hysterische. Körper als Medium und das Interface. In: *Die Wiederkehr des Anderen (Interventionen 5)*, Jörg Huber / Alois Martin Müller, Eds., Basel / Frankfurt am Main / Zürich, 245–263 **Freud, Sigmund** (1964): The Ego and the Id. In: *The Standard Edition of the Complete Psychological Works of Sigmund Freud*, Vol. XIX, James Strachey, Ed., transl. J. Strachey, London **Freud, Sigmund** (1969): Vorlesungen zur Einführung in die Psychoanalyse. In: *Studienausgabe, Bd. I*, Alexander Mitscherlich / Angela Richards / James Strachey, Eds., Frankfurt am Main **Freud, Sigmund** (1975): Jenseits des Lustprinzips. In: *Studienausgabe, Bd. III*, Alexander Mitscherlich / Angela Richards / James Strachey, Eds., Frankfurt am Main, 224ff. **Gasché, Rodolphe** (1998): Über chiastische Umkehrbarkeit. In: *Die paradoxe Metapher*, Anselm Haverkamp, Ed., Frankfurt am Main, 437–455 **Hayles, N. Katherine** (1999): *How We Became Posthuman. Virtual Bodies in Cybernetics, Literature, and Informatics*, Chicago / London **Lacan, Jacques** (1977): The Agency of the Letter in the Unconscious or Reason since Freud. In: *Écrits. A Selection*, New York / London **Lacan, Jacques** (1991): *The Seminar Book II (The Ego in Freud's Theory and in the Technique of Psychoanalysis 1954–1955)*, New York / London, 294–326, (Psychoanalysis and Cybernetics, or on the Nature of Language) **Lacan, Jacques** (1998): *The Seminar Book XI*, New York / London, 62f., (The Four Fundamental Concepts of Psychoanalysis) **Parker, Andrew / Sedgwick,**

Eve Kosofsky, Eds. (1995): *Performativity and Performance*, New York / London **Reiche, Claudia** (1998): Feminism is digital. In: *First Cyberfeminist International, 20.-28. September 1997 Kassel*, Cornelia Sollfrank / Old Boys Network, Eds., Hamburg, 24–32 **Reiche, Claudia / Kuni, Verena / Old Boys Network**, Eds. (1999): Call for Papers: CYBERFEMINISM: Next Protocols, published in the mailing lists 'Faces', 'Nettime' etc. (in this volume) **Reiche, Claudia** (2000): Tödliche Muster mit Aussetzern. Mutationen des Wissens und der Geschlechter in Jon Amiel's 'Copycat'. In: *Serialität: Reihen und Netze*, Elke Bippus / Andrea Sick, Eds., (CD-ROM), Bremen **Sedgwick, Eve Kosofsky** (1993): Queer Performativity. Henry James's The Art of the Novel. In: *GLQ. A Journal of Lesbian and Gay Studies 1.1*, 1–16 **Strowick, Elisabeth** (1999): *Passagen der Wiederholung. Kierkegaard – Lacan – Freud*, Stuttgart / Weimar **Strowick, Elisabeth** (2000): Wiederholung und Performativität. Rhetorik des Seriellen. In: Bippus/Sick 2000 (=Strowick 2000a) **Strowick, Elisabeth** (2000): Körper von Evidenz. Zur Performativität hysterischer Geschlechter. In: *Hysterie und Wahnsinn*, Silke Leopold / Agnes Speck, Eds., Heidelberg (=Strowick 2000b) **Strowick, Elisabeth** (2001): Singularität des Aktes. Zur Performanz des Lesens. In: *Singularitäten. Literatur – Wissenschaft – Verantwortung*, Marianne Schuller / Elisabeth Strowick, Eds., Freiburg i. Br., 59–72 **Tholen, Georg Christoph** (1994): Platzverweis. Unmögliche Zwischenspiele von Mensch und Maschine. In: *Computer als Medium*, Norbert Bolz / Friedrich A. Kittler / Georg Christoph Tholen, Eds., Munich **Tholen, Georg Christoph** (1997): Digitale Differenz. Zur Phantasmatik und Topik des Medialen. In: *HyperKult. Geschichte, Theorie und Kontext digitaler Medien*, Martin Warnke / Wolfgang Coy / Georg Christoph Tholen, Eds., Basel, 99–118 **Tholen, Georg Christoph** (1999): Der blinde Fleck des Sehens: Über das raumzeitliche Geflecht des Imaginären. In: *Konstruktionen Sichtbarkeiten* (Interventionen 8), Jörg Huber / Martin Heller, Eds., Vienna / New York, 191–214 **Tholen, Georg Christoph** (2001): Der Ort des Abwesenden. Konturen des Differenz-Denkens bei Derrida, Lacan und Levinas. In: *Singularitäten*, Schuller / Strowick, Eds., Freiburg i. Br. **Weber, Samuel M.** (1991): *Return to Freud. Jacques Lacan's Dislocation of Psychoanalysis*, Cambridge **Wiener, Norbert** (1948): *Cybernetics; or, Control and Communication in the Animal and the Machine*, Cambridge

Illustration   **01 Lacan, Jacques** (1977): The Agency of the Letter in the Unconscious or Reason since Freud. In: *Écrits. A Selection*, transl. Alan Sheridan, New York / London, 152

VERENA KUNI

[IF, else, next.]

> What is the meaning of issuing a "call for contributions" to a book that, in terms of the working title announced, aims to collect the "next protocols of cyberfeminism"?[1] If the quest for "next protocols" – a formula as such maybe already absurd enough – was not meant as mere rhetoric, but as a serious task: How could we ask for sketches or even descriptions of something that, as hereby proclaimed or at least suggested, did not yet exist nor should be framed at any time within fixed contours?

If the latter was not only suggested, but even stated within the very first lines of the "call" – as in the demand for new and controversial approaches – what about our own positions? What was our idea of future cyberfeminisms, yet to be explored – but close enough to be processed by words and/or images, caught in a vocabulary at least familiar enough to be negotiated by way of a medium belonging to the good old Gutenberg galaxy? If we claimed to be in need for related perspectives ourselves, how could we dare to ask others to contribute them? Else, if we were seriously calling for "new and controversial approaches" – how could we expect to provide – or even: suggest to call our own – criteria to decide which approaches would lead to "cyberfeminist perspectives"?

How could we be able to decide what kind of contribution deserved to be called a "next protocol of cyberfeminism" – and not? How could we dare to find criteria not only to select contributions for inclusion, but also refuse others and thereby exclude them from the book?

Else – whom did the "we" embrace that used to appear so prominently in the "call"? "The Old Boys Network", as a whole? But how many voices would this "Old Boys Network" embrace – not only in terms of numbers, but also in terms of cyberfeminist standpoints and positions? Were all of them – all of "us" – included within this "we"? But if so – were these members of the network indeed the ones calling or weren't they rather the ones being called? Else, if they were calling, why was there the need for a "call" for contributions anyway? Wouldn't it have been enough to communicate the project within the existing network of communication and collaboration? If not, if only the four Boys that temporarily signed as "editorial team"[2] were calling – whom did this particular (and partial) "we" expect to reach with the "call"?

Else, if we announced an "editorial team" instead of the network to be responsible for the project, what would follow from this? How could four people determine criteria for inclusion into something promising like cyberfeminism's "next protocols" – and therefore also create principles of exclusion from it? If this was legitimate, was it possible? And if this was possible, what was the reason two of us quit the task?

---

1   The title "Cyberfeminism. next protocols" was given by Claudia Reiche and accepted by the first editorial team after some weeks of questioning its literal and intellectual comprehensibility; the 'call for contributions' consists of two parts, written by Faith Wilding (first part, " READ.ME FIRST") and by Claudia Reiche (second part, "READ.ME: IF/ELSE"). [C.R.]

2   Members of the first editorial team of the "Cyberfeminism. next protocols" project have been: Verena Kuni, Claudia Reiche, Yvonne Volkart, and Faith Wilding in 1999. Yvonne Volkart and Faith Wilding left the project in 2000, before the choice of contributions to be included in the book was made. This choice was made by Verena Kuni and Claudia Reiche, as well as the editorial correspondence with the authors was started. Since 2002 Claudia Reiche was the one to carry out all of the editorial tasks and worked with Tina Horne, Brigitte Helbling, Margaret Morse, and mainly Sabine Melchert for the English translations and proofreadings and with the layout artist Janine Sack to finish the project. [C.R.]

3   Have there really been so few images in this book? [C.R.]

Next: If we wished to consider a broad variety of texts and non-textu-
al projects, regarding the mere fact that cyberfeminism had not only been
born and nurtured in a multi-media environment, but so far seemed to
have its nucleus in electronic media-based networks, why did we choose
the format of a book – instead of the World Wide Web – as a multi-
media environment? Wouldn't an internet-based publication have
promised to reach a far broader public, especially when combined with
free access to its contents? In other words: If we, the Old Boys, were calling ourselves a network – wouldn't a net-based network of "next protocols" not only provide better means to spread the message, but also be
more appropriate to the spirit of cyberfeminist networking anyway? Else,
weren't we aware that the format of a book would probably appear to be
calling more to text-workers and those familiar with print formats than to
all those who would prefer to work in other media? Hence, wouldn't the
"call" for a book as such exclude a broad variety of possible "next protocols of cyberfeminism" already?

If not, why was a majority of those who responded to our call text-
workers – most of them with an academic background in the humanities?
Why had only few artists responded, not to mention people with other
professions? Was it because we had failed to spread our call widely
enough? If not, was it easier for writers to think, and to invent "next protocols"? Or was it just easier for them to contribute, because it is simpler
to drop the word "cyberfeminism" in the framework of a text – while it
might be far more complicated to imagine a cyberfeminist imagery?
Hence, were there indeed too many constraints in the format chosen? Or
was it the way the call itself was written – which from our part was con-
siderably "open" (and ourselves as curious and open-minded), nevethe-
less containing mutual gestures of enclosure and exclusion, confinements
and limitations that for whatever reasons – a functional blindness maybe
– remained invisible for us? If not, what else could be concluded from
this result?

If, after all, "next protocols of cyberfeminism" were expected to consist of texts and images, or better: a few images and many texts[3] – what
would this mean in terms of reflecting "the actual (and future) state of art
of thinking about, and inventing, the digital medium in its capacity to
subvert cultural practices a cyberfeminist perspective can provide"? Has
cyberfeminism already become a cultural practice, reflected by its own
academic theory, history, and art? [If]...[else] – what will be [next]?   <

marie-luise_angerer

efemera_clone_2/ricardo_dominguez

ephemera/diane_lundin

kate_o'riordan

shu_lea_cheang

ulrike_bergermann

prema_murthy

helene_von_oldenburg

liquid_nation/francesca_da_rimini

christina_goestl

claudia_reiche

elisabeth_strowick

yvonne_volkart

ingeborg_reichle

irina_aristarkhova

julie_doyle

janine_sack

discordia/agnese_trocchi

anne-marie_schleiner

andrea_sick

contributors

Marie-Luise Angerer is professor of Gender and Media Studies at the Kunsthochschule für Medien, Cologne. Her specialist subjects in teaching and research
are the body, sexuality, feminist and psychoanalytic theory, film, TV, new
technologies and art. Her publications include: (2002) *Future Bodies*, Marie-
Luise Angerer/Kathrin Peters/Zoe Sofoulis, Eds., Wien/New York; (2000)
body options. Körper. Spuren. Medien. Bilder, Vienna; (1995) *The Body of
Gender*, Ed., Vienna; (1999) Life as Screen? Or how to grasp the
Virtuality of the Body. In: *Filozofski Vestnik*, vol. 2, Ljubljana, 153–164;
(1999) Space does Matter. On Cyberbodies and Other Bodies. In: European
Journal of Cultural Studies, vol. 2 (2), 202–229 (Sage); (1998) Medien und
Mediales, Überlegungen zur 'medialen Verfassung des Subjekts' (Media and
Media Matters, Thoughts on 'The Media Concept of the Subject'). In: *metis.
Zeitschrift für historische Frauenforschung und feministische Praxis*, vol. 7, no.
13, 64 –79; (1997) Medien-körper/Körper-Medien, Erinnerungsspuren im
Zeitalter der 'digitalen Evolution'. In: *Körper – Gedächtnis – Schrift. Der Körper
als Medium kultureller Erinnerung*, Berlin, 270–292; (1997) alt.feminism/alt.
sex/alt.identity/alt.theory/alt.art. Anmerkungen zur theoretischen und
medialen Zelebrierung virtueller Geschlechter und ihrer Körper. In:
Springerin, Hefte für Gegenwartskunst, vol.1, no. 2/3, 32–41.

Irina Aristarkhova (Moscow/Singapore) has been writing and teaching on Feminist
Theory and Aesthetics, Cyberart and Cyberculture, and Russian national
identity, among other topics. Currently she is teaching a course in Cyberarts
and heading the Cyberarts Research Initiative at the National University of
Singapore. (**http://www.cyberartsweb.org**) She is also completing a Russian
publication of Luce Irigaray's *L'Ethique de la difference sexuelle* to be published in Moscow. **Email**: uspia@nus.edu.sg

Ulrike Bergermann teaches media studies at the University of Paderborn, Germany, works at Thealit, the Women's Cultural Lab in Bremen, and lives in Hamburg. Dissertation on the notation of sign language and academic's disciplinary boundaries between 'writing' and 'image' (*Ein Bild von einer Sprache*, Fink 2001). Topics of interest are media theory, popular culture, gender studies, and most recently the history of science, focusing on the relations between science's and media's notion of "information" in genetics and cybernetics. Homepage: **www.uni-paderborn.de/~bergerma**, **Email**: bergerma@upb.de

Shu Lea Cheang self-styled digital nomadic artist. Her Net installation works have been commissioned and in the permanent collections of Walker Art Center (Bowling Alley, 1995), NTT[ICC], Tokyo (*Buy One Get One*, 1997) and the Guggenheim Museum (*Brandon*, 1998–1999). Her recent work includes I.K.U. (scifi digi porn, Tokyo 2000), *Baby Play* (NTT[ICC], Tokyo 2001), *DRIVE BY DINING* (Browserday, Amsterdam 2002). Her current projects include *St(r)eaming the fields* <**www.rich-air.com**> in New York and Theatrum Digitalis for Waag Society, Amsterdam.

Discordia/Agnese Trocchi (Rome, Italy), was born as **macchina**, a digital entity, in AVaNABBS (Bulletin Board System, part of the European Counter Network, settled in "Forte Prenestino", the squatted community center in Rome), **http://www.forteprenestino.net/laboratori/avana/index.html**. She has been an active participant in the development of counter-networks in Rome, including **http://www.thething.it**. She grew up in techno-organized disorder from the cradle of necrotic European culture and she created with Francesco Macarone Palmieri a website focused on the illegal rave scene in Italy: *Ordanomade, Children of The Noise Age* **http://www.kyuzz.org/ordanomade**. She is co-editor of *Torazine Magazine: pills of pop-countercoulture, aesthetic terrorism, detournment and plagiarism*: **http://www.kyuzz.org/ordanomade/tora.htm**. She is co-founder of CANDIDA TV a group of Video Hacktivist and Visual Dements, a project of infestation of the mainstream television channels: **http://candida.thing.net**. From 1999 she has been collaborating with Diane Ludin and Francesca Da Rimini at the net-project *Identity_Runners* http://z.parsons.edu/~ludin/final_pages/

Julie Doyle is a Media Studies lecturer at the University of Brighton. Her doctoral thesis examined the historical intersections between art, surgery and technology in medical discourses of the gendered body. More specifically, the role of image and imagination in the production of anatomical knowledge was explored. She has published on the cultural history of surgery and its influence upon contemporary understandings of gender, sexuality and the sexed body, including narratives of the transsexual and cyborg body. Her research interests are around the relations between medical science, technology and visual aesthetics in constructions of gender identity and embodiment.

Efemera_Clone_2/Ricardo Dominguez is a co-founder of The Electronic Disturbance Theater (EDT), the group that developed Virtual-Sit In technologies in 1998 in solidarity with the Zapatista communities in Chiapas, Mexico. He is Senior Editor of *The Thing* (bbs.thing.net). He is a former member of Critical Art Ensemble (1986 to 1995, the originators of the theory of Electronic Civil Disobedience). Currently he is a Fake_Fakeshop Worker (**http://www. fakeshop.com**), a hybrid performance group presented at the Whitney Biennial 2000. Dominguez has collaborated on a number of international net_art projects: among them are *Dollspace*, produced with Francesca da Rimini (**http://www.thing.net/~dollyoko**), and the *Somatic_Architecture* Project with Diane Ludin (**http://www.thing.net/~diane**), in which he is OS_slave for *i_drunners* (a Mistresses of Technology Project) – (**http://www. idrunners.net**). He has also collaborated with Jennifer and Kevin McCoy (**http://www.airworld.net**) on a number of projects, and participated in *The Warhol Hijack* with the Verbal group. Ricardo is a founding member of nettime latino (**http://www.nettime.org**). He presented EDT's SWARM action at Ars Electronica's InfoWar Festival in 1998 (Linz, Austria). His first digital zapatismo project took place in 1996–97, a three month RealVideo/Audio network project: *The Zapatista/Port* Action at (MIT). His essays have appeared at *Ctheory* (**http://www.ctheory.org**) and in *Corpus Delecti: Performance Art of the Americas*, (Routledge, 2000), edited by Coco Fusco. He edited EDT's forthcoming book *Hacktivism: network_art_activism*, (Autonomedia Press, 2002). Homepage: **http://www.thing.net/~rdom**

Ephemera/Diane Ludin recycles media into electronic blood and ether. She then frames counter events to mix her etherblood with others. These random encounters access memory of unspoken or neglected persons with the details of violence thrust upon them and discarded by the public, monocultural imaginary. Her growing roots entangle with those of the output of Discordia and Liquid Nation in a circulatory communication opening the source of hidden realities that haunt us all.

Christina Goestl is an artist, sexpert and communication designer, foundrix of *SEX - a positive guide*, **http://sex.t0.or.at**, creatrix of *matrix.64*, **http://www.matrix 64.net** and, most recently, *s.EXE interactives*, a visual real time sequencer for VJs and other playful people **http://www.clitoressa.net**. She is a netizen, living in the EU, and holding a M.A. degree. You can contact her via **Email**: clitoressa@t0.or.at

Marina Grzinic works as researcher at the Institute of Philosophy at the ZRC SAZU (Scientific and Research Center of the Slovenian Academy of Science and Art) in Ljubljana. She received her Ph.D. in Philosophy on the topic of Philosphical Aspects of Virtual Reality and Changed Time and Space Paradigms in the 1990's at the University of Ljubljana. She also works as a freelance media theorist, art critic and curator. Marina Grzinic has been involved with video art since 1982. In collaboration with Aina Smid she has produced more than 30 video art projects, a short film, numerous video and media installations, Internet websites and an interactive CD-ROM (ZKM, Karlsruhe, Germany). Grzinic and Smid have received several major international awards for their video works, including Videonale, Bonn 1992; Deutscher Videokunst Preis /Multimediale 3, ZKM, Karlsruhe 1993; San Francisco International Film Festival, 1994 and 1995; FIV Buenos Aires, 1995. Marina Grzinic has published hundreds of articles and essays and edited eight books. During the 1997–98 academic year, she held the Postdoctoral Fellowship for Research of the Japan Society for the Advancement of Science in Tokyo. Her last book is *Fiction Reconstructed. Eastern Europe, Post-socialism and The Retro-avantgarde*, Edition selene in collaboration with Springerin,Vienna, 2000. **Email**: margrz@zrc-sazu.si

Verena Kuni (D, Frankfurt/M) art historian and media theorist (M.A.). Currently working as assistant at the Department of Art History at the University of Trier, where she is also coordinator for the interdisciplinary and intercultural Gender Studies Programme (**http://www.uni-trier.de/zig**). Besides, she is working for the project <*gender/media/art*> at HfG Offenbach and the Center for Gender Studies in the Arts at the HfMDK Frankfurt/M. (**http://www.gendersenses.net/gmk**). From 1996 to 2001 she was assistant at the Department of Art Theory at the Johannes Gutenberg-University of Mainz, and co-organized a special lecture and teaching program for women artists (**http://www.kuni.org/v/frau24**). Teaching assignments at several universities and art academies since 1997. Ph.D. project on the (self)staging of the artist's persona and the creation of artists' myths in contemporary art. Besides working as a freelance curator organizing exhibitions, video screenings, webspaces and conferences (**http://www.kuni.org/v/curat.htm**); as well as a freelance author and critic for several art magazines (**http://www. kuni.org/v/public.htm**). Since 1995 co-curator of video programs for the Kasseler Dokumentarfilm und Videofest (**http://www.filmladen.de/dokfest**); where since 1999 she has also organized the Interfiction workhop (**http://www. interfiction.net**). Co-founder of the Filiale Zeitgenössische Kunst Gender Vermittlung (**http://www.thing.de/filiale**). Member of the Old Boys Network (**http://www.obn.org**). Homepage: **http://www.kuni.org/v/**. **Email**: verena@kuni.org

Liquid_Nation/Francesca da Rimini burning her own prophesies in her jaws of fire. Histories and potentialities smash, attract, recreate themselves. Her sister in the detention camp writes, "Beauty lies between the pen and her hand in this harsh red desert." *Oracle* (**http://www.thing.net/~dollyoko/ID/TEXT/ LN01.HTM**) born of *ghost* (**http://www.thing.net/~dollyoko**), born of *Puppet Mistress* (**http://www.suspectthoughts.com/puppet.htm**). And now, covered in nuclear dust (**http://www.thing.net/~dollyoko/TA**), her face damp with the tears of the *Invisibles* (**http://autonomous.org/refugee/**

TEXT/BLOOD00.HTM). Many of Francesca da Rimini's projects can be found at http://sysx.org/gashgirl

Sabine Melchert (Bremen, born 1966) works as a freelance translator and foreign language assistant in a neurobiological research group at the University of Bremen, Germany. After her graduation in English and Russian at the University of the Saarland in Saarbrücken, Germany, she has worked as a translator in computer sciences, information technology and software programming as well as in economics and jurisprudence. She has contributed to an academic project supporting women in computer sciences and in the past three years has concentrated on translating texts relating to feminist, educational and gender issues. She has also taken up teaching obligations and devotes her time to the translation of contemporary literature.

Prema Murthy is a digital artist based in New York. She received her M.A. in Fine Arts from Goldsmith's College, London. Using various forms of digital media, she explores intersections between culture, technology and modes of embodiment. Her work has been exhibited at museums, galleries and festivals in the US and abroad including the Walker Center (MN), List Center for Visual Arts at MIT, The Studio Museum in Harlem (NY), and the Generali Foundation (Vienna). From 1997 to 2001, she was a core member of the artgroup Fakeshop, which has exhibited at the N5M Festival, the Ars Electronica Festival, and the Whitney Biennial 2000.

Helene von Oldenburg (Rastede/Hamburg) holds a doctor's degree in Agricultural Science and a Diploma in Visual Arts. Her work – presented in lectures, performances and installations – centers on research of appearances and effects digital media force on perception, society and the future. She is member of the Old Boys Network (http://www.obn.org), curator of *UFO-Strategies*, Edith-Ruß-Haus für Medienkunst, Oldenburg (2000) and with Rosanne Altstatt of *Cyberfem Spirit –Sprit of Data*, Edith-Ruß-Haus für Medienkunst, Oldenburg (2001), (http://www.edith-russ-haus.de), and with Claudia Reiche founder of the first interplanetary exhibition site on Mars, THE MARS PATENT (http://www.mars-patent.org).

PLASTIQUE/j.u.l.i.e.t.a (1975 to date): filmmaker, artist, writer, recently turned genetics researcher. Founding contributor of *MOHO* magazine, interested in turning the impossible and the invisible into moving images. Traces of her can be found in various magazines, books and screens both in New York and Mexico City, and at science labs in Europe and the US.

Claudia Reiche (Hamburg) media theorist, artist, curator. Her work focuses on (cyber)feminist approaches to the question of how man/machine relations are designed with words and images. Selected publications in English: (1996) PIXEL: Experiences with the Elements. In: *Medicine Meets Virtual*

Reality: 4, Suzanne J. Weghorst, et al., Eds., Amsterdam/Oxford/Tokyo/ Washington DC; (1998) Feminism is digital. In: *First cyberfeminist international, documenta x, kassel*, Cornelia Sollfrank/Old Boys Network, Eds., Hamburg; (1999) Bio(r)Evolution™, On the Contemporary Military-Medical Complex. In: *The Spectralization of Technology: From Elsewhere to Cyberfeminism and Back*, Marina Grzinic, Ed., Maribor; (2002) Technics of Ambivalence and Telepresence. In: *technics of cyber◇feminism*. *<mode=message>*, Claudia Reiche/Andrea Sick, Eds., Bremen; (2002) The Visible Human Project. Accessing an Obscene Image Body. In: *Biotechnology, Philosophy and Sex*, [Special issue *maska, Journal for Performing Arts*, vol. XVII, no. 76–77], Marina Grzinic, Ed., Ljubljana. More publications, see: **http://www.rrz.uni- hamburg.de/koerperbilder**. Member of the Thealit Frauen.Kultur.Labor, Bremen, **http://www.thealit.de**, and of the cyberfeminist alliance Old Boys Network. Curating with Helene von Oldenburg THE MARS PATENT, the first exhibition site on Mars **http://www. mars-patent. org**. **Email**: Claudia.Reiche@hamburg.de

Ingeborg Reichle, M.A., studied art history, philosophy, sociology and archaeology in Freiburg i. Br., London, and Hamburg. Since 1998, lecturer at the art history department and gender studies department at the Humboldt University in Berlin. Her research focuses on gender and new media art (cyberfeminism) and the field where art and science meet (artificial life art, transgenic art). A special field of interest is the development of content management systems and image databases for art history education: system_kgs (**http://www. kunstgeschichte.de**), Prometheus - Das verteilte digitale Bildarchiv für Forschung und Lehre (**http://www.prometheus-bildarchiv.de**). Publications: (2000) Bild und Bildlichkeit. In: *Jahrbuch des Collegium Budapest, Institute for Advanced Studies*, 124–131; (2001) Kunst und Biomasse: Zur Verschränkung von Biotechnologie und Medienkunst in den 90er Jahren. In: *kritische berichte*, no. 1/2001, 23–33; (2000) Neue Medien in der Bildung: PROMETHEUS - Das verteilte digitale Bildarchiv für Forschung und Lehre. In: *kritische berichte*, no. 2/2000, 87–89; (2001) Keine Angst vor dem Cyberspace: Frauen und Neue Medien in der Bildung. In: *Die Philosophin. Forum für feministische Theorie und Philosophie*, no. 23, vol. 12,137–139; (2001) Kunst und Genetik: Zur Rezeption der Gentechnik in der zeitgenössischen Kunst. In: *Die Philosophin*, no. 23, vol. 12, Tübingen, 28–42; (2002) TechnoSphere: Körper und Kommunikation im Cyberspace. In: *Bildhandeln*, Klaus Sachs-Hombach/ Klaus Rehkämper, Eds., Reihe Bildwissenschaft, vol. 3, Magdeburg, 193–204; (2002) Medienbrüche. In: *Kritische Berichte*, no. 1, 41–56; (2002) Artificial Life Art - Transgenic Art: Zur Verschränkung von Kunst und Biotechnologie in der Medienkunst der Neunzigerjahre. In: *ZIF Bulletin 24: Cyberfeminismus. Feministische Visionen mit Netz und ohne Boden?* Zentrum für Interdisziplinäre Frauenforschung der HU, Berlin, 87–102. **http://www.arthistory.hu-berlin.de/mitarbeiter/reichle.html** **Email**: Ingeborg.Reichle@culture.hu-berlin.de

Kate O'Riordan is a Media Studies lecturer in Continuing Education at the University of Sussex, U.K. Her research interests are around sexuality and gender in relation to information and communication technologies. She has previously published on: female icons in computer games (Lara Croft), female cyber-bodies such as 'virtual idols,' the framing of the body through web cameras, lesbian identity and community online, and the ethics of Internet research. Her DPhil thesis is an examination of the representation of female bodies in relation to discourses of cyberspace. She is also an active member of the Research Ethics Working Committee for the Association of Internet Researchers (**http://www.aoir.org**).

Janine Sack is a visual artist based in Stockholm and Hamburg. She graduated in Visual Communications at the HfbK in Hamburg and did one year of post-graduate studies at the Royal Art College in Stockholm. Her mainly time-based art investigates clichés of representation. Notions of identity and gender are analyzed in terms of their social construction and media representation. Along with her work as an individual artist, Janine Sack has been engaged in various collaborative practices. From 1992-93 she was involved in *frauen-und-technik*, a women artist collective that used performance and TV to discuss issues of feminism and media theory. She also was a founding member of *-Innen*, a group of four women working with multi-medial techniques, such as performance or tv-gameshows. She has been working for OBN on the video *Processing Cyberfeminism*, 1999 and documented the *very cyberfeminist international* in 2001. She is responsible for the graphic design of this book. **Email**: sackjanine@web.de

Anne-Marie Schleiner (San Francisco) is engaged in gaming and net culture in a variety of roles as a writer, critic, curator, and gaming artist/designer. Her work investigates avatar gender construction, computer gaming culture, and hacker art. She has curated online exhibits of game mods and add-ons including the exhibits: *Cracking the Maze: Game Patches and Plug-ins as Hacker Art, Mutation.fem*, and *Snow Blossom House*. She runs a site focused on game hacks and open source digital art forms called *opensorcery.net*. She is also co-founder of *playskins.com*, a game development house for innovative and sexy games and toys.

Andrea Sick (Bremen) Cultural science studies in Heidelberg, Bremen and Hamburg. Lecturing assignments in art theory and cultural science on pictoral theories and psychoanalysis at the University of Bremen. Ph.D. with a grant from the Heinrich Böll Stiftung at the University of Hamburg on *Kartenmuster. Bilder und Wissenschaft in der Kartographie (Map patterns. Pictures and Science in Cartography)*. Main study and research topics in the area of media and cultural theory, psychoanalysis, gender theory, and cartography. Especially interested in the interface between scientific, artistic, and curatorial work. In 1990 she founded the Thealit Frauen.Kultur.Labor (women.culture.laboratory) together with Anna Postmeyer. Since then, she has been general and conceptual manager. (**http://www.thealit.de**). **Email**: sick@thealit.de

Elisabeth Strowick studied German Language and Literature and Psychology at the University of Hamburg, wrote her doctoral dissertation on the topic of repetition in Kierkegaard, Lacan, Freud (published 1999, *Passagen der Wiederholung. Kierkegaard - Lacan - Freud*, Stuttgart/Weimar: Metzler), has been lecturing at the University of Hamburg and the University of Trier, and now holds a postdoc-position at the University of Greifswald, teaching German Literature. Fields of interest: literary criticism, rhetoric, gender studies, psychoanalysis.

Yvonne Volkart (Zurich) is curator, art critic, and writer. She lectures in German and New Media at the Hochschule of Art and Design in Zurich, and at several European art schools and universities. As a member of OBN she was one of the organizers of Next Cyberfeminist International, Rotterdam, March 1999. The latest exhibition projects were: 'Tenacity. Cultural Practices in the Age of Bio-and Information-technologies,' Swiss Institute New York/Shedhalle Zurich, 2000, 'Body as Byte. The Body as information flow,' Kunstmuseum Luzern, 2001, and the Internet and CD-ROM part of: 'Double Life. Identity and Transformation in Contemporary Arts,' Generali Foundation Vienna, 2001. She is currently writing a Ph.D. about gender and cyborg fantasies in new media art in Oldenburg. **http://www.xcult.org/volkart**

More Books from Autonomedia

Visit our web site for online ordering,
topical discussion, events listings,
book specials, and more.
www.autonomedia.org

Autonomedia • PO Box 568
Williamsburgh Station
Brooklyn, NY 11211-0568
T/F 718-963-2603
info@autonomedia.org